ANOTHER ASIA

Another Asia draws on the intersections of the late Meiji period in
Japan and the Swadeshi movement in Bengal. It weaves through
an intricate tapestry of ideas relating to pan-Asianism, nationalism,
cosmopolitanism, and friendship, and positions the early modernist
tensions of the period within—and against—the spectre of a unified
Asia that concealed considerable political differences.

'Tagore and Okakura were performers on the world stage, straddling
continents in a way that had not been possible before ... The story in
this book of how Tagore and Okakura struggled to make sense of their
international roles, and to find common ground, moved me greatly.'

—WILLIAM RADICE
Senior Lecturer in Bengali
SOAS, University of London

'A really fascinating and illuminating set of reflections on issues
such as the concept of Asia, nationalism, and notions of civilization.
The book speaks very much to some key concerns of the present
age on globalization and postcolonialism. It offers a carefully nuanced
perspective on previously neglected areas of cosmopolitanism and
opens up wider debate and reflections on the nature of friendship
in modern society.'

—TESSA MORRIS-SUZUKI
Professor of Japanese History
The Australian National University

ANOTHER ASIA

Rabindranath Tagore
& Okakura Tenshin

RUSTOM BHARUCHA

OXFORD
UNIVERSITY PRESS

OXFORD
UNIVERSITY PRESS

Oxford University Press is a department of the University of Oxford.
It furthers the University's objective of excellence in research, scholarship,
and education by publishing worldwide. Oxford is a registered trademark of
Oxford University Press in the UK and in certain other countries

Published in India by
Oxford University Press
22 Workspace, 2nd Floor, 1/22 Asaf Ali Road, New Delhi 110 002

First Edition published in 2006
Oxford India Paperbacks 2009
21st impression 2025

ISBN-13: 978-0-19-806281-3
ISBN-10: 0-19-806281-8

Typeset in Spectrum MT 11.5/13/5
at Le Studio Graphique, Gurgaon 122 001
Printed in India by Manipal Technologies Limited, Manipal

If you press me to tell why I loved him,
I feel this cannot be expressed, except by answering:
because it was he, because it was I.

Montaigne

Contents

Illustrations

All photographs of Rabindranath Tagore, Priyambada Devi Banerjee, and Surendranath Tagore have been drawn from the archives of the Rabindra-Bhavana, Santiniketan. My thanks to Pulak Dutta for his editing of these images, and to Arpan Mukherjee for his assistance.

I am grateful to Koizumi Shinya of the Izura Institute of Art and Culture for selecting Okakura's images, which were scanned by Sato Koji of the Japan Foundation, Tokyo.

Acknowledgements

The impulse of this book to reflect on Asia through the inter-Asian affinities (and differences) of Rabindranath Tagore and Okakura Tenshin was nurtured by a generous grant from the Japan Foundation. In the calm of the Japan Foundation Library in Tokyo, I was alerted to the enormous archive that has been generated around Japanese Studies, which opened me to a totally different body of knowledge within my field of interculturalism. This research could have become overwhelming had it not been for the pleasure that I derived from any number of meetings, dinners, and conversations organized by three officers of the Japan Foundation, notably Ogawa Tadashi, Sato Koji, and Kakuta Eri, whose love of India heightened the cross-cultural dimensions of my project.

Through the meticulous time-management of my Japanese hosts, I was able to meet diverse scholars like Matsumoto Kenichi, whose civilizational biases of Asia were quite different from the refreshingly blunt perspective on Japanese nationalism provided by Oguma Eiji. In the idyllic surroundings of Izura, I was also introduced to Koizumi Shinya of the Izura Institute of Art and Culture, a most perceptive guide of Okakura's artistic legacy, who facilitated the selection of the photographs relating to Okakura published in this book. My friends at the Japan Foundation also arranged for my manuscript to be read by two dedicated readers, Usuda Masayuki and

Hori Madoka, who alerted me to many details of Japanese history and language. The diverse publications of Inaga Shigemi from the International Research Centre for Japanese Studies were also useful inputs in my research.

My greatest debt as a writer for the Japanese component of my research is to Tessa Morris-Suzuki of the Australian National University, who offered to read my manuscript when it urgently needed to be 'checked out' by a seasoned researcher in the field of Japanese Studies. Her generous comments and insights made me aware of the possibilities of interdisciplinary scholarship and dialogue outside the strictures of Area Studies. In Tokyo I was also fortunate to be affiliated to my sponsor Uchino Tadashi at the Department of Interdisciplinary Studies in Tokyo University, who introduced me to my translator Sato Mika. My acknowledgements in Japan would be incomplete without mentioning Richard Emmert, whose knowledge of Noh theatre was elaborated over many animated discussions in his home, where I was fortunate to be his guest. His neighbourhood in Nakano-ku, Tokyo, a village nestled in a twenty-first century metropolis, remains one of my many homes in the world.

Shifting the base from Tokyo to Calcutta, I have many mentors to thank, notably Sankho Ghosh, whose pre-eminence as a scholar of Tagore I had occasion to experience through his very suggestive corrections of my text, always informed by precision and subtlety. Though she did not read the manuscript, Sukumari Bhattacharya has guided my reflections on Tagore with her inimitable candour in relation to his *oeuvre* and person. William Radice has also been gracious in his comments and critical insights into the framing of my text. Other readers who have gone through the manuscript with a discerning eye and helpful feedback include Jasodhara Bagchi, Subhoranjan Dasgupta, Pradip Datta, and Manas Ray, who provided me with pages of densely reflective notes. I am particularly indebted to Bhaskar Mukhopadhyay for his vigorous translation of Tagore's *Swadeshi Samaj*, in addition to many valuable theoretical citations relating to travel and friendship. Rajarshi Chakrabarty also helped me to engage with the task of translation.

No reference to Tagore is complete without Santiniketan. Here I wish to acknowledge Pulak Dutta, whose lyrical and intuitive knowledge of Rabindranath (and of Rabindrasangeet in particular) has been a constant counterpoint to the shaping of my cultural critique. I am grateful to his colleagues at Kala-Bhavana, and most of all to K.G. Subramanyan, whom I had the pleasure to meet only once, but whose conversation was more revealing than what can be derived from many books. To the officers of Rabindra-Bhavana at Visva-Bharati University, and to Supriya Roy in particular, I extend my thanks for their support in allowing me to research the archives and to select photographs reproduced in this book with their kind permission.

To Oxford University Press, I express my thanks for its faith in this book, which was first commissioned by Anil Chandy and subsequently supported by Priya Rana at every stage of the production process. The opportunity to research Rabindranath Tagore and Okakura Tenshin has been nothing short of a deep privilege, which, I trust, will be appropriately acknowledged in the ultimate test for any writer—the life of the book itself.

Preface

At the heart of this book is a friendship between two luminaries of Asia, the Bengali poet Rabindranath Tagore (1861–1941) and the Japanese curator Okakura Tenshin (1862–1913), whose relationship is idealized in almost direct proportion to its relative absence of documentation. We have no photographs of Tagore and Okakura together, notwithstanding many striking portraits of their individual personalities. Nor can we draw on records of their conversations and dialogues: nothing, for instance, on the lines of Tagore's philosophical exchange with Einstein. In the evidence that remains of their relationship, we are compelled to accept that Okakura and Tagore spoke about each other but not to each other. Moreover, they met only twice in their lives, once in Calcutta in 1902, and later, more fleetingly in Boston in 1913. During the intervening years, they did not seem to have corresponded with each other. Nor did they rigorously read each other's books or quote from each other's texts. Despite these lacunae, or perhaps because of this lack of academic accountability, their friendship has acquired an almost iconic quality, testifying to the endurance and intimacy of inter-Asian cultural dialogue.

My task in this book is not to disrupt this idealized friendship, even if this were possible or desirable, but rather to test it within, and against, a larger spectrum of contradictions, difficulties, and tensions that Tagore and Okakura, at least to the best of my knowledge, never once invoked in relation to each other. If they had differences, they were elided or silenced or subsumed within larger appreciations of each other's work and person. However, as time passes, and postcolonial theory breaks the complacency of earlier myths of inter-Asian unity, we are obliged to read the untold story of the Tagore–Okakura friendship in a somewhat different critical register. My purpose, therefore, is not to deepen the existing hagiography of Tagore and Okakura, but rather to draw an intellectual history out of their affinities to Asia, complicated by the politics of nationalism, cosmopolitanism, and friendship. This is not so much an academic history as a play of ideas linking Tagore and Okakura to the ideals of their times, and to the troubled legacy of those ideals today.

How do I position myself as a cultural critic in relation to this narrative? More precisely, how did I enter the Asia field in the first place? Neither a historian by training nor an Asian area studies specialist, I first encountered the discursive field of Asia indirectly through my intercultural work in the theatre. By the 1990s, I was beginning to participate in a series of inter-Asian theatre workshops and productions that were for the most part centred in Singapore.[1] What appeared a refreshing contrast to the Eurocentric discourse and practice of interculturalism, marked by appropriation, decontextualization, and cultural tourism, gradually began to take on more political dimensions, as I became aware of the heavy investment in 'Asia' as state-determined cultural capital. Over the years this capital has accumulated through accretions of intellectual and political discourse relating to Asian Values, the Asian Renaissance, and the more recent propagation of New Asia, under whose aegis the state of Singapore has attempted to sell itself as 'the global city of the arts'.[2]

As it became clearer to me that Asiacentricity could be the other side of the same coin as Eurocentricity, I was compelled to acknowledge that it could be even more insidious in its deceptions. To begin with, I was made uncomfortably aware that some form of Asian identity was being thrust upon me because I happened to live somewhere within that geographical expanse called Asia. The fact that I live in India and have marked myself as Indian in specific contexts, does not, I would emphasize, make me Asian. This is not entirely a matter of cultural choice, but an acknowledgment of specific historical considerations that go into the making of identities, independently of geography and its primordial associations linked to birth, blood, lineage, and race. If one accepts that identities are not unchanging 'givens' assumed as birthrights, but rather, are constructions that are shaped in and through larger discourses, then one must emphasize the absence of such an Asian discourse in the public domain of contemporary India. In this turbulent domain encompassing any number of identitarian debates around caste, community, religion, gender, region, language, and nation, the belongingness to a larger imagined community called Asia does not exist. The few civilizational critics in India who have attempted to invoke Asia can scarcely be said to form a constituency.[3]

The fact is that Asia does not have the same discursive weight or political valency in all parts of the continent designated as Asia. Indeed, one could argue in this context that Singapore needs 'Asia' in a way that India does not, in order to enhance its state-managed multiracialism in a metropolis that has thrived on eliminating local cultures, languages, traditions and communities in the interests of global capital and real estate. Ironically, it is in these denatured city–states where the capitalist foundations of the West have been so thoroughly assimilated that Asia should be emphatically flaunted as cultural capital: a capital that is at once legitimized and controlled by the discourse and mechanisms of New Asia.

In at least one of its manifestations, New Asia draws on the rich but messy cultural resources proliferating in 'Old Asia': the Asia of 'living traditions', with a mind-numbing diversity of folk, epic, ritual, and performance traditions, that continue to thrive in countries such as India. Spanning centuries and layers of time, ranging from the pre-modern to the postmodern, these traditions embody vital ingredients of the 'knowledge-based economy'[4] that the Singapore state prioritizes in its promotion of cultural capital and the intellectual property rights surrounding a specifically Asian cultural heritage. To my mind, what is troubling is not just the paternalistic rhetoric of this economy, buttressed by notions of Asian hospitality and family resemblances, but its coexistence with the use of labour from the poorer countries of Asia. This labour force, divested of rights and legal protection, is marked as irrevocably 'foreign', not Asian. Clearly, there are 'other' Asias that are *not quite* Asian which are subsumed within the hegemony of this New Asian framework.

Having expressed my discomfort with New Asianism, let me emphasize that it is not the subject of this book. It serves at best as a provocation insofar as it has made me aware that the apparently beneficent category of Asia, with or without its prefixes, can also be politically loaded and manipulative. Even so, while it may be easy to reject the demagoguery of New Asia, is it that simple to let go of the idea of Asia itself? In confronting this question, I had no other choice but to recall a landmark essay written by Fukuzawa Yukichi (1834–1901), the quintessential pragmatist of the Meiji period in Japan. In 1885, he published an essay audaciously entitled *Datsu-a Ron* (On Saying Goodbye to Asia).[5] This belligerent clarion call has lent itself to numerous translations: 'escaping from Asia', 'leaving Asia', 'dissociating from Asia', 'de-Asianization', and most pugnaciously, 'Goodbye Asia'. In his embrace of 'world civilization', which was singularized and entirely linked to the enlightenment of the West, Fukuzawa embraced the possibilities of material and social progress. Castigating the old-worldly Confucianism and non-scientific behavioural systems of Korea and China, he affirmed his position devoid of all diplomacy: 'We do not have time to wait for the enlightenment of our neighbours so that we can work together toward the development of Asia. It is better for us to leave the ranks of Asian nations and cast our lot with the civilized nations of the West.' With a final flourish of his relentless polemic, he added: 'We simply erase from our minds our bad friends in Asia.'[6]

Fukuzawa was very clear that if Japan had to get out of Asia, it had no other option but to join the West: *datsu-A nyu-O* (escaping from Asia and joining the West).[7] Significantly, he compared the process of 'joining' the West to catching measles, the disease that had spread all the way from Nagasaki to Tokyo, operating with a 'natural law' that could not be resisted. 'Get infected for your own good' was the subtext of Fukuzawa's bold recommendation. Since there was no way of 'preventing' a 'communicable disease', it was downright foolish to shut oneself in an enclosed room, the strategy that had been adopted by reactionary cultures like China and Korea. 'Without air, they suffocate to death,' declared Fukuzawa triumphantly, with no semblance of compassion for his Asian neighbours. The only option for modern nations like Japan was to open itself to the liberatory possibilities of contamination, the benefits of survival far outweighing the damages. Tellingly, Fukuzawa never once considered the consequences of actually dying from the measles of civilization, though he acknowledged, like a hard-nosed globalist, that a risk factor of death was a possibility.

Today, Fukuzawa's plea to escape Asia and join the West has been subject to contemporary reinterpretations. In a series of epigrammatic assertions, the Japanese civilizational critic Matsumoto Kenichi has described Fukuzawa's strategy as playing into the 'territory game', whereby Japan adopted a militarist position competing with the West only to end with its humiliating defeat in the Second World War. The post-war period in Japan, according to Matsumoto, could be described as *datsu-A nyu-Bei* (escaping from Asia and joining America),[8] in which the 'wealth game' dominated over politics. Now, in the post-Cold War period, when the unilateralism of the United States is pre-eminent, Matsumoto echoes the increasingly widespread global sentiment that it is time to 'escape America' by relinquishing the 'world history games' of the past in search of a rejuvenated Asia.[9]

The question however is: Escape the US to join what? Wallowing in an ahistorical, if not revivalist, assumption that it is possible for Asia to recover 'our shared common essence', which he describes somewhat too fatuously as 'symbiosis', Matsumoto assumes that something like an 'Asian common house' exists for all peoples in the region fleeing the new unilateral imperialism of our times.[10] Even within the constraints of metaphor, this hypothesis demands a suspension of disbelief, given the tightening of borders across Asian nations, beginning with Japan, whose immigration policy has scarcely been liberalized since the Second World War. Besides, one need not reiterate the intensification of many other wars, genocides, border disputes, and nuclear threats that have afflicted Asia in recent years. Arguably the continent with the widest economic disparities and increasingly restrictive immigration policies, Asia offers no common 'house' or 'home' to which migrants or refugees can be guaranteed the comfort of a shelter. Against this stark reality, Fukuzawa Yukichi's candid reference to China and Korea as 'bad friends' at least had the virtue of concealing an oxymoron, if not inner contradiction or lapsed intimacy. In contrast, Matsumoto's assumption that all Asians are essentially friends, if not members of the same civilizational family, is at best a blissful denial of contemporary history.

The more I probed the idea of Asia on Fukuzawa's instigation and Matsumoto's elaborations, I found that that it was not easy to get out of it, either intellectually or politically. Even as I had no illusions about seeking refuge in its proverbially timeless wisdom traditions, I was provoked into considering other ways of thinking about it. Was there another Asia worth thinking about capable of countering the crass bombast of civilizational rhetoric? One of Singapore's New Asia advocates, Kishore Mahbubani, mimicking the tough-talking US stance of his admirer Samuel Huntington, has entitled one of his books, *Can Asians think?* (1998). Perhaps, a more challenging question would be, 'How Does One Think Asia?'

With this question in mind, I found myself turning to the one major Indian thinker who, indeed, had spent considerable time thinking about, and through, Asia at the turn of the twentieth century into the devastation of the Second World War: Rabindranath Tagore. Dying shortly before the war ended with the devastation of Hiroshima, he was spared further disillusionment in his awareness of the 'crisis in civilization'. With Tagore, I realized that one could travel deeply into another Asia, which for all its fuzzy ideals and political simplifications had greater emotional depth and humanitarian insight than the arrogant assertions of Asian ideologues, whose flaunting of the New Asia 'success story' has simply played into the demagoguery of Huntington's 'clash of civilizations' (1996).

As I entered Tagore's Asian universe, I encountered for the first time a charismatic Japanese traveller called Okakura Tenshin, who could be said to have catalysed the very idea of Asia for Tagore and many Indians at the turn of the last century. An exposition of his journey, not only from Japan to India but to Boston as well, revealed more vistas of how 'Asia' can travel, both as an idea and as an ideal of world civilization. From entering Asia via the backdoor of inter-Asian theatre workshops, therefore, I now find myself reflecting in this book on an Asia from another time, sparked by the Tagore–Okakura meeting, but with many cultural and political resonances today.

Not all these resonances are pleasant. Japanese imperialism and competing Asian nationalisms were seethingly alive by the late nineteenth century, with the Sino-Japanese War of 1894–5 leaving a legacy of xenophobia and racism with violent repercussions in the first half of the twentieth century. Okakura, who was branded an ultra-nationalist by the late 1930s, had died before the start of the First World War, and therefore, his arguably jingoist affirmation of Asia is somewhat more 'New Asian' in its triumphalist tone and register than the defeated 'Old Asia' that Tagore appears to incarnate. However, neither of these manifestations of the two men is unequivocally intact, as indeed, the 'new' and the 'old' are strange bedfellows in the intimate affinities animating Asian differences. In Okakura's apparent New Asian persona there are contradictions and vulnerabilities relating to the present, and in the Old Asia of Tagore there are echoes of the Orient and a prescient envisioning of the future.

At this point I should stress that I have not turned to Tagore or Okakura to seek a utopian alternative to the New Asia that needs to be rejected. As the very title of this book suggests, *Another Asia* will always conceal an other to itself. Indeed, the 'unified' Asia of which Tagore and Okakura appeared to dream together was imagined on significantly different grounds. It is with this paradox in mind that I seek to complicate the idea of Asia both in its conflicting epistemologies and in its actual articulations of cultural theory and practice. While this complication of the idea of Asia contributes towards the theoretical thrust of the book, enhanced by an interlinking of ideas relating to pan-Asianism, nationalism, cosmopolitanism, and friendship, I trust that these ideas will not overwhelm the telling of a story—or, more precisely, a history of two remarkable men.

Let me stress that it is not hagiography that concerns me here, though, arguably, it is a genre in its own right that can be a useful source of reference so long as one can work against the grain of its narrative. Nor am I interested in anything so large as a cross-comparative history of India and Japan through a reading of the Meiji and Taisho periods vis-à-vis the *swadeshi* movement in Bengal and the early years of Indian Independence. If there is history in this book, it exists in fragments and details, through illuminations of 'historicality' and the cultures of everyday life, rather than through dense overviews of historical events. I should also add that I am not attempting to write art history, notwithstanding my reflections on Okakura as a curator and his museumization of Asia. My approach has been to contextualize what is necessary for my analysis, prioritizing facticity over factuality, the flow of the narrative over the aura of comprehensiveness. The copious notes at the back of the book, some of which are lengthy and technical, attempt to direct the reader to other sources that can provide a larger picture of what has been left out in my narrative.

In short, instead of attempting to summarize the totality of some fictitious 'Asian perspective' represented by Tagore and Okakura, I have focused only on the *intersection* of those ideas that are relevant to my discussion. Here I should acknowledge that many of these ideas are not merely pertinent in their own temporal contexts, they are strangely linked to critical debates today, more specifically in relation to revisionist readings of postcolonial and subaltern theory. Indeed, I have been struck by the almost uncanny ways in which the ideas that preoccupied Tagore and Okakura have catalysed my own rethinking of dominant tropes and norms relating to the Orient, the rewriting of history outside the limits of world history, vernacular cosmopolitanism, and the politics of friendship in relation to the indeterminacies of homosociality in non-Western contexts. Without trying to 'contemporize' either Tagore or Okakura, I cannot deny that what initially seemed to be a cluster of archaic sensibilities and ideals embodied in their magnetic personalities, has turned out to be nothing less than an intellectual provocation. Far from being an exercise in nostalgia, this book has compelled me to question how one can think about Asia today through its conflicting modernities, wars, and a spectrum of differences, that nonetheless coexist with legacies of kinship and intimacy that are becoming increasingly harder to define in the age of globalization.

Tagore and Okakura may not be our contemporaries, but they have the capacity to make us think about our times through the filter of shattered ideals, many of which may have been flawed in their inception. Inevitably, in structuring any narrative around the bodies of thought relating to two individuals, there is the risk of imbalance, of favouring one over the other. I have tried to be as alert as possible to this risk, but without succumbing to any kind of specious impartiality driven by notions of political correctness. Avoiding the traps of a 'compare-and-contrast' methodology as far as possible, I have allowed the ideas to shape the narrative, without feeling the need to break it constantly in the interests of equally balanced reportage. Thus, the reader will find long stretches in the book where Okakura seems to dominate, and then Tagore takes over. Towards the end, there is greater *jugalbandi*, to use a metaphor drawn from classical music in India, a playful contest of skills. I will leave it to the reader to decide where I stand in relation to Tagore and Okakura, though it is obvious that there are considerable differences in the sheer impact of their public personae: Tagore is India's foremost national poet, notwithstanding his condemnation of nationalism as an ideology, while Okakura remains something of a cult figure in Japan, despite his influence on certain sectors of Japanese artists and civilizational thinkers.

While a comparative assessment of their respective legacies is inevitable, it is important not to reduce the multidimensional lives and careers of Tagore and Okakura to singular positions. If Tagore, for instance, protested on many occasions that he was a poet—'*Ami kobi*' ('I am a poet')—he was basically saying, as William Radice points out, that 'his thought wasn't a complete or coherent system but a constantly developing and unfolding *sadhana* (self-realization), with quite a number of false turnings along the way'.[11] The same could be said for Okakura, whose transformation of sensibility and consciousness between 1902–13 encompassed many contradictory strands of nationalism, imperialism, cosmopolitanism, and love.

Significantly, there are several temporalities at work in this narrative, coalescing and separating at different junctures in my argument. The first decade of the twentieth century, which provides the primary time framework of the narrative, is also the meeting ground of the ideals and affinities shared by Tagore and Okakura. Underlying these apparently uncomplicated affinities, however, are unspoken dissonances and tensions relating to war and xenophobia, cultural superiority and racism, one Asia over another. While some of these dissonances and tensions are prefigured in past histories, they remained virulently alive to haunt the future. As I have mentioned earlier, Tagore lived to witness the unresolved crisis and destruction of the Second World War, when Okakura's spectre of Asia was resurrected posthumously in some kind of perverse recognition of his ideals. Within such volatile temporalities, this book is compelled to move back and forth between past and future, even as it appears to work through a chronological sequence. Lives can be lived chronologically; ideas are more mutable.

Inevitably, biographical details, both real and imagined, play a significant role in the unravelling of these ideas. I should stress, however, that this book has not been structured or designed as a biography, which is a separate genre altogether from the intellectual history that I choose to write. For some readers, this may be a disappointing choice because the lives of Tagore and Okakura certainly have the makings of a juicy narrative, as the numerous biographies around these personalities can testify, though with varying degrees of success. I favour the genre of intellectual history for the simple reason that this book could be the first such study of Tagore and Okakura within a larger canvas of ideas relating to Asia, nationalism, cosmopolitanism, and friendship. These ideas, I would emphasize, are 'juicy' in their own right. Moreover, I should add that even though I am not writing a biography, it will become clear that certain ideas, particularly those relating to the nebulous domain of friendship, cannot be envisioned without the illumination of people's everyday lives caught in moments of being.

As a non-Area Studies cultural critic, with some experience in the field of interculturalism at both theoretical and practical levels, I am well aware that this book can be seen as an amateur transgression insofar as I cannot claim any authority as a specialist of 'Bengali culture', and still less so, of 'Japanese culture', insofar as these monolithic essentializations make sense. In writing this book, I have become only too aware that even within the frameworks of particular academic departments, the Asias don't meet. South Asia doesn't talk to Southeast Asia, and East Asia is so exclusive that it is almost relegated to the status of a 'rich relative', whose excess of funding and capital seems totally out of proportion to the other Asias, the 'poorer cousins' as it were, who are finding it increasingly difficult to sustain their pristine disciplines. Perhaps I stress the familial metaphor too much, but I do believe that it would make a lot of sense if these Asias (and many others that are not yet officially recognized) could talk to each other in a more familiar but informed mode, not to restore imagined family resemblances but to initiate a more nuanced cross-cultural conversation across borders. This book is by no means the last word on the meeting of Tagore and Okakura, but perhaps it is a small contribution to the already existing conversations that attempt to cut across disciplinary protocols and political divides.

With these comments, let us turn now to the prologue in which I have sketched the epic scale of the narrative that lies ahead. The process of writing this book has been a constant source of surprise, and I can only hope that some of this quality of wonder, or *adbhuta rasa*, will resonate in the pleasure of the text.

Prologue

In the Kano school of Japanese painting, the student is never allowed to breakfast before he has finished his book of sketches. And these are all to be thrown away, these are only memoranda for him to remember. When he creates, it is with the aid of this knowledge, but not by actually using it.[1]

In this prologue, I will attempt to sketch with broad strokes the larger contours of the narrative in this book—epic in scale but minimalist in structure. Like all sketches, which can be discarded after being scrawled, but whose memory serves to stimulate the creative process of a drawing or painting, this one is incomplete, with glaring gaps and jump-cuts in time. It is a mere impression of the energies that hold the larger narrative together. I settle, therefore, not for chronology but for a somewhat random counterpoint of personalities and events, all of which help to frame the larger narrative. While this particular book assumes the form of an extended essay in four parts, combining cultural critique and theory, its material could also be rendered and transformed as an opera or a Hollywood blockbuster in its other incarnations.

With a semblance of history, therefore, let us begin at the turn of the last century, during the late Meiji period, just three years before the Partition of Bengal in 1905, when a Japanese traveller by the name of Okakura Kakuzo landed up in my home city of Calcutta on 6 January 1902.[2] No mere tourist, he stayed on for close to nine months, travelling to different parts of India, visiting Buddhist sites, completing a pan-Asian history of Japanese art in English entitled *The Ideals of the East*, and drafting a xenophobic tract tentatively entitled *We are One*. While keeping himself busy, Okakura also found time to socialize intimately with the cultural circle of the Tagores, Bengal's most illustrious landowning family with Renaissance aspirations and achievements. Poetry, drama, music, philosophy, linguistics, mathematics, fashion, and, above all, social reform of ritual-bound orthodox Hinduism were merely some of the radical, if not iconoclastic, interventions of this altogether striking family. Tellingly, their very branding as outcaste Pirali Brahmins, whose ancestors had lost their caste status ostensibly for smelling beef cooked by Muslims, contributed towards their openness to experimentation and engagement with the world.[3]

Thus far Rabindranath, the fourteenth child and *wunderkind* in a large family, had not become a 'world poet' (*visva kobi*),[4] even though he had already distinguished himself through collections of poems, plays, and essays on social and political themes. When Okakura visited Calcutta in 1902, Tagore was a prolific composer of songs, though he had not yet contributed some of his most intensely patriotic songs to the *swadeshi* movement, revolving around the boycott of foreign goods and indigenous enterprise, precipitated by the colonial government's notorious 'divide and rule' policy.[5] In addition to his literary experiments, Tagore had also started his Brahmacharya Ashram for alternative education and holistic living in the village of Santiniketan, which gradually metamorphosed into a university with a utopian vision based on the interculturality of the universe: *yatra visva bhabati ekanidam*, 'where the world finds its home in one nest'.

Before Okakura came to India, it would be safe to assume that he might never have heard of Tagore's experiments in education or his more radical interventions in the Bengali language. Instead of this relatively unknown poet called Tagore, Okakura had come to India in search of a far more internationally recognized luminary, arguably the leading god-man of that time, Swami Vivekananda (1863–1902), whose discourse at the Parliament of World Religions in Chicago in 1893 had inspired a worldwide following of disciples. It was one such spiritual seeker in globetrotting cosmopolitan circles, a wealthy American woman named Josephine MacLeod, who, while passing through Tokyo, had initiated Okakura's meeting with Vivekananda in Calcutta. Indeed, the top priority of Okakura's unstated Indian agenda was to invite Vivekananda to Japan for yet another conference on world religions with a more specific inter-Asian focus.

This invitation fell through because Vivekananda died in June 1902, just months after Okakura had met him in Belur and later travelled with him to Bodh Gaya, Benares, and Sarnath. Arguably, even if Vivekananda had lived, it is not certain that the Indian monk would have followed up on the Japanese invitation. Against the grain of the hagiography surrounding these two charismatic men from Asia, one should acknowledge Vivekananda's misgivings, perhaps even a trace of jealousy, regarding Okakura's mesmerizing control over his most ardent disciple, Margaret Noble, whom he had renamed Sister Nivedita (1867–1911). A fiery Irish nationalist, she had relocated to Bengal in 1898 and had promptly converted to Hinduism and joined the Ramakrishna Order, advocating a united India with religio-nationalist fervour. Under Okakura's influence, however, she seemed to be more enamoured of the pan-Asian unity underlying Oriental art, a unity that she emphatically endorsed in her preface to Okakura's *The Ideals of the East*, which was completed in Calcutta under her editorial supervision.

It appears that Vivekananda nurtured some scepticism about Okakura's spiritual affinities and once asked his Japanese compatriot, 'Will you join us?', whereupon Okakura responded with due candour, 'No, I haven't finished with this world yet'.[6] Worldliness was Okakura's natural state, even though he was apotheosized as some kind of a spiritual revolutionary. On cue, as it were, he performed this role with theatrical aplomb, playing to the gallery with consummate ease. From a vivid first-contact reminiscence provided by Surendranath Tagore, Rabindranath's nephew, we have a glimpse of Okakura's histrionics at a party held in the residence of the American Consulate in Calcutta:

My first impression of him is still vivid. Seated by our hostess was a sturdy figure of medium height, clad in a black silk *kimono*. ...In his hand was a bamboo-and-paper fan, decorated with a sprig of foliage done in sepia, and on his feet were Japanese cloth socks and grass sandals. His face was more of Chinese than Japanese type, with heavy eyelids and spare moustache, but his complexion was ruddy. He sat at ease, with a profound gravity of expression, incessantly smoking Egyptian cigarettes.[7]

At a later point in the evening, it appears that Okakura disappeared into the verandah, ostensibly for some more meditative chain-smoking. Then, Nivedita, with a 'mysterious air', beckoned Surendranath to enter the secluded space where Okakura offered his young Bengali friend a cigarette on the open palm of his hand, while revealing, Houdini-like, an entire tin of cigarettes tucked into one of the capacious sleeves of his kimono. He then fixed Surendranath with a gaze and asked abruptly: 'What are you thinking of doing for your country?' Unable to disguise his unabashed upper-class *bhadralok* (gentrified) diffidence, Surendranath equivocated only to be reprimanded by the older man on the 'despondency' of Bengali youth. This was followed by Okakura recalling an incident from his own childhood in Japan, when 'hearing sounds of altercation in the next room, he peeped through a chink to find the headless trunk of his uncle still in a sitting posture, the arteries of his neck spurting fountains of blood'.[8]

The archival evidence of this samurai story is dubious, but, clearly, it does not stop Okakura from playing up his heroic past, and getting away with it. No samurai himself, though hailing from a somewhat undistinguished samurai family, whose father had settled for the silk business in the boom town of Yokohama before seeking a career as an innkeeper in Tokyo, Okakura (whose first name was Kakuzo, which literally means 'corner warehouse')[9] was far from being a samurai hero. Indeed, he could be more accurately described at this point in his life as a self-exiled Orientalist art critic and historian, who was in search of himself as much as he was in search of the East. Cynics would add that he was a man facing a midlife crisis in search of a job.

It is true that when Okakura came to Calcutta, he was hailed as the founder of a radical art school called the Nihon Bijutsuin, which advocated a Japanese neo-traditionalist art that was 'true to Self' and which celebrated 'not the thing as it was, but the infinitude it suggested'.[10] Contrary to Bengali hagiography, however, Nihon Bijutsuin was not the summation of his artistic vision, the Oriental equivalent of Merton Abbey commemorating the Arts and Crafts movement of William Morris, as Sister Nivedita had rhapsodized, but a substitute for a failed career. Indeed, even today it is not sufficiently acknowledged among Okakura's admirers in Bengal that he had been forced to resign from all his previous appointments by 1898. Officially, by that time, he was *persona non grata*, ostracized by the establishment that had nurtured him. This could be described as a classic case of a quick burnout following a meteoric career.

Around ten years earlier, in January 1889, Okakura had been appointed the leading curator of the Japanese section in the Imperial Museum of Japan, which was followed by yet another prestigious post in October 1890, when he became the principal of the Tokyo Bijutsu Gakko (Tokyo School of Fine Arts). The fact that Okakura was just twenty-eight years old at that time makes his achievement all the more astonishing. Indeed, by the time he had graduated from the Imperial University of Tokyo, Okakura had already become an advisor for the state in matters relating to education, art policy, and the deciphering and registration of 'national treasures', which he investigated along with his former mentor and professor of philosophy, the American Orientalist Ernest Fenollosa (1853–1908). As the founder of Japan's leading art magazine *Kokka*, Okakura also shaped the discipline of Japanese art history at its most formative levels. Complementing his eloquent lectures on Japanese art history, he gradually established himself as a curator, not least through his spectacular design for the interior of the Japanese pavilion at the World Fair in Chicago in 1893. This was just one indication of Okakura's status as a cosmopolitan superstar.[11]

Then, around 1896, with the death of his father, when he enigmatically assumed the honorific pseudonym (*gagou*) of Tenshin or 'Heart of Heaven', Okakura's career began to fall apart. Now he would be better known as Okakura Tenshin rather than Okakura Kakuzo. Gradually, his drinking got out of hand; he continued to flaunt a scandalous affair with the estranged wife of his former boss, Kuki Ryuichi, from the Ministry of Education; he alienated his own family, and was generally irresponsible in running institutions. While he could take pride in the fact that a large number of his former associates had followed him to Nihon Bijutsuin, notably the painters Yokoyama Taikan and Hishida Shunso, Okakura's new institution was a shaky enterprise. Rather than attempting to build it with the liberal financial support of his rich American friend, William Sturgis Bigelow, a prodigious collector of Japanese art and a patron of the Museum of Fine Arts, Boston, Okakura chose to opt out of this task by retreating to India. The East was already his career, but within a year it became clear that this career would have to be built elsewhere, not in Japan (where he had burnt his boats), nor in India (which was, at best, a refreshing detour in his journey). Okakura's career would be built at the Chinese and Japanese department of the Museum of Fine Arts, Boston, where he served as an Advisor between 1904–9, and as a curator from 1910 onwards till his premature death in 1913.

It was in February 1913, a cold and bleak month in Boston, that Okakura met his friend Rabindranath for the second, and the last time, in his life. Following the poet's visit, Okakura is said to have felt a 'sudden loneliness',[12] on which we will speculate later in the book. Moving back to Japan for the last months of his life, Okakura died of Bright's disease, which he has described with a droll sense of humour as 'the usual complaint of the twentieth century... I have eaten things in various parts of the globe — too varied for the hereditary notions of my stomach and kidneys'.[13] The nationalist had clearly mellowed, if not succumbed, to the pleasures of global cosmopolitanism.

What of Tagore? Between 1904–13, while Okakura was jet-setting around the world as Asia's foremost curator, the relatively unknown Bengali poet Rabindranath was dividing his time between building his experimental school in Santiniketan on a shoestring budget and writing incessantly, even while craving his nomadic yearning for travel. At a personal level, these years were devastating, because the poet had to deal with an almost macabre series of four deaths in his family. Between 1902–7 he lost his wife, his second daughter, his father, and younger son. These deaths corresponded with Tagore's immersion in the swadeshi movement, followed by a gradual withdrawal from its politics, and subsequent introspection on the possibilities of a universal self, transcending the sectarian demands of caste, community, and nation. This vision was crystallized in the writing of his monumental novel *Gora*, serialized and eventually published in its entirety in 1910. Arguably the most powerful national allegory of the Indian subcontinent, it remains deeply pertinent in an age of growing fundamentalism and communal conflict. *Gora* was followed by Rabindranath's most intense offering of songs to the *jiban-debata* ('life-god'), *Gitanjali* which, even in a perfunctory English translation in 1912, so enamoured the poets W.B. Yeats and Ezra Pound, among a growing numbers of international admirers, that Tagore was nominated for nothing less than the Nobel Prize.

Barely two months after Okakura died in September 1913, Rabindranath Tagore, a poet with an unpronounceable name from Bengal, was awarded the Nobel Prize for Literature, the first Asian to win this honour. Now, indeed, he was a superstar, if not a world celebrity, who had to keep reminding his international audiences that he was essentially a poet. Three years later, in 1916, Tagore visited Japan for the first time in his life and delivered his famous lectures on — or, more precisely, against — nationalism. There were over 20,000 cheering fans to meet him when he arrived at Tokyo Station, but when he returned to Japan on his way back from the United States later that year, there were two people to greet him at the port.[14] Something had obviously gone wrong in his address to the Japanese people; the poet had touched a nerve, as he always did, fearlessly, and with an uncompromising need to tell the truth.

I often wonder: had Okakura been alive, how would these lectures have affected their friendship? Would it have been possible for Tagore to modulate his virulent anti-nationalism against Okakura's closet nationalism, if not scarcely disguised Japanese imperialism? Or would a tacit avoidance of politics have been the only means of sustaining their friendship? Indeed, could their friendship have survived the politics of their times?

On these questions, I will interrupt this sketch, which, as I had indicated earlier, leaves many gaps in the intersection of strikingly individual lives, cutting across three very different cosmopolitan cities: Tokyo, Calcutta, Boston. One such gap needs to be filled, however parenthetically, because it plays a crucial element in this narrative. When Okakura returned to India in 1912 for a brief visit, Rabindranath was not around, but the now somewhat world-weary Japanese traveller had come into contact with the Bengali widow and poet, Priyambada Devi Banerjee (1871–1935), with whom he exchanged love-letters almost till the last day of his life. I had indicated the possibilities of an opera in my early comments on the narrative, and later in this book I hope not to disappoint the reader in addressing this dimension of long-distance love, from Boston to Calcutta to Izura and back to Calcutta.

For the moment, let me acknowledge that among the motifs that resonate most strongly for me in the shaping of this particular narrative—nationalism, cosmopolitanism and friendship—it is the spectre of Asia that is the most haunting, and indeed, the most difficult to demystify. It is through Asia that the motifs of this narrative are most intricately linked, serving to fuel its thought and content. For all the problems in dealing with the construction of Asia—its legacy of illusions and shattered ideals is the underlying leitmotif of this book—there was something palpable about it, which brought Tagore and Okakura together. Without Asia, they might not have met.

In 1929, on his third visit to Japan, Tagore openly acknowledged the mediation of Asia in a moving posthumous tribute to Okakura, which he addressed to the Indo-Japanese Association.[15] (It is telling, indeed, that Tagore never once mentioned Okakura's name in his public lectures on nationalism in Japan during his 1916 visit. An enigma that we shall examine later in the book.) However, in 1929, farther removed in time, Tagore invoked Okakura as the 'voice of the East' whose tumultuous effect on 'the young men of those days', including the early proponents of 'the art movement in Bengal', could still be felt (604). 'And I assure you, my friends,' Tagore went on to say, 'that this meeting had the effect of drawing the heart of our people in Bengal towards your country [Japan] more than any other fact that has happened since then, or before that time. It was that personal relationship, personal influence, in which he represented the best of Japan' (605). Openly acknowledging that it was 'that great man' Okakura, his 'intimate friend' who had introduced him to both Japan and China, Tagore then proceeded to rhapsodize about the future possibilities of that early meeting: '[I]f this association of culture and sympathy is allowed to grow, then some day will be developed, not merely national culture, national minds, but a continental mind of Asia, greatly needed and long waiting to be revealed' (606).

With these remarks, the sketch that I have presented here can be temporarily forgotten as we focus on the spectres of Asia that haunt this book.

1

Asia

WHAT IS ASIA?

'A continental mind of Asia?' Tagore's construct has a different premise from the more banal proposition that I first faced in geography class in elementary school, when I encountered Asia as a continent, a mass of land, one among six, each of which had to be marked with a different colour. This land seemed to have no mind; it was a mere territory. Even at that level, Asia posed a problem because it was a hopelessly large continent that was almost impossible to map. It resisted the most rudimentary art of sketching. While its eastern extremities (at least, from the location of India) were clear enough, its western borders were more nebulous. Indeed, the reverse could be said for Europe, which is almost conjoined like a Siamese twin to its Asian other half. They are bound somewhere in the middle. While Europe has attempted to bureaucratize its eastern borders within the homogenization of the European Union, despite problematic exclusions such as Turkey, Asia's attempts to push its boundaries westwards towards Afghanistan, Iran, and Iraq are fraught with charges of expansionism and coercive inclusion.

Today, with the growing disenchantment surrounding Area Studies, despite some recent attempts to salvage its historical and linguistic expertise against postmodern charges of territorial essentialization and uninflected nationalism,[1] there are more sustained attempts to view Asia outside of the strictures of the continent. While the collusion of academic and Cold War politics is increasingly being exposed through the deconstruction of categories like the Far East, Southeast Asia, and South Asia, the globalizing advantages in upholding so-called 'regional' configurations of power like ASEAN (the Association of Southeast Asian Nations) continue to be strongly upheld. As it becomes lucrative for new partners in trade and commerce to enter such caucuses, with mutually beneficial strategic partnerships in search of free trade zones, it is likely that these 'regional' configurations will become more diffused. To what extent this will result in the de-ideologization of Asia is a question that lies beyond the scope of this book, which is more concerned with the ways in which the cultural geography of Asia was envisioned at the beginning of the twentieth century.

In her preface to Okakura's *The Ideals of the East* (1903), Nivedita had specifically pitched her Asian nationalist rhetoric against a mere juxtaposition of geographical regions. Even Bengal, the most intense repository of the swadeshi movement, had to be seen as a part of 'United India', which was in turn part of the larger expanse of Asia. This Asia was less a political entity than a metaphysical and spiritual realm, transcending the cultures of distinct histories and nations. In envisioning this realm, Nivedita acknowledged the seminal guidance of Okakura, who represented Asia not as 'the congeries of geographical fragments', but rather as a 'united living organism, each part dependent on all the others, the whole breathing a single complex life'.[2] While the word 'congeries' suggests an agglomeration, a mere heap of scattered elements, the cultural geography of Asia, as envisioned by Okakura, was an imaginary unity of shared ideals.

Countering the notion of a mere continent, therefore, this advocacy of Asia as an Idea, and more specifically, as a summation of Ideals, runs against the received wisdom on the origins of Asia as a name and sign. The philosopher Naoki Sakai encapsulates this wisdom succinctly when he reminds us that 'the name Asia originated outside Asia'.[3] It is a 'word' invented by Europeans in order to 'distinguish Europe from its eastern others' (213). Without positing Asia, Europe could never have marked itself as a 'distinct and distinguishable unity' (213). Highlighting the postcolonial truism that 'Asia could never be conscious of itself before it was invaded by the West', Sakai spells out a disturbing truth, which, in all probability would have been anathema to Okakura (and perhaps, to Tagore as well): 'the defeat [of Asia] is registered in the genealogy of the name itself' (215).

Rejecting any notion of an authentic Asian self, or a naturalized collective identity based on 'some presumably immutable properties of a person or a group,' (235) Sakai is willing to acknowledge some notion of Asian 'self-consciousness' only with the advent of European colonization. Prior to that time it would seem that Asia did not exist. Echoing the views of the Japanese Sinologist Takeuchi Yoshimi (1910–77), whose name is often too rashly associated with Okakura, despite his far more ambivalent and self-critical reading of pan-Asianism, Sakai emphasizes: 'Only through the acknowledgement of its lost autonomy, of its dependence on the West, or only in the mirror of the West, so to say, could Asia reflectively acquire its civilizational, cultural, ethnic, or national self-consciousness' (215).

Against the unequivocal enunciation of this position, one is compelled to ask how the prehistory of Asia, the history preceding the age of colonization, can be most appropriately named. If Asia comes into being only with modernity—and its resistance to modernity only further enhances its inscription within the delusions of world history monopolized by Europe—then how does one name Asia prior to that time? Can the prehistory of Asia exist only under the firm erasure of its name? This is a hard question that historians and philosophers of history are compelled to tackle, rather than to succumb to the notion of an always already existing Asia whose origins can never be quite erased in the traces of its ever-evolving, omnipresent history.

Yet another, somewhat more subtle trap, would be to succumb to utopian unselfconsciousness by which Ashis Nandy, for instance, posits 'an Asia which does not probably even see itself as Asia'.[4] While critically aware of Asia's historical genesis through colonization, Nandy cannot quite suspend the redemptionist possibilities of the intrinsic civilizational values embedded in the very ethos of Asia; so much so, that this Asia becomes a messianic repository of resources for saving the West. In an almost atavistic register, appealing in its rhetoric of inclusivity, yet territorial in its claim over an indigenous Asian identity, Nandy elaborates:

We might even be holding as part of a cultural gene-bank aspects of traditional Western concepts of nature (as in St Francis of Assissi or William Blake) and social relationships (as in Ralph Emerson and Henry Thoreau) to which the West itself might some day have to return through Asia.[5]

The organicist and biological underpinnings of the metaphor of the 'gene-bank' contribute to the notion of Asia as some kind of a living reality, which displaces the crucial notion that it is as much of a construction as the so-called West. As for 'returning through Asia', ostensibly to find one's authentic self, this is an Orientalist trope that continues to haunt readings of Asia today.

There have been other ways in which Asia's signification has been suspended, yet problematized, in less utopian registers. Rejecting any association of an 'already existing Asia', some cultural analysts have preferred to shift its meaning into the future, towards an 'Asia that is to be', even while acknowledging that Asia was, and continues to be, 'a synonym for the oppressed'.[6] In this sense, Asia can only meaningfully exist in a dialogic and processual mode through a series of connections between different cultures, not necessarily centred in Asia. In a more political register, other critics have called attention to the 'Asia within', or more precisely, 'the other within',[7] the Asia that exists through the filter of 'cultural difference' but which is rendered invisible and implicitly denied basic rights. Koreans and other foreign residents in Japan, for instance, may be indigenized, but they remain othered. In this context, one needs to emphasize the critical truism that Asia is not merely othered by the West; it is othered within its own boundaries.

While the process of 'othering' minorities in the Indian subcontinent has a long history, culminating in recent communal riots and genocides that bear a painful resemblance to the religious sectarian violence surrounding the Partition, the point is that it has never been articulated around the cultural supremacy or preservation of an 'Asian' identity. If anything, with the formation of extremist

Hindu organizations like the Rashtriya Swayamsevak Sangh by the late 1920s, the authentication of Indianness has been established primarily through the assertion of upper-caste brahmanical Hindu cultural values. Within this mindset, 'Asia' is as much of a *mleccha* (barbarian) as any other non-Hindu foreigner.

In contrast, the foreigner in Japan has been marked and positioned over the centuries against a complex series of assertions affirming Japan's isolation from the rest of the world, and its subsequent nationalism and claim over preserving an authentic Asian identity. By the late nineteenth century, for instance, when Okakura was already at the peak of his career and in close social contact with American patrons of Japanese art, there were heated debates on the issue of 'mixed residence' (*naichi zakkyo*).[8] By 1889, the official scholar of the state, Inoue Tetsujiro (1856–1944), who later wrote a commentary on the Imperial Rescript on Education, had specifically warned against the cohabitation of Japanese and foreigners, following the withdrawal of earlier sanctions negotiated with colonial powers. With the revised treaties, foreigners were free to live and trade anywhere in the country, without restrictions. Based on the alarmist premise that the entire world was a potential enemy, Inoue revealed an almost pathological inferiority complex by speculating that the Japanese would not survive foreign competition on account of their smaller cranial capacity in relation to the brains of Europeans.[9] The fact that he upheld this position on specifically 'scientific' grounds, as opposed to the 'ignorance' underlying the earlier plea to 'expel the barbarians', merely reinforces his racist insularity. For Inoue, 'the only place in the whole world where the Japanese can live is Japan and Japan alone... [I]f we allow foreigners to live with us, the people of Europe and America will enter Japan and will take possession of our land.'[10]

The paranoia underlying this inferiority complex deepens when one considers that it was possible to debate the consequences of living with the foreigner, but, at the same time, it was perfectly justifiable for Japan to wage war against its Asian neighbours. Even as the debate around mixed residence abated with the victory of Japan in the Russo-Japanese War of 1904–5, the fear of the foreigner was replaced by a more systematic demeaning of his or her status. Thus, after the war, there was a new abusive category to designate the 'half-Japanese' (*han-Nihonjin*), which was later replaced by the more chilling neutrality of 'non-nationals' (*hikokumin*).[11] More terrifying evidence of anti-Asian Japanese xenophobia is to be found in the massacre of over 2,000 Koreans and 400 Chinese residents in Japan following the Great Kanto Earthquake of 1923: the victims of genocide accused of sedition.[12] Those singled out for slaughter were killed on the basis of 'their ability or inability to speak Japanese'.[13] This is a classic communal predicament faced by minorities even today: damned if you speak the language, damned if you don't. One way or the other, with or without credentials of belongingness, you are a foreigner and fit to be killed.

When one confronts the historical density of how such constructions of foreigners vis-à-vis Asians have mutated over time, contributing to different forms of xenophobia and racism today, it becomes almost fatuous to view Asia outside of national, ethnic, linguistic, and religious differences. Even so, that is precisely the plea put forward by Naoki Sakai in his eminently postmodern suggestion that the fluidity of the very distinctions between Asia and its others should be enhanced. For Sakai, a normative definition of 'Asian' should be applied 'whenever we find some effect of social adversity or a trait of alienation from the alleged ideal image of a Westerner in that person, regardless of his or her physiognomy, linguistic heritage, claimed ethnicity or habitual characteristics'.[14] In a gesture that would have to be considered hopelessly cosmopolitan, Sakai suggests that the atavistic binding of 'We Asians' should be substituted by the open invitation of 'You Asians'. At the risk of being rejected, this vocative should be addressed to those who 'customarily fashion themselves as Westerners', in order to 'break through the putative exclusiveness of our cultural, civilizational and racial identity'.[15] As in many such postmodern reversals of fixed categories operating at a purely theoretical level, the actual task of shifting identitarian constructions leaves a lot to be desired at levels of social and political practice.

This book is not concerned with contemporary readings of being 'Asian', or of jettisoning the category of 'Asia' altogether, or of foisting it on others. It engages more specifically with the cultural history of the early modernist period when 'Asia' had an undeniable liberatory resonance that it does not have today, linked to the first glimmers of Independence in India through failed insurrections such as the swadeshi movement, and the more self-confident leadership of Asia provided by the ideologues of the late Meiji period in Japan. In this period of emergent nationalisms, there are different things being said about Asia even when they appear to be saying the same things. Indeed, in the echoes of similar sounding tropes and sentiments in pan-Asian discourse, there are also refractions and distortions. Even as Tagore and Okakura met through Asia, they constructed it in radically different idioms, and on substantially different grounds. At a discursive level, this book attempts to elaborate on these idioms and grounds in which significantly different imaginaries of Asia are embodied, shared, and set against one another.

Following these general insights on the conflicting genealogies and epistemologies of Asia, it would be useful now to concretize the discussion by focusing on Okakura's pan-Asianism through a reading of his seminal texts in relation to his curatorial practice. Even as his Asian ideals are asserted with uncomplicated bravado, we shall see how they are submerged in the deceptions of an insufficiently acknowledged, if febrile form of Japanese nationalism.

One Asia

Predictably, Okakura makes a grand entrance in this narrative, upholding the magisterial discourse of his opening paragraph of *The Ideals of the East*, which has an uncanny capacity to defy any number of deconstructive readings through the sheer eloquence of its rhetoric. Against my will, this obligatory beginning has to be heard one more time before we begin to unearth its somewhat ignominious subtext:

Asia is one. The Himalayas divide, only to accentuate, two mighty civilizations, the Chinese with its communism of Confucius, and the Indian with its individualism of the Vedas. But not even the snowy barriers can interrupt for one moment that broad expanse of love for the Ultimate and the Universal, which is the common thought-inheritance of every Asiatic race, enabling them to produce the great religions of the world, and distinguishing them from those maritime peoples of the Mediterranean and the Baltic, who love to dwell on the Particular, and to search out the means, not the end, of life.[16]

The canonical opening sentence of this aria-like paragraph almost flaunts its non-negotiable, axiomatic truth: 'Asia is one.' Perhaps, it would have been less provocative if Okakura had declared that Asia is three, or at least three-in-one, because his entire discourse rests on a triangular structure of three 'mighty' Asian civilizations: India, China, and the as-yet-unnamed Japan.

Okakura seemed to be fond of triangles. His artistic pedagogy, for instance, could be summed up in what has been described as the 'magnetic triangle',[17] where three crucial elements — tradition, nature, and originality — are closely intersected, with no one element dominating over another. In Okakura's Asian Triangle, however, there is no such inner dynamism, with Japan positioned at the apex of the triangle, embodying in its artistic heritage the synthesis of Indian religion (represented by the 'individualism of the Vedas') and Chinese communitarian ethics (represented, somewhat misleadingly, by the 'communism of Confucius'). Unlike the 'magnetic triangle' of Okakura's aesthetic model, where tradition, nature, and originality impact on each other, there is no such interaction in Okakura's civilizational model. Within its hierarchical framing, the civilizations of India and China are primary sources of knowledge, but, in the final analysis, rather like tributaries of a river, they flow into the mainstream of Japanese art, where Asia in all its diversity is 'protected' and 'restored'.

There are at least two deceptions in Okakura's rhetorical structure of Asia that need to be exposed at the very outset of the discussion. At one level, he simply plays into a tenacious trope that 'Japan is and is not a part of Asia'; a trope that Tessa Morris-Suzuki has correctly traced in Fukuzawa Yukichi's slogan *Datsu-a Ron*, which I have examined earlier. In attempting to 'escape from Asia', Fukuzawa would seem to suggest that Asia is 'something already external or at least separated from Japan by some dividing membrane'.[18] In this sense, Asia is more of an 'environment' than an 'inextricable part' of

Japan, thereby enabling Japan to 'leave or return to it without doing violence to its own national integrity'.[19] While Japan's separation from Asia in *The Ideals of the East* is not quite so explicit, Okakura reveals his position more candidly in a later text when he affirms that '*we* must regard Asia as the true source of *our* inspiration. *She* it was who transmitted to *us* her ancient culture, and planted the seed of *our* regeneration.'[20] Whereas this is an obvious tribute to Asia as the repository of rejuvenating sources, in contrast to Fukuzawa's dismissal of Asia as the site of desuetude and stasis, both constructions are premised on an implicit difference between 'them' (Asia) and 'us' (Japan').

The second deception of *The Ideals of the East* lies in the truncated title by which this pan-Asian text is most widely known, acquiring a quasi-philosophical status. In all fairness to Okakura, the original title of the book is more emphatically qualified: *The Ideals of the East with Special Reference to the Art of Japan*. The subtitle is what the book is essentially about, with the ideals of the East constituting, at best, the prologue and epilogue of the narrative. 'Asia', it could be argued, is at best a wrapping for the 'Japanese art' addressed at length in the book. While the idea of 'wrapping' lends itself to postmodern figuration, it is perhaps more accurately read in this context as a strategic means of empowering a series of rhetorical impressions of Japanese art through the ages. The prologue and epilogue in which 'Asia' resounds with grandiloquence elevate Okakura's rewritten lecture notes on Japanese art history within a framework of pan-Asian philosophy.

Let us turn now to *The Ideals of the East* in greater detail to expose some of its assumptions. Against the 'broad expanse of love for the Ultimate and the Universal, which is the common thought-inheritance of every Asiatic race' (13), Okakura spells out the credentials of Japan's unquestioned leadership in Asia:

1. Foremost among all criteria, Okakura emphasizes the mixed 'Indo-Tartaric' *blood* of the 'Yamato race', which, paradoxically, justifies the purity of Japan's claim to represent all Asian races (14–15). In this mixed 'heritage',

there are infusions of sources from other gene-pools, including the 'Akkadians', the 'Turkish hordes' who settled in the 'Indo-Pacific', and 'Aryan emigrants who pushed through the Kashmirian passes, to be lost amongst the Turanian tribes', among other nebulous migratory groups. Significantly, there is no place in Okakura's cultural genealogy for the aboriginal Ainu, who were driven away by the Yamato race, which in turn absorbed other ethnic groups to consolidate 'the Empire of the Rising Sun'. Tellingly, the specific aboriginal genealogy of the Ainu (still a source of contention in contemporary Japan) is excised from Okakura's vision of 'One Asia'. The indigenous is clearly alien, and not fit to be nationalized or Asianized.

2. Japan's leadership of Asia, for Okakura, also rests on the undisputed fact that it remains 'an unconquered race' with 'unbroken sovereignty', unlike the colonized states of India and China (15). Okakura substantiates its *sovereignty* on grounds of the 'tenacity' of the Japanese race, which not only ensures its political independence, but which has the power to 'preserve' Chinese and Indian 'ideals' even after they have been ostensibly abandoned by their mother countries. Clearly, Japan's sovereignty over the rest of Asia is not imposed because it rests on the belief that Japan is the 'real *repository* of the *trust* of Asiatic thought and culture' (15, emphases mine). Needless to say, Okakura provides no historical evidence of this trust; it is sublimely assumed.

3. The most concrete of Okakura's metaphoric verifications of Japan's leadership is linked to his specific description of Japan as 'a *museum* of Asiatic civilization' (16, my emphasis). Of course, this pithy statement has to be followed by a more grandiose elaboration in a spiritual register. Japan, as Okakura emphasizes, is 'more than a museum, because the singular genius of the race leads it to dwell on all phases of the ideals of the past, in that spirit of living Advaitism, which welcomes the new without losing the old' (16). While the reference to Advaitism is not substantiated in the rest of

the text, it contributes a certain Oriental aura of profundity, which at one level can be read as an appropriation of Hindu spirituality.[21] In a neat interpretation provided in a footnote, Okakura claims that 'this state of not being two' (Advaita) enables 'all truth' to be 'discoverable in any single differentiation, the whole universe involved in every detail' (128). In *The Ideals of the East*, however, it is Japan that embodies the state of 'living Advaitism'; Okakura has nothing to say about the origins and continuing legacies and differing interpretations of Advaita in India itself, where it is presumed to be dead as a philosophy. Once again, it is Japan that has the singular capacity to interrelate the 'old' and the 'new' in its refiguration of Asia's wisdom.

THE NATION AS MUSEUM

Returning to Okakura's cogent description of Japan as 'a museum of Asiatic civilization', I would now like to focus on his arresting analogy of the Nation as Museum—a museum that could be more accurately described as the Japanese Museum of Asian Civilization. At one level, this metaphor is grounded in Okakura's pioneering role as an art historian of Japan, and arguably, the most influential international curator of 'Asia' at the turn of the twentieth century. At another level, the metaphor is a reminder of how Japan continues to be invoked today as a 'living museum' in broad civilizational terms, beyond the disciplinary regime of art history. One such fervent plea for transforming Japan as a 'living museum of the world' rests on the assumption that 'if the Japanese can establish Japan's identity as a space in which many civilizations coexist', then it can turn into a 'mediating force activating the diverse cultures of the world'.[22] This privileging of Japan's capacities of mediation within the framework of a 'uniquely universal Japanese civilization',[23] is indeed a troubling sign of how its leadership of Asia continues to be assumed and reinvented.

In *The Ideals of the East*, in which the metaphor of nation as museum is first articulated, it could be argued that Okakura's text is most effectively read as a museumization of the history of Japan through the periodization of its art in an unbroken chronology extending over centuries. For all his disdain for the 'dissecting knife of the chronologist' (16), Okakura submits to this regimen with poetic flair, transforming the disjunctive linearity of chronology into a continuum of time, 'clear and continuous as a mala, a rosary of crystals' (131). Tellingly, Okakura's periodization of Japanese art and history forms a perfect continuum, with the Asuka period leading inexorably to the contemporary Meiji via the Nara, Heian, Fujiwara, Kamakura, Ashikaga, Toyotomi, and Tokugawa periods.

All of these periods are evoked through artistic images and attributes rather than historical facts. Thus, in one section of the book, while romanticizing the 'tenacity' of the Yamato race and its 'art-instincts', we are exposed to the 'delicacy of Fujiwara culture', the 'martial ardour of Kamakura, which tolerates the gorgeous pageantry of Toyotomi', and the 'austere purity of the Ashikagas' (121–2). Towards the end of the book, we are subjected to yet another round of epithets, but this time the Fujiwara period is characterized by 'unmeasured devotion', Kamakura is marked by its 'heroic reaction', while Ashikaga remains true to the 'knighthood' of 'stern enthusiasm and lofty abstinence' (132). In a more impressionistic section in the book, the different ages and their corresponding aesthetics are evoked through colours: 'now gleaming in the amber twilight of idealistic Nara, now glowing with the crimson autumn of Fujiwara, again losing itself in the green sea waves of Kamakura, or shimmering in the silver moonshine of Ashikaga' (114).

Underlying this picturesque mode of what could be described as 'catalogue writing' today, one has to assume that there was some very precise historical knowledge informing these nebulous and conflicting descriptions. The point is that Okakura did not intend his work to be assessed on scholarly grounds, even while it would be presumptuous to assume that he was anything other than the master Sensei. Rather, he was more interested in projecting certain 'ideals' of Japanese art to a predominantly Western audience, both within their specific periods, and through its evolution. Most critically, this pseudo-Hegelian evolution of art, which at some level has been too rashly attributed to his reading of philosophy under Fenollosa's tutelage, was totally coterminous in all its phases with the 'evolution of the nation' which, as Okakura affirms in the epilogue, is 'clear and unconfused, like that of a single personality' (132).

While the listing of 'ages' would seem to be a reductive tool in the mapping of art history today, it was a radical innovation in Japan around the late 1880s. Indeed, as the principal of Tokyo Bijutsu Gakko, Okakura lectured extensively in Tokyo on Japanese art history from 1890 onwards, outlining chronological narratives of painting and sculpture from 'ancient' (*kodai*) through 'medieval' (*chuko*) to 'recent' (*kindai*) periods.[24] These categories themselves were responses to the disciplinary demands and codes of Western art history and curatorial practice, which were impacting on Japan at that time. For example, the word for 'art' (*bijutsu*) had come into being as early as 1873 to distinguish 'fine art', such as sculpture and painting, from other art objects, specifically to conform to the criteria of the Vienna World Exposition (1873) in which Japanese art was featured.[25] Without discriminating between artistic categories in an academic mode, *The Ideals of the East* clearly focuses on 'art' (*bijutsu*) in all its aesthetic layering, with the nation rendered as beautifully as possible without any submission to the demands of social utility or populism.

In additition to the organic evolution of Japanese art, Okakura prioritized a listing of its 'masterpieces', each masterpiece representing the essence of each period. In the process, a hierarchy was built into his assessment of each age, revealing assumptions of taste and aesthetics based on authentic knowledge and indigenous expertise. The unspoken assumption here was that such knowledge and expertise were in the long run the only ones worth accessing. European assessments of 'Asian art' were intrinsically unreliable in their derivative and second-hand exposure to the 'real' sources of aesthetic illumination. For all his advocacy of modernist values like 'individuality' and 'originality', Okakura legislated the criteria on the basis of which Japanese art had to be *authenticated* for the rest of the world through the mediation of experts like himself.

Significantly, even as Okakura was evolving his own criteria of art history within the context of Japan, the museological practices of the West were themselves passing through a transition at conceptual, architectural, and curatorial levels. When Okakura joined the Department of Chinese and Japanese Art at the Museum of Fine Arts, Boston, as an advisor in 1904, there was a significant shift from the earlier South Kensington model of displaying art according to 'material and techniques so that the public could be instructed in design'.[26] Rejecting this random assemblage of objects, the new mode of display favoured an arrangement of art according to 'culture and date rather than by material'. Most important of all was the 'primacy' given to the 'masterpiece', appropriately lit and displayed in 'small permanent galleries'. All these positions were clearly asserted in the polemical stance adopted by one of the officials of the museum, Matthew S. Prichard, who railed against the 'indiscriminate' display of all the museum's holdings: 'The public does not look at Greek vases. The public does not look at Japanese pottery. The public does not look at any long series of small objects' (145, all caps in original).[27] Almost in total congruence with Okakura's view, the 'masterpiece' was upheld over the collection at large, and the somewhat anonymous 'public' was replaced by a more aesthetic notion of the individual spectator.

I insert these details to emphasize that there is an almost uncanny duplication of this museological model of displaying the 'masterpiece' of a single culture, essentialized through certain qualities, and Okakura's rhetorical model in *The Ideals of the East* whereby the art of Japan is *displayed* as it were for the readership of aspiring Western connoisseurs. While it could be argued that Okakura did not directly influence the curatorial innovations at the Museum of Fine Arts, Boston, the point is that he was already participating in a cross-cultural conversation with his American friends in Japan, most of whom, like William Bigelow and Ernest Fenollosa, were closely connected with the museum's developments. I would suggest in this regard that there is nothing like a conceptual rupture between how Okakura perceived Japanese art and how the Museum of Fine Arts, Boston, was in the process of re-envisioning Japan. They are part of the same episteme, in which Japan is not separated from the West any more so than the West is separated from Japan.[28] They share the same premises, and even speak the same language. Arguably, the multilingual Okakura had an epistemological advantage over his American colleagues insofar as he was in a position to play the authentic native and provide the expertise of traditional knowledge, even while packaging it for his admirers apparently on their own terms. I shall elaborate on these strategies later in the book while dealing with the capitalist underpinnings of Asian cosmopolitanism.

IMPLICIT HIERARCHIES

Shifting the discussion away from the nexus between international curatorial practice and the building of Japanese art history, let us explore some other possible analogies for the evolutionary perspective of art and the nation assumed by Okakura. Though this connection is not specifically invoked, or even suggested by Okakura, there is yet another parallel to be found in the folklore and ethnography of Yanagita Kunio (1875–1962),[29] whose normative assertions of 'Japanese culture' (*nihon bunka*) were formulated long after Okakura had died. Tellingly, and almost with a sense of *déjà vu*, there are correspondences in their respective thought processes, which ultimately converge around the notion of national exclusivism in and through their seeming openness to the diverse cultures of the nation and the world.

Briefly, Yanagita believed that while each age in Japanese history has its own culture, these specific cultures are part of the larger evolutionary process of the Japanese nation.[30] One could, therefore, speak of Kamakura culture or Meiji culture, which had their own processes of evolution, contributing cumulatively to the growth of the nation at large by transcending local and regional particularities. Yanagita was, however, increasingly troubled by the intransigence of local cultures, and over the years, developed a defensive, if not hostile stance, toward the valorization of cultural difference. Fearing the erosion of 'social cohesion' through 'the delusion that it is acceptable for a variety of different cultures to exist in the same nation at the same time',[31] Yanagita shifted his priorities towards outlining a more 'national', distinctively 'Japanese' culture, as opposed to its diverse manifestations in regional and local contexts.

According to Tessa Morris-Suzuki, Yangita's definition of culture 'slip[ped] quietly from being a description of *actual* social beliefs and practices in all their dynamic complexity, to being a description of *the beliefs and practices which must be created*'.[32] In the process, a certain prescriptiveness entered his endorsement of the normative over the empirical. However, there were interesting contradictions, if not a cut-off point, in his evolutionary understanding of culture: While ethnic groups 'possessed their own trajectory of historical evolution, within which some regions or subsections might be more "primitive" or "ancient" than others', the bottom line was that 'national trajectories were independent of one another and could not be lined up into a single linear system of human development'.[33]

Without directly engaging with this premise, it is significant how closely Okakura's aesthetics corresponded to this model. Within the framework of the nation, it was possible, and indeed, mandatory, to imagine a single evolutionary course of artistic progress. However, having arrived at a notion of national culture through local and regional trajectories, there was no attempt to compare the Japanese summation of art with that of its European counterparts. This did not, of course, stop Okakura from adopting a generally superior attitude towards the West, which was, at one level, an understandably resentful reaction to the academic European art that had been imposed in the early Meiji period. Okakura did not attempt to conceal his contempt for this 'Western imitation':

The art which reached us was European at its lowest ebb—before the *fin-de-siècle* aestheticism had redeemed its atrocities, before Delacroix had uplifted the veil of hardened academic *chiaroscuro*, before Millet and the Barbizons brought their message of light and colour, before Ruskin had interpreted the purity of pre-Raphaelite nobleness.[34]

Even as this polemic seems legitimate in the context of the Eurocentric imposition of academic standards on the sheer diversity of Japanese art traditions, the point is that Okakura did very little to revise his views on European art even when he was in a position to engage with its aesthetics and cultural politics on a more equitable basis.

Ignoring the artistic breakthroughs of the French Impressionists, for instance, Okakura did not enter the complex debates surrounding the apparent 'Japanese' affinities of Monet in his 'juxtaposition of bright primary and secondary colours', among other imagined visual correspondences, which compelled the famous French critic Theodore Duret to idealize the 'unique' qualities of the 'Japanese eye'.[35] Nor did Okakura directly participate in the polemic surrounding the European valorization of *ukiyo-e* printmakers, notably Hokusai, whose sketches were compared to 'Watteau in their elegance, to Daumier in their energy, to Goya in their fantasy, and to Eugene Delacroix in their movement'.[36] It was Okakura's American colleague Fenollosa who entered the international debate, defending the traditional Japanese masters while barely concealing his contempt for the French for upholding Hokusai, a mere 'artisan artist' whose 'vulgarity' was at best worth studying as a 'sociological phenomenon'.[37] In retrospect, it would seem that Fenollosa somewhat missed the point, because Hokusai's 'vulgarity' was being strategized by the French precisely to undermine the dominance of academic art, the very repository of mediocrity which Okakura and Fenollosa were rejecting in Japan.

While Okakura scrupulously avoided entering the international debate, he at best condescended to acknowledge that the Rimpa school in Japanese art had preceded the Impressionists by two centuries.[38] Arguably, this rewewed attention given to the Rimpa school had been initiated in Europe itself through Louis Gonse's inflected appreciation of the individual style of the painter Korin, which in its combination of 'supple, sinuous and serene' brushwork seemed to evoke the 'summit of Impressionism'.[39] As the art historian Inaga Shigemi has pointed out, it was 'the European appreciation of the Rimpa school' that led to Baron Kuki Ryuichi's endorsement of the 'decorative' aspects of the school, which was later echoed by Okakura in *The Ideals of the East*.[40] However, apart from his passing comment on the Rimpa school, Okakura made no attempt to analyse its Impressionist connections, if only to debunk them. Not only was he singularly disinterested in cross-cultural aesthetics, it almost seemed as if he was determined not to acknowledge the artistic breakthroughs of modernity in *fin-de-siècle* Europe.

When his friend and art benefactor William Bigelow, for instance, showed him a catalogue of photographs representing a Cubist exhibition, it is said that Okakura commented, 'I stretch out my mind toward [these images], I can touch nothing'.[41] These dismissals of European art, I would submit, are cursory and somewhat disingenuous given Okakura's considerable exposure to the art world represented in some of the leading museums and galleries in Europe and the United States. Yet, he strategically opted to excise all considerations of European art from his larger understanding of art, carving a niche for himself in the West as an Oriental art expert.

Tellingly, this failure to engage with the breakthroughs of European art at the turn of the century did not stop Okakura from adopting a comparative perspective within Asia itself. In *The Ideals of the East*, the comparisons are cast in a highly poetic language, where the denigration of Indian and Chinese art is so subtle that it is almost imperceptible. At one point, Okakura invokes the spirit of Fudo, an amalgam of culture and climate, in which Japan triumphs over its neighbours through its unique combination of diverse ethno-geographical elements. Many years later, the philosopher and cultural historian, Watsuji Tetsuro (1889–1960) would conceptualize his *magnum opus* on Fudo, in which 'aesthetic orientations' and 'human relationships' were naturalized.[42] Within this conceptual grid, India, represented by the monsoon climate, was destined to be oppressed by resignationism and defeat; the Middle East, represented by the desert, had no other choice but to be aggressive in the face of a hostile environment; the European Mediterranean, represented by grassland environments and a regular cycle of seasons, was more prone towards rationality. Japan alone had a specific blend of variables.[43]

In *The Ideals of the East*, Okakura skilfully camouflages his sense of Japanese cultural superiority by embedding his discourse in the grain and texture of a uniquely Japanese sense of nature. In the following passage, which I will quote at length to capture the sheer seduction of his prose, Japan is a veritable paradise:

The waters of the waving rice-fields, the variegated contours of the archipelago, so conducive to individuality, the constant play of its soft-tinted seasons, the shimmer of its silver air, the verdure of its cascaded hills, and the voice of the ocean echoing about its pine-girt shores — of all these was born that tender simplicity, that romantic purity, which so tempers the soul of Japanese art, differentiating it at once from the leaning to monotonous breadth of the Chinese, and from the tendency to overburdened richness of Indian art.[44]

Following the thick description of Japan's natural beauty, which contributes inexorably to the 'soul of Japanese art', the references to the 'monotonous breadth' and the 'overburdened richness' of Chinese and Indian art, respectively, are subtly disparaging. Even in the course of asserting the innate cultural and artistic superiority of the Japanese, Okakura is scrupulously refined, and yet, peremptory, in his artistic assessment. Nature, in this regard, is his accomplice in undermining the rest of Asia.

In his later writings, Okakura was much more assertive about declaring the artistic superiority of Japan. At a lecture delivered at the World Trade Fair in St Louis in 1904, he had vehemently affirmed: 'We feel ourselves to be the sole guardians of the art-inheritance of Asia.'[45] Indeed, the problem for Okakura, as he elaborated in *The Awakening of Japan* (1904), a nationalist defence of the ongoing Russo-Japanese War, was that 'we no longer have the benefit of a living art in China to excite our rivalry and urge us on to fresh endeavours'.[46] As for India, all that remained were lost ruins, which had already been evoked in *The Ideals of the East* through the 'crumbling stones of Bharhut and Bodh Gaya', remnants of violence that had survived the 'rough-handedness of the Hunas, the fanatical iconoclasm of the Musulman, and the unconscious vandalism of mercenary Europe'.[47] At the very peak of his self-confidence, Okakura seemed to wallow in resplendent solitude, exemplified in categorical statements such as, '*Japanese art* stands *alone* in the world'.[48] This self-opinionated verdict could be allowed to pass were it not for a chilling slippage in Okakura's rhetoric a few sentences later: '*Japan* stands *alone against* all the world.'[49] The elision in these two sentences, as represented in 'Japanese art'/'Japan', and 'alone'/'alone against', reveals some of the central tensions in Okakura's conflation of art and politics, solitude and exclusivity.

THE AWAKENING OF THE EAST

It should be clear by now that in Okakura's discourse, there are signs of the most deadly trope in Japanese studies: *nihonjinron*, or Japanese uniqueness. To engage with this category is to risk entering into the 'schema of co-figuration',[50] as Naoki Sakai has formulated the problem, whereby the authentication of one's own imagined cultural uniqueness is highlighted vis-à-vis what is considered to be a specifically exotic Japanese otherness. Avoiding this tendency to play into 'national and cultural exceptionalism', I will call attention to a particularly troubled text in which different Asian identities are mixed and confused. The title of this text, which was written by Okakura while he was living in Calcutta, remains a mystery because it was never published in his lifetime. Indeed, it was an abandoned text until it was retrieved in 1938 by members of the Okakura family, who facilitated its publication first in Japanese translation, and then in 1940, in its original English draft as *The Awakening of the East*. It is said that Okakura had toyed with the idea of entitling his tract *We are One*. Whatever the title, the publication of this text simply played into the propaganda of Japanese ultra-nationalists, who succeeded in appropriating Okakura's pan-Asianism within the imperialist tenets of the Greater East Asian Co-Prosperity Sphere.

Certainly, it would be disingenuous to deny that Okakura's text lends itself to this appropriation, as I will elaborate at some length in the following pages, working through the discursive formations of Okakura's imperialist affinities with Asia. On the one hand, he wanted to believe that 'we are one', but on the other hand, his Japanese identity kept disrupting this unity in startling ways. The rupturing of 'we', therefore, is one of the recurring leitmotifs in the text, where an apparent empathy for the colonized can suddenly shift into registers of denigration, if not contempt. For example:

The gaunt image of India, here, rises before me with an inexpressible sadness. ... I see before me today an orphaned child of Asia seeking in vain that parental care which she has lost forever. ...The Himalayas bow their heads down to the plains in this mute agony.[51]

Following this grandiose elegiac mode of registering India's loss, Okakura then shifts into a journalistic register:

Do not the Englishmen's own statistics prove that the daily income of Indians was two pence in 1850? And is only three farthings in 1900?   [141]

Then follows a sudden reversal of his apparent empathy with colonized countries:

What can they expect? Wolves are made to devour, sheep can but bleat. We have still the shadow of grandeur, they have only a memory of mutiny.
[141]

The sudden inscription of 'they' comes as a jolt, because all along it has been subsumed in 'we'. Indeed, the all-inclusive Asian 'we' is further ruptured by specific assertions of 'we, in China': 'We, in China, felt the White Disaster in the Opium War...' (138); 'We, in China, have welcomed Buddhism and Zoroastrianism, the Nestorians and the Mohammedans in an equal spirit of toleration' (152). How can Okakura presume to affirm this affinity, if not belongingness, to China in the aftermath of the Sino-Japanese war of 1894–5? As the historian Carol Gluck has elaborated in her detailed history of that period, the cowardly 'Chinamen' from 'pigtail land', who 'ran from battle disguised in women's clothes', were demeaned in a series of Japanese woodblock prints, war songs, magic-lantern shows, and New Year's games, among other manifestations of xenophobic cultural practice.[52]

The Sinicized 'we' is further complicated in its explicit marking ('we in China') and then its disappearance into a more generalized 'we' in which Japan is curiously absented from the rest of Asia: 'Who of us, except Japan, sad survivors of ancient empires, can really call himself independent?' (139). What does it mean for Okakura to claim 'us' by tacitly excluding himself through his filiation to Japan? Once again, it would seem that we are revisiting the trope that 'Japan is and is not a part of Asia'.

More tantalizingly, even while acknowledging how '*our impressions of neighbouring countries*' in Asia are inevitably derived from 'European sources', there is a sudden upsurge of indignation directed at the reader: 'Do *you* not suspect that China lives on horrors, that Turkey dwells in atrocities, that India sits in voluptuous torpor?' (145). Who is the 'you' here? Where is Okakura's unspecified reader to be located? In Asia, or the West? The affinities are further muddied when Okakura adds that, '[A] Fifth-Avenue scandal [in New York] causes greater excitement amongst us than a rebellion in Honan' (145). Does the 'us' refer to a global cosmopolitan élite familiar with the scandals of Fifth Avenue, or to a radicalized Asian élite that might not have heard of the rebellion in Honan?

The palpable volatility of Okakura's subject position borders, I would suggest, on cultural schizophrenia. My purpose is not merely to illustrate this point through sharp and occasionally bizarre juxtapositions within his discourse. Rather, I am equally interested in suggesting how these shifts reveal some unresolved complexities that are still intrinsically a part of what gets inscribed in today's postcolonial discourse. Through the very roughness of his text— let us bear in mind that it was not intended to be published in its present form—Okakura exposes himself to a certain vulnerablity, if not ridicule. Most tellingly, he enables us (professionals, ostensibly trained to read postcoloniality) to confront our own blind spots, as we vacillate between identifying with what he's talking about, and rejecting his position.

To substantiate this vacillation, I would like to read in some detail a section from *The Awakening of the East*, which begins with an almost copybook echo of the Saidian critique of Orientalism, though Okakura does not speak with an academic voice. Rather, he adopts an unabashedly polemical tone as he outlines the phenomenon of non-Western knowledge being authenticated in Europe through self-serving endorsements:

Sanskrit is barbarous if not Germanic, the Taj is a blot if not Italian, *Sakuntala* is a wonder because Goethe admired [it], Vedantism is a treasure because Schopenhauer borrowed [from it].   [142]

More provocatively, Okakura locates the actual laboratory of Orientalism in Anglo-European universities, whose intellectual production he is, perhaps, too hasty in deriding:

[W]ho in Oxford or Heidelberg can compete with a second-rate sastri in his knowledge of Brahminical lore? Who in Berlin or the Sorbonne can compare with a third-rate mandarin in his grasp of Confucian classics?

[145]

Opportunistically, he hints at his own expertise as a scholar of Asian art by belittling the 'mottled talk of curio dealers', on whom American and European museums depended for their purchases. Despite its blatant opportunism, this no-holds-barred critique of the Orient produced in the West is juxtaposed with a far more ambivalent passage that self-consciously wallows in archaic Orientalia:

Come, trot out the merry bowl, my favourite hookah, my opium-pipe of jade! These at least will last my time. The millennium never arrives while we are living. Let the sleek *samnyasin* feast in his cozy cell, let the jolly fakir carol under his shady tree, let the maundering mandarin write his bad poetry, as much as ever! The world is for the survival of the fittest, — why should we interfere?

[142]

At one level, this histrionic outburst can be read ironically, almost self-mockingly, as if Okakura is deriding the passivity and waste of time in the Orient, lost in its dreams. How can Orientalism not exist in the context of such a 'real' Orient? The stereotypes are only too real, and they are heightened by the very arch 'Englishness' of Okakura's Victorian idiom ('let the jolly fakir carol under his shady tree').

Surely this is a different Englishness from that adopted by Okakura's contemporary, Nitobe Inazo, the author of the best-selling *Bushido* (1899), who compares 'the Way of the Samurai to the moral code of Tom Brown, whose ambition was "to leave behind him the name of a fellow who never bullied a little boy or turned his back on a big one"'.[53] In contrast to this 'mildly exoticized version of the British public school ethos', as Tessa Morris-Suzuki puts it very neatly,[54] Okakura would seem to be mocking the Orient through Englishness, not playing into its stereotypes.

This reading, however, is further complicated when, a few paragraphs later, Okakura affirms, with no irony whatsoever, that, ' The Oriental is at home at one with the Oriental' (146). In this assertion of a fundamental unity across different cultures of the

Orient, Okakura traverses a panorama of differences, ranging from examples drawn from material culture like the 'shape of a turban or the cut of a pyjama' to the different dietary habits of the 'pastoral north' and the 'fishing south' (146). Underlying all these differences, there are fundamental similarities in the socializing patterns across Asia, which Okakura sketches with flamboyant exaggeration: '[T]he matrimonial troubles of Bangkok are those of Cairo, the street scenes of Bombay are those of Canton...' (146). In the very next sentence, the rhetoric shifts to a more sober compilation of all the basic tropes associated with the Asiatic mode of life:

We all owe and own to an agricultural communism where the family is the social unit, where woman is worshipped as mother, where labor is harmonized by interchange of duty, where freedom is gauged by tolerance, where virtue is sought in self-sacrifice.   [146]

Family, mother, duty, tolerance, self-sacrifice: all these tropes, as we shall examine in the next section, resonate in Tagore's discourse on swadeshi, though with significantly different implications. What connects these tropes is the primacy of kinship, which somehow holds Okakura's scattered thoughts together. Even a 'moment's contact with any Oriental, a single visit to any Asiatic country now', according to Okakura, ensures 'our irrevocable kinship' (147).

Indeed, wasn't it a strange kind of 'kinship' that made young Bengali men of the early twentieth century imagine that Okakura was 'one of them', almost an honorary Bengali? Certainly, this would seem to be the case when one reads Surendranath Tagore's evocative description of Okakura as he was in the process of writing his inflammatory tract on *The Awakening of the East* in Calcutta:

[He] works all day, sprawling over a bolster on his bedstead; while we spend wildly exhilarating evenings, sitting round his table, listening to his glowing passages deploring the white disaster spreading over the East, in its intellectual and spiritual surrender to the western cult of Mammon. Okakura would invite, nay, insist on our criticism, and appeared gratefully to incorporate such harsher words or blatant epigram as any us thought fit to suggest.[55]

This description has all the ingredients of a juicy *adda*,[56] which could take place only between the closest friends in Bengal, sharing the deepest possible connections through gossip, fantasy, humour, histrionics, and a seemingly limitless amount of time to discuss the state of the world.

ENCOUNTERING NIVEDITA

From kinship, uninhibitedly ensconced within the homosocial word of Asian men, Okakura turns to women: 'Shame to our mothers that they bore a race of slaves! Shame to our daughters that they shall wed a race of cowards!' (142–3). The rhetoric here is insidious in its abrupt targeting of women as mothers and daughters, who are inexorably blamed for perpetuating the humiliation of Asia. 'Women are not born to bear heroes nowadays,' is Okakura's unqualified verdict (135).

From where does this misogyny emerge? How is it to be located within the multiple patriarchies dominating Asia? To what degree does homosocial male bonding produce an unacknowledged self-hatred that gets transferred on to a minority within the already minoritized Asians, notably Asian women? How did Sister Nivedita react to this passage and allow it to pass, if it did not feed at some level her own Orientalization of Indian women, apotheosized in the self-sacrificing mode of quiet devotion and servitude, extending to the exaltation of sati?

We see before us a woman, beautiful indeed, and adorned like a bride, with her whole mind set on the moment of triumph, yet without the slightest consciousness of her own glory. The form is pure Sattva, without one particle of Rajas. ...The spire-like flames leap up. She kneels throned on a summit of fire. Yet there is no fear. ...The moment is one of union. She knows nothing of separation. ...In this perfect fearlessness, this absence of any self-consciousness, what a witness we find to the Indian Conception of the Glory of woman.[57]

Perhaps, Nivedita's deification of the Indian woman and Okakura's denunciation of the Oriental female race are two sides of the same coin.

Contrary to received opinion, Sister Nivedita is not, to my mind, merely the editor of *The Awakening of the East*, whose scribbles, corrections, and comments in the margins and the body of the text were allegedly taken into account when the handwritten manuscript of *We are One* was published in Japanese translation in 1938. Nor would I accept Inaga Shigemi's sentimental reading that the manuscript was written for her sake and personally addressed to her as 'the modern incarnation of the spiritual Mother of India'?[58] Far from being the Muse or the Ideal Reader, I would suggest that Nivedita is the ghost-writer of the text who eventually fell out with Okakura on the sensitive issue of the authorial ownership of Asia itself. Indeed, her rhetorical influence pervades the writing of the text and, at times, it is directly interventionist.

How can one not, for instance, read her ventriloquizing her own Swamiji in his famous opening address in Chicago in 1893 with the first sentence of *The Awakening of Asia*: 'Brothers and Sisters of Asia!' (135)? Nor can one ignore the masculinist ring of exhortations like 'I call you not to violence but to manhood. I call you not to aggression but to self-consciousness. The glory of Europe is the humiliation of Asia!' (136). Is this Okakura speaking, or is Nivedita speaking through Vivekananda's voice to him? Later, there is a more direct inscription of Nivedita's devotion to the Mother: 'We await the Durga bestriding the lion and spearing the Asura on her invincible course (165)', followed by the more insidious invocations of 'Om to the Steel of honour! Om to the Strong! Om to the Invincible!' (166). These 'Oms' are directly lifted from one of Nivedita's letters to Josephine MacLeod where Okakura is affectionately regarded as the 'Banner-Chief'.[59]

In a more historical register, these invocations to the Sword in the name of Om need to be contextualized within the political climate of the swadeshi movement. Similar sounding oaths were already being made in clandestine extremist revolutionary cells in and around Calcutta. Indeed, in the very year 1902, when *We are One* was being improvised in freewheeling *adda* sessions with gentlemen of leisure attached to the Tagore household, the swadeshi revolutionary activist Hemchandra Kanungo was swearing a religious vow administered to him by Aurobindo, who had not yet become a guru. This vow, as

Sumit Sarkar informs us in his valuable historiography of the swadeshi movement, involved 'the laying of hands on a sword and a Gita, and the recitation of certain Sanskrit mantras'.[60] In 1905, the iconic figure of Nivedita's *Kali, the Mother* was incarnated in the sword, while Aurobindo was envisioning the cultivation of Sakti through a temple dedicated to Bhawani, 'the Mother of Strength, the Mother of India'. Already, as Sarkar informs us through his reading of Hemchandra Kanungo's revolutionary notes, 'the means to the end of political emancipation [namely, religion]...was turning into an end in itself'. The fierce religiosity of 'Om to the Steel of honour' in Okakura's text suggests an uncanny resemblance to these oaths, notwithstanding Nivedita's Anglicized translation.

Why *The Awakening of the East* was not published during Okakura's lifetime is, in all probability, linked to his falling out with Nivedita, which is itself subject to conjecture. At the most lurid level of speculation, one popular interpretation is that Okakura and Nivedita were emotionally involved—a fact that was not lost on Vivekananda, who even nicknamed Okakura *khudo* (the Bengali word for 'uncle'),[61] thereby indicating his droll sense of humour in what could be read as an increasingly volatile *ménage à trois*. Following Vivekandanda's death, Okakura and Nivedita, two foreigners in India in quest of a revitalized Asia, found solace in each other's company, though there is no reason to believe that their relationship ended in a flare-up following Okakura's sexual advances. This fiction, embroidered with all the appropriate *masala* (spice) by Sunil Gangopadhyay in his celebrated novel *Prothom Alo* (First Light, 1996), lacks the credibility of historical evidence.[62]

More to the point, one could argue that Okakura had lost interest in *The Awakening of the East* and was already thinking about Boston while he was in Calcutta. The traveller was already on the move, and Nivedita must have sensed that her mission was not going to be fulfilled through him. The possibility of inviting her to Kyoto for the Second International Parliament of Religions fell through, as Okakura's future career in Boston became more viable. Her erstwhile 'little one', whom she had nicknamed 'Nigu', 'Rhinoceros', 'Chieftain', and whom adoring 'local boys' in Calcutta had regarded

as Krishna and Kalki, was now 'Mr OK'. And, if the records of
the Ramakrishna Mission are to be trusted, Nivedita eventually
came to believe that Okakura was 'a Japanese agent'.[63] So much for
inter-Asian trust.

The real reason for the falling out, as I had indicated earlier, could
be related to problems relating to authorship. At a cultural–ethical
level, there was the crucial issue of acknowledgement. Nivedita
fervently believed that all her books, beginning with the 'little Kali-
book' and *The Ideals of the East* (which she almost passed as her own),
and her more widely circulated *The Web of Indian Life*, all had manifested
themselves through the blessings of Vivekananda. He was 'the real
author'.[64] Needless to say, Okakura never shared this devotional zeal,
despite his very real regard for Vivekananda as a seer of Asia—a
regard that never succumbed to the deference of discipleship.
Indeed, the Japanese traveller had no illusions that the rigours
of monastic austerity could be sustained in his embrace of art and
the sensuous pleasures of life.

A more specific bone of contention between Okakura and
Nivedita could be related to their conflicting politics, most specifically
in relation to the institution of royalty. For all his problems with the
bureaucracy of the Japanese government, Okakura was unequivocally
loyal to the institution of the state and the unbroken imperial
tradition and symbolic embodiment of the nation in the emperor.
This invisible hallowed figure exists, in Okakura's words, 'not by
divine right, but by divine law'; he 'may cease to govern, but he always
reigns'.[65] The constitution is his 'voluntary gift' to the nation, rather
than 'forced from the sovereign by the people', as in Europe, where
the regulations of liberty curb the possibilities of inner freedom.[66]
Indeed, so seductive is his portrayal of royalty that even the radical
Nivedita was almost persuaded that 'sovereigns have not always and
everywhere been vulgar and rich and self-indulgent and grasping at
the show of power'.[67] According to Okakura,

The glory of Asia...lies in that vibration of peace that beats in every heart;
that harmony that brings together emperor and peasant; that sublime
intuition of oneness which commands all sympathy...making Takakura,

Emperor of Japan, remove his sleeping-robes on a winter night, because the frost lay cold on the hearths of his poor; or Taiso [T'ai-tsung] of T'ang, forgo food, because his people were feeling the pinch of famine.   [130]

While this rhetoric was persuasive, it was not strong enough to deflect Nivedita's unflinching rejection, if not hatred, of royalty, for which she was held in great esteem in India, even by those who had reason to distrust her. As she put it in one of her many forthright statements: 'Our Royal Family seems to me the most entirely appropriate summit of our Imperialistic system that could possibly be imagined.'[68]

The politics of imperialism apart, it was the ownership of Asia itself that contributed to the politics, particularly its subterranean relationship to religion in defining the supremacy of nations in Asia. Nivedita's stakes are clearly evident in her Preface to *The Ideals of the East*, where she envisions an emphatically Hindu India. First, she incorporates Buddhism into Hinduism, affirming that 'the thing we call Buddhism cannot in itself have been a defined and formulated creed'.[69] Brazenly, she then proceeds to affirm 'not the Buddhaizing, but the *Indianizing* of the Mongolian mind',[70] which ultimately reveals itself in the Great Mother of Asia, which is 'forever One.'[71] Indeed, this is a highly loaded and politicized One, which would make Okakura's 'one Asia' seem almost ecumenical in comparison.

Against the reality of these conflicting Asias, which Okakura and Nivedita never fully thrashed out, it was inevitable that the legacy of their unresolved conflict would haunt the resurrection of *We are One*, when it was eventually published as *The Awakening of the East*. In a melodramatic register, it would be tempting to imagine the unacknowledged ghost-writer Nivedita cursing the narrative for daring to excise her authorship of 'Asia' in its imagined 'awakening'. For all their affinities, her Asia and Okakura's were never reconciled, neither in the historical moment of their meeting of minds, nor in the future when Okakura's Asia became a surrogate for defending Japan's war against the rest of Asia. In critical hindsight, it would not be incorrect to claim that the enduring subtext of *The Awakening of the East* could be more accurately rendered as 'We are Not One': this is the political unconscious of the text, a palimpsest that refuses to be erased.

PROBLEMATIZING THE POSTCOLONIAL

Having provided sufficient evidence from *The Ideals of the East* and *The Awakening of the East* to substantiate Okakura's singularly non-reflexive nationalism and imperialism, I would now like to complicate the argument somewhat by turning the screws, as it were, on the postcolonial critique that has thus far informed my analysis. The anti-essentialist axioms on which we thrive these days need to be troubled, not because their pluralist or deconstructionist premises relating to nation, race, and culture need to be rejected. Rather, they need to be stretched and opened to other possibilities of critical consideration, so that we do not lapse into what could be described as postcolonial enlightenment.

With this qualification in mind, let me particularize one instance of such enlightenment by referring to Leo Ching's provocative essay entitled 'Yellow Skin, White Masks' (1998) in which he plays with Fanonian constructs, while problematizing Okakura's notorious assertion that 'Asia is One'.[72] Ching raises a pertinent issue: Okakura travelled to China for five months in 1893, after which he wrote a series of articles in Japanese, differentiating Japan from China, which seemed to resemble Europe more closely. Significantly, after travelling to Europe in 1886 on an official tour relating to art and museology, Okakura had been compelled to acknowledge that Europe is *not* one. Indeed, he was not even sure what Europe *is*. However, while visiting China, memories of Europe surfaced for Okakura in unexpected ways—for instance, on seeing the silhouettes of herders on horseback, highlighted by the sunset of Luoyang.[73] In this vignette Okakura was reminded inexplicably of Rome, and likewise, in his random but perceptive observation of objects in everyday life, like chairs and tables, and the incorporation of bricks and tiles in the architecture of homes, he was alerted to the fact that these objects are not part of Japan's social landscape. The farther China retreated from Japan in Okakura's travel-imaginary, the closer it gravitated in the direction of Europe.

Beyond the cultures of everyday life, Ching emphasizes that Okakura had listed numerous regional differences and local complexities between north and south China. Why then does

Okakura declare that 'Asia is one', when even within specific regions of particular countries there are perceptible differences in the ways people live and relate to each other? 'How is Asia one?' demands Leo Ching. 'Why must Asia be one, and more importantly, what entitles Okakura, a Japanese, to speak of Asia as one?'[74] These questions resonate with all the familiar indignation that characterizes postcolonial theory (including my own comments in the previous sections), preoccupied with destabilizing monolithic perspectives of unitary culture at national, continental and global levels. Does Okakura's 'one' constitute a deception or a strategic lie or a transcendent essentialization which has been created specifically for the mystification of the Western reader?

While I declare my postcolonial affinities through this question, I would also acknowledge that 'one' coexists with difference, and indeed, it underlies all differences, not unlike the 'creative unity'[75] embraced by Tagore. This 'unity', which was essentially a poetic category, celebrates the oneness underlying both the self and the universe, in addition to the communion relating these distinct entities. There are also more metaphysical readings of 'one' drawn from the philosophy of Vedanta, on which Tagore drew extensively with unabashed poetic license. Okakura may not have been particularly knowledgeable about Advaita, as we have already indicated, but is it sufficient to simply dismiss his derivative discourse as a self-serving element of Indian philosophy, which merely legitimized his own magisterial discourse? Alternatively, is there something more to be said about 'one'? Is there another layer in Okakura's idealization of Asia as an imaginary unity which Ching cannot read in the absence of an alternative epistemological paradigm for 'one'? The point is that there is more than one 'one'.

Drawing on the wisdom of the Upanishads, which he freely translated and transformed within his poetic vision, Tagore constantly returned to One in his embrace of the diversities and differences of the universe. In his meditation on *sadhana* (self-realization) for instance, which had been sparked by spiritual dialogue with Unitarians and later delivered as a series of lectures at Harvard University, Tagore had tried to elaborate on 'one' as accessibly as possible:

The Upanishads says with great emphasis: *Know thou the One, the Soul. It is the bridge leading to the immortal being.*

This is the ultimate end of man, to find the *One* which is in him; which is his truth, which is his soul... But that which is *one* in him is ever seeking for unity—unity in knowledge, unity in love, unity in purposes of will; its highest joy is when he reaches the infinite one, within its eternal unity.[76]

At the risk of crude paraphrase, the 'one' of the soul is constantly seeking another unity, which would seem to be a paradox: if you are one, why would you seek anything? What would there be to seek? However, this yearning for unity is with the infinite one, the Supreme One, through 'all the diversities of the world'.[77] Driven by a 'direct and immediate intuition' rather than by any 'ratiocination or demonstration', the 'one in us' gravitates towards 'the one in all', affirming in the process its 'nature' and 'joy'.[78]

Clearly, there are gradations, mutations, and embodiments at work by which unitary constructions of 'one' can assume highly differentiated states of being, not to mention different envisionings of God. Countering the Unitarian abstraction of One God, 'the pure impersonal Brahman of the Vedanta', Tagore upheld a personalized *jiban-debata* ('life-god'), which was itself a revelation of the 'unity of God and his creation', also described as 'the unity of a creative personality'.[79] 'Just as God governs and penetrates and harmonizes all aspects of an endlessly varied universe, so this *jiban-debata* governed and penetrated and harmonized Tagore's own varied creative activites';[80] in this formulation, it becomes clear how the notion of 'one' dissolves into the act of creativity itself.

While it could be argued that the subtleties of this context do not apply to Okakura, who was, at best, appropriating Advaita for political purposes, I would suggest that the critique of 'one' in relation to Asia could be more layered and reflexive if it could incorporate diverse philosophical frameworks that open up other epistemological readings of 'one'. The problem with Ching's critique is that it is apparently oblivious of, or indifferent to, these other readings, and consequently, it becomes far too immersed within the epistemological securities of Euro-American postcolonial theory. In the process, he reiterates the axioms with no element of doubt or questioning, as, for example, in this forthright passage:

Asia is neither a cultural, religious or linguistic unity, nor a unified world. The principle of its identity lies outside itself, in relation to (an)Other. If one can ascribe to Asia any vague sense of unity, it is that which is excluded and objectified by the West in the service of its historical progress. Asia is, and can be one, only under the imperial eyes of the West.[81]

Predictably, this irrefutable, arguably imperialist, critique is cast within a larger rejection of binarism in which 'the putative unity of Asia, or the East, is "invented" or "imagined" in direct opposition to another putative unity of the West'.[82] This binarism is in turn 'firmly entrenched in the geopolitical configuration of the world in which the West has constantly to exclude, suppress, and eliminate Others in order to ceaselessly transform its self-image'.[83] Within the relentless thrust of the argument, there is no acknowledgement that binaries need to be culturally grounded, or that their oppositional dynamics can vary considerably from one culture to another. Nor is there any suggestion that binaries can be inadvertently betrayed or transgressed, even by those who uphold them. Instead, binarism is fetishized into a constant, and the assumption is that its articulation somehow frees the postcolonial critic from succumbing to its reductionism.

Likewise, in invoking the problem of 'reverse discourse', Ching accuses Okakura far too easily of falling into the trap in which 'the terms of resistance are already given us, and our contestation is entrapped within the Western cultural conjuncture we effect to dispute'.[84] One wonders whether Ching is not duplicating the same problem, as he submits to an already determined (Western) hegemonic system in which the terms of theoretical resistance to Okakura have already been predetermined. I should emphasize here that I am not disputing so much the validity of Ching's postcolonial tropes of argumentation, as I am somewhat troubled by their lack of reflexivity. His ultimate verdict on Okakura strikes me as being far too closed: 'In the end, Okakura's defiant rhetoric and nativist assertion only serve to reconfirm and reinforce the universalist position of the West.'[85]

My own submission is that Okakura's rhetoric, insidious as it was in many aspects that I have already discussed, does many other things apart from legitimizing 'the universalist position of the West' (insofar as there is one). Nor do I see his assertion of Asianness functioning in a predominantly 'nativist' mode, which doesn't mean that his rhetoric didn't lend itself to racism. There are more complexities at work here, for which Okakura shouldn't be let off the hook, but neither should he be reduced to some kind of bigot who was unaware that his critique was at least partially bound and shaped by the discourse of the West. The fact that he did not theorize this point, in the postcolonial mode that is now *de rigueur*, is another matter.

The Complication of Beauty

Even if one accepts that Okakura was a nativist and imperialist, then how do we account for the fact that he was intensely loved and admired even by those who had every reason to be alert about the excesses of Empire? Dipesh Chakrabarty raises this point in his own brief comments on Leo Ching's critique of Okakura, where he points out that his *bhadralok* contemporaries in West Bengal have a 'tremendous affection' for Okakura, who 'increased our sense of our own aesthetic richness'.[86] While this cultural affinity for a specifically Bengali aesthetics is not free of its own cultural essentialization, it indicates that there are different perceptual locations and routes through which a figure like Okakura can be claimed, just as there are different trajectories by which he has been vilified and rejected.

In addition to acknowledging a diversity of epistemological contexts for defining Asian affinities and differences, one should also be attentive to those elements that contribute to the tangibility and intimacy of abstract categories like Asia. In the process, these elements complicate the heuristic truths of dominant categories. One such element is beauty, which I would like to insert briefly into the discussion here. While it is a leitmotif that runs through the book in different descriptive and critical registers, I offer here a few preliminary observations.

Beauty, it could be argued, is one of the least interrogated dimensions in postcolonial discourse, more often than not regarded with some embarrassment as a remnant of formalist theory. Yet, beauty—not just the idea of Beauty, but the experience of beauty in works of art and in everyday life—was the primary animating force that brought Tagore and Okakura together. Bearing this context in mind, to what degree can beauty be said to destabilize questions of power? If one attempts to assess the impact of Okakura on contemporary painters and artists in Bengal today, particularly in Santiniketan, one realizes that he is remembered against the grain of his imperialist and nationalist background, to which there continues to be relative disinterest, if not indifference. What matters is his contribution to principles of art practice linked to the Bengal and Santiniketan schools of painting, which have contributed to what Chakrabarty has described as 'our own aesthetic richness'.

Foremost among Okakura's aesthetic principles was his eminently useful insight into what I have earlier described as the 'magnetic triangle' of tradition, originality, and nature, which he perceived as essential elements in the composition of painting. In a well-documented story, he had graphically conveyed the interactivity of these three elements to the leading figures of the Bengal school like Abanindranath Tagore and Nandalal Bose by using matchsticks to demonstrate the dynamics of his aesthetic model. If 'tradition' was not impacted by the 'personality' of the artist determining his or her 'originality', and if it was not challenged by the observations of the world embodied in 'nature', then it would simply petrify into 'convention'. Such simple but valuable pedagogical insights continue to be invoked in Santiniketan today, not least because they are sufficiently broad and flexible in their definition to be interpreted in highly individual ways. Without the interactivity of tradition, nature, and originality, however, an artwork would cease to have inner dynamism and life. 'A weak composition was like a reptile,' as Okakura succinctly put it. 'It survived even if cut into pieces, whereas a strong composition was like the human body: the tiniest pin-prick alerted the whole nervous system.'[87]

It is precisely this kind of insight that needs to be taken into account when surveying Okakura's larger legacy. Otherwise it becomes far too easy to evaluate his contribution in purely ideological terms, without acknowledging the creative impact of his tutelage. For instance, one's assessment of his sensibility would be thoroughly incomplete if we disregarded the enormous value that he placed in Nature, which was not just a matter of aesthetics in relation to the landscapes and drawings represented by 'East Asiatic painting'.[88] What mattered to Okakura, and in this regard, his affinities to Tagore are only too palpable, was not just the construction of nature through the technical processes of art, but its embeddedness in the observations and relationships of everyday life.

So, for example, we are reminded of the great Japanese painter Sesshu from the eighteenth century who returned from China during the Ming dynasty without being able to find a guru. Yet, he comforted himself by saying, 'I found excellent masters in the mountains and rivers of China' (146). Likewise, Okakura reveals startling anecdotes by linking the biological and material dimensions of nature and the animal world to the somewhat bizarre creative practices of particular artists. We learn, for instance, of an artist who walks on all fours and growls like a tiger in his studio in order to draw tigers more effectively, while another lies in the bushes among insects so that he can identify himself with these creatures (151). Indeed, so finely tuned was the Chinese painter Ts'ao-pu-h'ing's observation of insect life that he is said to have 'dropped a spot of ink on his picture by accident, and in order to cover this blemish, turned the blot into a fly with such success that people would later try to blow it off the painting' (146). If this seems like an affirmation of naturalistic virtuosity, one needs to bear in mind that the essential quality by which painting had to be judged according to Okakura was not its versimilitude to nature, but its capacity to evoke the 'inner spirit' underlying the 'outward form' (146). Therefore, what mattered in the representation of horses, for instance, was neither the colour nor the musculature of the horse, but its inner agility or 'real fleetness' that can be discerned only by artists who are trained to see the invisible (147).

For Okakura, it is clear that the technique of rendering the invisible rests on memory, and not on models which can merely be copied without being transfigured. As we shall examine later in the book, this thorough scepticism, if not disdain, for the literality of imitation, is one of Okakura's deepest affinities with Tagore. Both of them tended to essentialize the mnemonic and imaginative resources of artists as opposed to their technical ability in reproducing the real. For both of them, the pleasure of art was to be found in the wonder of 'recognition', in 'rediscovery' of what had already been 'felt' (149). This recognition could extend from the sensation of watching bamboo sway in the breeze, as reproduced in a painting, to the sense of walking through a landscape rather than looking at it (149).

At times, the aesthetic affinities between Okakura and Tagore are highlighted through subtle distinctions, as, for instance, in Okakura's acknowledgement that 'the quest of art is not the beautiful but the interesting' (148). Drawing on the Japanese word for 'artistic', *omoshiroi*, he proceeds to trace the genealogical roots of this multivalent word to the 'white-faced' visage of the gods. The 'story of the word', as told by Okakura, is well worth retelling:

The Sun-Goddess once became disgusted with the world. There were many things which vexed her, and she withdrew into a cavern, leaving the whole world in darkness. The gods assembled and tried to entice her out of her retreat. They danced and sang until the Sun-Goddess emerged, and as the first ray broke upon the darkness, the gods, who had seen nothing before, recognized that their faces were white.   [149]

In this recognition, Okakura attempts to evoke the sensation of 'artistic delight', which resonates in one of the many meanings of the word *omoshiroi*, which seems relatively free from the ethical and moral weight that Tagore inscribed in his 'sense of beauty' (*soundaryabodh*).[89]

While these differentiations with Tagore's aesthetics will become clearer in the course of the narrative, what needs to be emphasized here is that while Okakura's sense of beauty complicates his political legacy, one needs to resist any romanticization of his artistic legacy on its own terms. Chakrabarty clearly goes overboard when he acknowledges the wonder of the wash techniques of painting from Japan and China entering '[his] Bengali romantic inheritance': 'How do I suddenly open myself up to somebody else's aesthetic? How do I suddenly find something that is unfamiliar, beautiful and want it in my life?'[90] Highlighting the act of 'opening up to the world' prior to the closure of 'conceptualization', Chakrabarty claims that the master of the Bengal School of painting, Abanindranth Tagore, could open himself to the beauty of wash painting precisely because he was trained to do so 'prior to words' and 'prior to representation'.[91]

Some facts need to be inserted into the discussion here to demystify the artistic process, which can all too easily serve as a falsely intuitive counter to the constraints of theory, as if art is devoid of its own thought processes and theoretical grounding. First of all, contrary to popular myth, it is wrong to assume, as Chakrabarty does, that Okakura introduced the 'wash' technique to the Bengal school of painting. Okakura was no painter himself, and his influence was primarily philosophical, not technical. Following Okakura's departure from India, it was the painters Yokoyama Taikan (1868– 1958) and Hishida Shunso (1874–1911) who passed on some rudimentary techniques to Abanindranath Tagore through their close interactions in his studio in Jorasanko. However, at no point, were these techniques duplicated, even at a purely mechanical level: while Taikan would periodically moisten the material of his painting with 'liberal splashes of water' even in the process of working on it, Abanindranath would dip the paper in water before painting on it.[92]

Contrary to Partha Mitter's impressionistic view that the Japanese technique of *morotai*, or the hazy style, was 'ideal for the Indian artists' mellow elegiac landscapes',[93] the truth is that Abanindranath's carefully regulated 'wash' was far removed from Taikan's prodigious risks in almost allowing his canvas to disappear through smudges, traces, and an almost evanescent sense of blurred outlines. Indeed, as the artist–scholar K.G. Subramanyan has pointed out to me, Abanindranath's so-called atmospheric effects could be more closely related to the European practices of glazing and 'scumbling'.[94] Here again, one is not asserting a duplication of techniques but a painterly resemblance. Likewise, even as the genres of landscape, calligraphic drawing, and scroll painting have been recognized as distinctively 'Japanese' contributions to the Bengal school, one has to acknowledge the freewheeling and highly personalized uses of these genres, which became actual elements of an evolving grammar in the articulation of the individual styles of Bengali artists.

Perhaps, the 'Japanese-ness' that Chakrabarty discerns in the Bengal school is a projection of foreignness on what is essentially the inner mutations of a native tradition. There is a long history of such (mis)perceptions which can be traced to, say, the French Orientalist constructions of *Japonism* in Impressionist paintings. In these paintings, 'Japanese' elements were falsely valorized in what was essentially an European avant-garde rejection of academic norms relating to colour, tone, and density of light. The art historian Inaga Shigemi has pointed out how Japan-returned European illustrators were busy 'modifying their "impressions" of ukiyo-e prints by applying Western perspective modelling and chiaroscuro to create illusionistic images of Japan, while Japanese printmakers in Yokohama were busy imitating these Western techniques'.[95] More ironically, it appears that the 'distinctively' bright Japanese colours of the ukiyo-e prints were scarcely indigenous; rather, they were a direct response to the importation of Western-manufactured colours, notably Prussian blue and aniline red.[96] In addition, the essentialization of ostensibly 'Japanese' principles like '*disymmetrie*', affirmed by French critics in their reading of prints like Hokusai's *Mt Fuji off the Coast of Kanagawa*, was more accurately an assertion of their own aesthetic priorities. In the Hokusai image, now globally serialized through any number of postcards and posters in the global tourist industry, there is a 'dynamic contrast between a great wave in the foreground and the small cone-like form in the background', but, as Inaga succinctly puts it, it is possible that this apparent disymmetrie between the wave and the cone-like form can also be viewed as a 'free and exaggerated interpretation of Western linear perspective'.[97]

While such observations demand a technical grounding in the grammar of painting, they compel cultural critics to be somewhat more cautious in making generalizations, as Chakrabarty does, about the transportation of the wash technique 'from a Chinese/Japanese inheritance into my Bengal romantic inheritance'.[98] Perhaps, between the interstitial transference of these two Asian inheritances, the most potent influence could be Europe, and more specifically, Britain. After all, it is this colonial mediation to which Abanindranath was deeply indebted, not least through the conceptual and aesthetic guidance of his English 'guru' E.B. Havell (1864–1937), the superintendent of the Government School of Art, Calcutta, on whose 'new orientalist' educational and artistic reforms much has been written.[99] Such mediations need to be addressed in order to illuminate a fuller picture of the complexities at work in the Bengali–Japanese cross-fertilization of art practice and aesthetics.

While this illumination lies outside the boundaries of this book, it is important that we acknowledge the role of art practice in reflecting/inflecting/deflecting the larger issues of power and cultural politics surrounding interculturality. This brings me back to the question that I had raised earlier: To what degree does beauty destabilize issues relating to power? In the course of this book, we will be examing some of the tensions at work in this dynamic, and, as we shall see, beauty can reinforce power in virulent ways, if not be totally identified with it. Beauty is not necessarily an ethical alternative to the violence of war and politics. Nor is it an escape route leading to the possibilities of a facile, if not illusory, transcendence. As we shall see in the last section of this book, the realities of war can break all possibilities of sharing aesthetic affinities. However, for the moment, let us inscribe a captivating moment in the inter-Asian exchange of Taikan and Abanindranath at the level of actual art practice. The art historian Partha Mitter tells the story well:

Abanindranath asked the Japanese to treat the theme of *Ras-Lila*, the love play of Radha and Krishna, on a full-moon night. Taikan began with sketches of Radha's sari. After this, he spread a silk scroll on the floor and made preliminary drawings. Days went by but Taikan could not make any progress. One day he came across a dish of white flowers left by the ladies of the house, some of which had spilled on to his scroll lying on the floor. He was utterly riveted by the scene and started scattering flowers all over the painting. At last he stumbled upon what was lacking in it.[100]

In this realization, the missing element of *bhava*, the outpouring of emotion and feeling, suddenly comes alive in the painting.

At one level, this experiment could be dismissed as romantic and far too bound within the subjectivity of a particular artist to resonate at more worldly and political levels. It is, however, precisely such stories that perpetuate cultural legacies, and we need to bear them in mind in order to complicate the postcolonial readings of nationalism and imperialism that can so easily be hegemonized around controversial figures like Okakura. At one level, as we have examined in this section on 'Asia', there is something terrifying about his aestheticization of the nation in his envisioning of Japan as a 'museum of Asiatic civilization', because this idealized reading totally camouflages the violence of war, racism, and xenophobia. However, at another level, his sense of beauty has the possibility of filtering into many non-discursive contexts of personal and social relationships, which resist hegemonic readings of the political. Having inserted the complication of beauty into the discussion, we can now proceed to deal with nationalism in a more directly confrontationist mode.

2

Nationalism

THE ENIGMA OF SILENCE

At this point in the narrative, Rabindranath Tagore, who has been
waiting in the wings of this book for far too long, makes a long-delayed
entrance. Instead of allowing the poet to sing, I would prefer to raise
some critical questions around his silence in relation to Okakura's
representation of Asia. How could the poet tolerate Okakura's
advocacy of one Asia, when its representation was so conflictual,
hierarchical, if not occasionally racist and culturally superior? How
could a great poet like Tagore, so attentive to the nuances of language,
not have been disturbed by these obvious problems in Okakura's
writing?

It could be argued that *The Awakening of the East* was an emotional,
inflammatory, and blatantly polemical work of its times, best
forgotten or else remembered as an indulgence. Then what about
the more measured and implicit defence of Japanese imperialism
offered by Okakura in *The Awakening of Japan,* which was published in
1904, in almost direct counterpoint to the actual outbreak of the
Russo-Japanese War? Here, his case against Korea, for instance, is
presented with the clarity of a military strategist:

1. Eternal threat: 'Korea lies like a dagger ever pointed
   towards the heart of Japan.'[1]

2. Legitimate outlet: '[S]tarvation awaits our ever-increasing population if it be deprived of its legitimate outlet in the sparsely cultivated areas of these countries [Korea and Manchuria].'[2]

3. National defence: 'Today the Muscovites have laid their hands on these territories, with none but us to offer any resistance.'[3]

4. Historic spirit: 'Korea was originally a Japanese province.'[4]

Clearly, this is an imperialism that failed to recognize its own complicity in waging a 'just war' against Asia for the sake of Asia—indeed, for the love of Asia. The critic Karatani Kojin has illuminated the problem in the larger context of Japanese imperialism: '[T]he Japanese annexation of Korea [in 1910] was viewed not as a Western-style colonization but rather as an attempt to transform Koreans into Japanese through "love". This was the height of self-deception. Japanese colonial domination is detested even today precisely because of this "love".'[5]

With all his visionary insight, how could Tagore not have seen through this 'love', were it not for the simple and crucial fact that he loved his friend more? Perhaps this is too evasive an argument that plays into the dilemma of being caught between love for one's own country and the love for one's friend. In such a crisis, it was assumed by pacifist liberals like E.M. Forster that one should have the courage to betray nationalist sentiments in favour of sustaining the ideals of a particular friendship. As we shall examine in the last section of the book, the modalities of friendship around the Tagore–Okakura relationship open up a different spectrum of considerations relating to homosociality. For the moment, I would emphasize that Tagore did see through the duplicities of imperialism masquerading as 'love', but at no point did he want to implicate Okakura in his critique. Perhaps, this is one reason why Okakura was never mentioned in his public lectures in Japan in 1916, which does seem to be a strange omission given the idealization of their friendship; a subject that Tagore had no difficulty in acknowledging, and indeed, valorizing, on his later trips to Japan. However, on his first trip in 1916—Okakura had been dead for barely three years—when one would have expected him to dedicate his lectures to Okakura's memory, Tagore is silent.

There is a more literal reason that can be provided for Tagore's failure to respond to the problematic aspects of Okakura's thinking in *The Awakening of the East* and *The Awakening of Japan*. As mentioned earlier, the first text was published posthumously in 1938, first in a Japanese translation, thereby reversing the normal trend of Okakura's publications, which were written in English and then translated into Japanese many years later. We need to keep in mind this significant time-lag in the reception to Okakura's key texts in the Japanese-speaking world. These English texts were not read in Japan during his lifetime, even though he was an iconic figure, an exile in and out of Japan. In not attempting to get his texts translated into Japanese, Okakura was merely reaffirming his critical choice to exclusively address 'the West'. That was his target audience.

If *The Awakening of the East* was not published till 1938, thereby justifying Tagore's silence on the xenophobic content of the book, the same cannot be said for *The Awakening of Japan* published in 1904, shortly after *The Ideals of the East* (1903), in at least two English editions. One would expect Okakura to have sent his Indian friends a copy of his new book. However, archival evidence confirms that this was not the case, and indeed it is clear that Tagore had not read the text.[6] Once again, there is an alibi for the poet's silence on Okakura's vindication of Japanese imperialism. At another level, however, one is compelled to ask why Okakura never felt the need to share his book in the first place with his most admired Indian friend. Had they already lost touch with each other? Alternatively, in not gifting the book, was Okakura withholding something?

To translate this problem in more contemporary terms—and I address this question specifically to the postcolonial writer—when you write something and choose not to share it with a friend, what are the possible interpretations of the choice ('I don't want you to read me')? This is a predicament that postcolonial writers are compelled to confront and negotiate in different ways, as they switch back and forth between different languages and theoretical idioms, for significantly different audiences in different locations. One may not want to be read 'at home' because the writing may seem too simplistic; a capitulation to the nativist burden of information retrieval. Or else, the writing may be considered too obscure (postmodern?) for one's friends, still troubled by the colonial legacy of modernity. Conversely, one may not want to share one's writing with friends abroad, on the dubious grounds that 'they wouldn't understand it anyway'.

None of these ambivalent formulations, I would submit, can be applied so readily to Okakura. His strategy was more clearly marked: *The Awakening of Japan* was not being addressed to the Japanese, still less to Indians; it was being written very consciously with an American audience in mind. Boston was Okakura's new 'home', or 'second home'; it is for this destination that he had left Japan in the company of his associates Yokoyoma Taikan, Hishida Shunso, and Rokkaku Shisui on the very day that the Russo-Japanese War began. *The Awakening of Japan* has to be read as part of this journey to the US; a point of departure from rather than a sequel to Okakura's Indian trip.

Tagore's erasure of Okakura in his 1916 lectures may also need to be seen in the larger context of his own erasure, and transformation, of the swadeshi movement, as he distanced himself from its politics to reflect on its troubled ethos. The presence of Okakura was inseparable from the premonitions of the swadeshi movement, which, in 1902, was already febrile in its energies and assertions of nationalism against colonial rule. In most established readings of Tagore's biography, this was his most 'nationalist' phase as a poet, from which he later distanced himself, politically and artistically, as we shall examine in this section. Tagore's erasure of Okakura needs to be seen in the context of his larger 'distancing' from nationalist politics. Indeed, even as Okakura was firing the revolutionary imagination of his young Bengali comrades—Surendranath claims that 'it was *our* awakening that the astute Okakura was really after'[7]—it is hard to imagine Rabindranath participating in that fervor. Even as he seemed to be contributing to the rhetoric of excess, he was imagining swadeshi differently.

SWADESHI SAMAJ

I will now read Tagore's envisioning of swadeshi through one of his most powerful essays, *Swadeshi Samaj*, which was first delivered as a lecture in 1904 at the Minerva Theatre in Calcutta, and then rendered once again for a rapt audience at the Curzon Theatre. Though Tagore had distanced himself from the politics of swadeshi by 1908, this essay remains a landmark in his oeuvre, a *tour de force* of a heightened poetic polemic combining grand rhetoric with colloquial utterance. While it is stylistically antithetical to Gandhi's inflammatory but cryptic *Hind Swaraj*, which was written a few years later in 1908, both these texts can be regarded as contrapuntal registers of the same historical moment. Both writers are addressing the politics of the self—Gandhi through *swaraj* (self-rule) and Tagore through *atmashakti* (self-reliance). Both writers base their argument for indigenous (swadeshi) culture in the fundamentally rural context of an India that is still in the process of being imagined. Both of them emphasize the necessity of sacrifice for freedom. Both are equally aware that political freedom is not sufficient.

Needless to say, the methods prescribed by Gandhi and Tagore for India's self-realization are radically different. At the level of political practice, Gandhi's grasp of grass-roots economics, cooperative enterprises, and mass movement mobilization virtually obliterates the poet's more cultural solutions to awakening people's consciousness through the religious and folk mediations of *melas* and magic-lantern shows. While Gandhi's politics are grounded in the organizational demands of social practice, Tagore's vision has a more symbolic and performative resonance. In terms of leadership, there is something distressingly naïve, and perhaps even dangerous, in the poet's faith in the *samajpati* (leader of the samaj), whose criteria of election are left nebulous, even as it is assumed that his appointment has to precede the formation of a free society. How this is likely to happen, Tagore does not elaborate.

Given the difference between Gandhi's faith in radical action and the potency of non-violence, and Tagore's more reticent affirmation of 'constructive swadeshi',[8] it was inevitable that the Great Sentinel and the Mahatma, as they called each other, could not agree on how Independence was to be achieved. Despite, or perhaps because of their deeply intimate disagreements, it became clear that Tagore would not accept Gandhi's concept of swaraj, either at an ideational level or as a model for political practice. This clash of ideals has been elaborated in numerous texts and interpretations, which I will not reiterate here.[9] Rather, my purpose is to open the canonical text of *Swadeshi Samaj* against the backdrop of Asian politics presented so far in this book. Indeed, *Swadeshi Samaj* and Okakura's *The Awakening of the East* are contemporaneous texts, which seem to share a common agenda, and yet they are almost diametrically opposed.

Against the continental sweep of Okakura's ostensibly revolutionary Asia, Tagore locates the spirit of swaraj in that eternal repository of Indian civilization, as he envisioned it at that time: *samaj*. A polysemic term, rather like *jati* (caste), with shades of meaning and subtle differentiation in relation to context and modes of address, samaj is closer to primordial notions of 'community' and face-to-face interactions of localized groups of people than to 'society', which is how it is normally translated. Even so, in its texture of multivalent associations, it lies somewhere between 'society' and 'community', with Tagore endowing it with a significance that resists, yet hovers uneasily between the orientalist retrieval of primitive societies and the nationalist appropriation of community for militant ends.

If the ontology of samaj is left somewhat undefined, even as it is seductively evoked in the course of the essay, Tagore is only too clear what samaj is not. Most emphatically, it is positioned against the modern institutions of the nation and the state—indeed, Tagore would deny that India has a 'state', even though it has something like a 'government' (*sarkar*). Indeed, he even refuses to translate the English word for 'politics' into Bengali, retaining its foreignness; or else, with acute self-consciousness, he juxtaposes the 'political' against the indigenous category of *sadhana* (vocation), as in the construction, 'political sadhana'. In this critically reflexive use of language, it is clear that Tagore is seeking an alternative epistemology of samaj to the institutional languages informing colonial civic and social institutions. He is fashioning, as it were, a society on indigenous and traditional grounds.

In this context, Tagore emphasizes that samaj is the locus of dharma, not merely in its religious, spiritual or ethical connotations, but in relation to the very sustenance of the structures of everyday life. From education to the provision of drinking-water, the construction of wells to the organization of *kirtans* and *kathas*, samaj provides for the needs of all its people, regardless of larger invasions and colonization, through an intricate web of social relationships based on kinship. Precisely because it has an in-built system for the support of each of its inhabitants, who in turn support each other through the implicit bonds of sociality, the people belonging to a samaj do not need the benevolence of the state, even during periods of crisis and emergency. The *prana-shakti* (life-force) of the samaj, which is at once autonomous and self-renewing, rejects the anonymity and functionality of the developmental aid provided by the state.

At a less abstract level, what holds the samaj together are the intimate ties of *kinship*, which Tagore evokes through one of his numerous neologisms in the essay: *atmiyasambandhasthapan* (literally, the 'establishment of the relationship of relatives', the word *atmiya* for 'relative' and *sambandha* for 'relationship', stimulating a complex web of social relations). In a memorable passage from *Swadeshi Samaj*, Tagore spells out the dynamics of his indigenous society:

The primary effort of Bharatbarsha has always been to implicate human beings in ties of relationality—of kinship. We are duty-bound to keep in touch even with distant relatives; when our children grow up, the relationship does not weaken. According to our *varna* and circumstances, we have to maintain appropriate kin-like ties with our neighbours in villages. There are customary ties between the householder and his guru and family priest, guest and beggar, landlord and subjects and servants. Let me emphasize that I am not talking about mere ritualistic, *shastra*-ordained roles—these are ties of heart (*hridayersambandha*). Some of these people are akin to one's own father, son, brother or friend. Whenever we get to know a person, we cannot help thinking of him or her outside of a broader relational matrix. That is why we cannot think of human beings as mere instruments, as parts of a larger machine, to serve our own ends. Maybe this has advantages as well as disadvantages, but this is truly what we are, and more importantly, this is what the Orient is all about.[10]

Tagore then goes on to make a startling connection between the relational bonds of the Orient and the capacity of Japanese soldiers to transcend their machine-like roles through their capacity to sacrifice themselves:

Undoubtedly, war is a technical, mechanical matter — soldiers must act like machines, they must become machines. Nonetheless, Japanese soldiers transcend the machine-role; they are not inanimate things, nor are they mere blood-thirsty animals. They are soldiers through their relationship with the Mikado who stands for the country at large. They regard and sacrifice themselves through this relationship. In our country, in ancient times, soldiers were no mere cogs in the wheel — they sacrificed themselves to their *dharma* as *kshatriyas*, implicated in their relationship to their lords. Thus, when they died, they died as fulfilled human beings and not as mere pawns. They died to attain *dharma*. As a result, wars often resembled mass-suicides, giving rise to bewildered Western commentary: 'This is wonderful, but this is not war.' By enlivening warfare with this sense of grace, Japan has attained glory. It has earned the praise of both the East and the West.   [631–2]

Needless to say, this pursuit of dharma in death has uncomfortable echoes of the rationales provided by Japanese ultranationalists, who urged young men to embrace the beauty of sacrifice during the Second World War. I cannot enter that discourse here, which has a significantly different context and time-frame from the essay in question. However, it is telling that the specific references to Japan in *Swadeshi Samaj* are not concerned with its economic or industrial supremacy in Asia, or its ability to stand up as a military power to Russia. Rather, its ethos of self-sacrifice in war is fundamentally related to its culture of kinship, in which the most ordinary soldier is linked to the Mikado, who assumes the aura of a larger beneficent Personality.

Despite these references, it could be argued that Tagore's invocation of the Mikado totally failed to grasp the ideology of the emperor system (*tennosei ideorogii*), in which the relationality of ordinary Japanese citizens to the emperor was consolidated through an ancestral lineage of the nation embodied in the term *kokutai*. Not only was this term frequently invoked during the late Meiji period, as the historian Carol Gluck informs us, it eventually became 'a symbolic rebus that, whatever its context, stood unmistakably, if indefinably, for the nation'[11]— or, more precisely, the unchanging *essence* of the nation, which prevailed over all its ideological uses and appropriations. While in its earlier incarnations, kokutai had served as a 'rationale for imperial restoration' and as a 'benchmark against which to measure institutional change',[12] it gradually acquired an increasingly sacrosanct, non-negotiable aura. Already by 1925, it was considered a crime against the state under the Peace Preservation Law to tamper with the idea of kokutai.[13] By the late 1930s, the propagandist use of kokutai by the military and the Ministry of Education further rigidified its signification to mean 'a conception of an essentialized and exceptionalistic culture capable of resisting historical change'.[14] Even after Japan lost the war, the emperor in his broadcast to the nation was compelled to acknowledge that kokutai had survived.[15]

Clearly, koktuai transcends the kind of personalized relationality that Tagore reads in his invocation of the Mikado, who cannot be compared to an ordinary feudal lord in whom *kshatriya dharma*, or the code of the warrior, resides. Indeed, the context becomes even more distorted when Tagore invokes the example of Japan as providing a model whereby the king can be reconciled with the country through the charismatic authority of the samajpati, on whose legitimacy and qualities of leadership, Tagore is extremely vague. He is on stronger ground when he shifts the attention away from these figures of authority to focus on the most indigenous and emotionally laden figure in the swadeshi imaginary: the archteypal Mother of the nation. Here, Tagore comes very close to echoing the religiosity of politics, as articulated by Aurobindo during the swadeshi movement: 'The Mother asks us for no schemes, no plans, no methods. She herself will provide the schemes, the plans, the methods better than any that we can devise.'[16] In this construction, nationalism 'is not politics but a religion, a creed, a faith'.[17]

Such was the ubiquity of the iconic figure of Bharat Mata in the late nineteenth century, that it was enriched not only by political discourse and fiction but by popular visual culture, ranging from Abanindranath Tagore's rendering of *Bharat Mata*, which was hailed by Sister Nivedita as the very landmark of modern Indian art, to political rallies resounding with cries of *Bande Mataram* (Hail to the Motherland).[18] So visceral was the cumulative impact of this image that nationalists like Bipin Pal insisted that the 'nation as mother', in the Indian context, 'had no metaphor behind it'.[19] Not 'a mere idea or fantasy', nor a 'mere civic sentiment' endorsing the 'secular patriotism of Europe', Bharat Mata was at once a 'physical and spiritual, geographical and social' entity, and even more so 'the cult of the Mother' was nothing less than an 'organic part of our ideal of the love of God'.[20]

Significantly, Tagore in *Swadeshi Samaj* does not go quite so far in highlighting the religiosity of the Mother; instead, he humanizes her in a hyperreal mode, so that she appears less as a symbol than an omnipresent reality. She first makes her entrance in the narrative unobtrusively, yet subversively, in a distinctly non-modern and essentially domesticated role, while Tagore is narrating his experience of attending provincial conferences of the Congress in cities like Dhaka. Here, despite the trappings of the protocol of the conference, there is an aura of a specifically Indian ethic of hospitality (*atithisatkar*) that cuts through the formality of the occasion; so much so that Rabindranath feels, though not without a touch of irony, that he is a member of the bridegroom's party attending a marriage ceremony.

Within this hubbub of conviviality and festivity, it would seem as if Bharatlakshmi herself had opened her dilapidated 'old long-unused guesthouse', and passed through the august assembly, distributing home-made sweets to all the delegates before disappearing into the inner chambers of the house.[21] She comes and goes, a bit of a misfit, very much in her own world, yet observing the curious spectacle of the English conference, where the speakers deliver political speeches in English and wear spectacles and carry elaborate watch-chains. Tagore adds that 'our old mother', vernacular and shamefaced, might have felt more comfortable if, instead of this English spectacle with its 'borrowed, convoluted, unassimilated rites of civic politics and citizenship', she could have been a part of an ancient Yagya, which could have been open to everybody without any distinctions of status or class or caste. A bigger gathering could have resulted in less food to be shared by all, but the entire atmosphere would have been permeated with joy (*ananda*) and maternal blessings.

Later in the essay, Tagore returns to the figure of the mother, with a direct exhortation to the reader: *Ekbar tora ma boliya dak* (Call your motherland Ma, at least once, 641). Cynics would say that this is unstinted emotional blackmail on Tagore's part, but he works through the emotionalism of the mother-figure, who has held 'our minds and souls' together, protecting us from 'complete destruction during the dark night of foreign domination' (641). This mother is today destitute, and demands our critical attention:

Can't we repair the dilapidated house of our mother? We never considered money to be very important, poverty was never looked down upon in our country—today will we genuflect before money and thereby disrespect our tradition? Can't we bring back our earlier simple way of living and engage ourselves in the service of our mother? In our country, it was never shameful to eat food from banana leaves, it was shameful to eat alone, without sharing food with others. Will we never get back that shame?

[641]

Seva, the concept of service, and *atmashakti* (self-reliance) are embedded in the ethic of sharing whatever exists. Instead of developing a false dependency on external sources of aid, the important thing is to recognize, respect, and build on communitarian resources. In this crucial sense, one could say that Tagore shared the fundamental premise of Gandhian self-sufficiency, even though he arrived at the concept through a different route and emotional register.

Should we who shared our hard-earned rice with distant relatives, treated their children as our own, and never considered it a great sacrifice, now say that we are unable to bear the responsibility of our own mother and motherland? Should we simply take it for granted that we will live off the crumbs thrown to us from time to time by an alien government? ...Never! We ourselves have to assume responsibility for our *swadesh*. Our *dharma* dictates that we do so, it is our glory to do so. Time has come when our *samaj* will become a true, all-encompassing *swadeshi samaj*. Time has come for everyone to think that I am not an isolated unit—no one has the right to abandon me even if I am small, and likewise, I have the responsibility to take care of even the weakest.   [633–4]

Perhaps, realizing that this rhetoric is too idealized, Tagore qualifies that these ties of heart may not extend beyond the boundaries of the village. For the country at large, it may be necessary to accept a larger 'machine-like impersonal structure', which has 'mechanical laws' (*kaler niyam*). However, 'Bharatbarsha', as Tagore reminds us, 'cannot be run by machines alone' (*sudhu kale bharatbarshey cholibe na*, 634).

Gora's *Bharatbarsha*

Bharatbarsha: this is yet another motif in Tagore's rhetoric that is drawn from the larger archetypes of the swadeshi movement. Rather like the Japanese concept of kokutai, it is almost impossible to define, but as its most ardent advocates would claim, it is something deeply connected to the essence of the motherland that has to be *felt*. At least, this is the position of Tagore's most swadeshi-obsessed character Gora, before he sees through the illusions of his overly idealized construction of Bharat, the indigenous name for India. Indeed, there are sections in *Gora* which almost seem to echo the emotional rhetoric of *Swadeshi Samaj*:

You must realize that Bharat possesses a special nature, a special power, a special truth — and only by the fullest manifestation of all these will Bharat be preserved and achieve its fulfilment.[22]

Like kokutai, Bharatbarsha is a mystical 'entity' that encompasses time itself, appropriating the distant past and the even more distant future, while 'weaving a particular thread in a particular pattern in the vast destiny of mankind' (135). The difference with the indivisible ancestral legacy of the kokutai is Bharatbarsha's connection with an ideational geographical time-space that exceeds the limits of a particular nation, though this is not immediately apparent to Gora. Nor is it embodied in any one person, as the kokutai is symbolically embodied in the emperor. *Bharatbarsha* is more expansive in its spread of power and beneficence.

Paradoxically, even as it transcends the country and supersedes its strength, it has to manifest itself through the materiality of a specific culture. Within this materiality, there may be many flaws and areas of deep suffering and injustice. However, for Gora, in his unrepentant phase as a traditional radical Hindu zealot, these flaws have to be embraced through the visceral bonds of 'emotional attachment':

I want the Bharatbarsha that I know. You may blame it, abuse it, but I want that and no other.... I want to share the seat of dishonour which Bharatbarsha occupies at present, forsaken by the rest of the world, humiliated—this is my Bharatbarsha of caste discrimination, of blind superstition, of idol worship.   [324]

While Tagore in *Swadeshi Samaj* does not go so far as Gora in embracing the flaws of orthodox Hinduism, his silence on matters relating to caste, superstition, and idol worship in his advocacy of the *samaj*, was sufficiently provocative for some leading intellectuals in Bengal to lambast him for his revivalist stance. As Prithwischandra Ray put it bitterly, 'It is enough to make one feel like dying of shame and sorrow to find a man like Rabibabu declaring that all opportunities for the cultivation of human qualities had been available to every villager under the traditional social organization.'[23] The doyen of the Sadharan Brahmo Samaj, Sibnath Sastri, was even more cutting: 'The patriotism which glorifies our past as ideal and beyond improvement and which rejects the need for further improvement is a disease.'[24] For Sastri, the 'disease' was specifically related to the obscurantism of tradition, and more generally, to the hatred of everything foreign that accompanies the veneration of the past.

Ironically, after seeming to champion the cause of samaj, Tagore provided its most layered and introspective critique in his monumental novel *Gora*. Here, almost till the end of the novel, he re-lives in a fictional mode the validity of *Swadeshi Samaj* through the ardent nationalism of his protagonist Gora. However, against his will, as Gora is compelled to acknowledge that 'divisive custom' and 'blind obedience' undermine 'the health, knowledge and work-culture of the people', the myth of the samaj is shattered (434). In words that

would probably be somewhat too harsh even for erstwhile critics like
Prithwischandra Ray and Sibnath Sastri, Tagore makes Gora observe
that 'with the weapons of custom and tradition, man was shedding
the blood of other men and ruthlessly denying them their human
rights' (433).

In an agonized *anagnorisis*, an opening of eyes that is as painful as it
is liberatory, Gora is spared the illusion of trying to become one with
ordinary people when he learns that he is not a Hindu but the
orphaned child of Irish parents killed in the Mutiny. This very severing
of blood-ties and brahmanic roots enables him to articulate the
universalist possibilities of an individual self, free of ritualistic ties and
bonds—indeed, so free that it almost detaches itself from any
communitarian bond whatsoever. Now Gora is no longer obliged to
circumvent the divisions of 'Hindu, Muslim, Khrishtan, Brahmo'
(476). In his freedom to respect all faiths, he becomes a true 'Bharatiya'
as he opens himself to a Bharatbarsha that is not the kingdom of
Hindus alone.

Tellingly, the moment of liberation comes with the realization
that he is 'nothing'. In words that resonate with the awareness of a
void, Tagore evokes the 'nothing' with memorable clarity, as the
foundations of Gora's life disintegrate and he is left confronting a
past that no longer has 'substance', and a future that 'disappears'
altogether:

He felt he was floating like a momentary dewdrop on a lotus leaf. He had
no mother, no father, no country, no race, no name, no lineage, no god.
All of him constituted a 'no'. What could he do? Hold on to what? Start
from where?   [471]

Contrary to nationalist readings of this positive despair, Gora's self-
realization is not the objective correlative of the birth of the nation.
It is, more enigmatically, yet precisely, the birth of an unconstituted
self; indeed, a self that both Gandhi and Tagore realized was necessary
for swaraj. Not a politically determined self, but an inner self, akin to
God (or Truth, as Gandhi preferred to name it), ready to embrace
the universe. For Tagore, who was to become the world's most
eloquent spokesperson for a poet's religion, this self was a 'life god'

(*jiban-debata*), as we have briefly indicated in the earlier section; a creative force that was the microcosm of a larger universal Personality.

NEGOTIATING 'NOTHING'

Against Gora's realization that he is 'nothing' I would like to intercept into the discussion here a somewhat startling input from a different context at the end of the Second World War, when, in the depths of Japan's post-war humiliation, Takeuchi Yoshimi, the great Japanese Sinologist and critical thinker of Asia, affirmed that his country was 'nothing'.[25] This 'nothing' was not a sign of nothingness affirming a credo of existential despair. It was more like a caesura; a moment of rest, an acknowledgement of dead space and time, indicating a temporary inability to act or even to think. At once profoundly bleak and yet promising, Takeuchi's 'nothing' suggested the lull before the storm, the withdrawing reflex that precipitates the blow.

Reflecting with considerable depth on this complex moment, Naoki Sakai has emphasized that Takeuchi refused to seek solace in any humanist solution, nor any transcendence of the self, for the simple reason that he was not in a position to claim the self. As the very resistance of the Orient to the West through the process of the modernization was 'integrated into the dominion of the West', the Orient could not 'occupy the position of a subject'.[26] Working through the complex ambiguities of this philosophical truth, Sakai explicates how Takeuchi arrived at the consciousness of 'nothing': 'For there is no *resistance*, that is, there is no wish to maintain the self (the self itself does not exist). The absence of resistance means that Japan is not Oriental. But at the same time, the absence of the self-maintenance wish (no self) means that Japan is not European. That is to say, Japan is nothing.'[27] Takeuchi's predicament approximated that of the slave, as envisioned by the Chinese revolutionary writer Lu Hsun: 'He rejects what he is, and at the same time he rejects any wish to be someone other than what he is.'[28]

I insert Takeuchi's apprehension of 'nothing' into the discussion here to highlight the significantly different implications of 'nothing' in the Tagorean context. While Tagore consciously ends *Gora* on the liberatory possibilities of this 'nothing', Takeuchi (who is, after all, not a character in a novel but a disillusioned political thinker in real life) is compelled to work out some kind of pragmatic political solution to 'nothing'. Even as he was deeply aware of the violence inherent in postures of pan-Asianism, he realized that Asia needed to rally its positive forces around a new collective agency of the non-Western nation, which would have to be the new subject of history, heterogeneous in its opposition to the West but homogeneous within. Rejecting the viability of 'overcoming the modern', Takeuchi settled for critical realism, as we learn from Naoki Sakai's succinct summary of his embattled position:

Takeuchi believed that Asian modernity could be accomplished only by appropriating the essence of Western modernity. But, in order to appropriate the essence of Western modernity, there had to be a collective agent 'nation', and an Asian nation had to resist the West without and overcome the reactionary heritage within. In other words, Asia was to modernize itself by negating both the West outside and its own past inside. For Asia as well as for the West, modernity meant a self-transcending project of struggle with the remnants of the past.[29]

Totally rejecting any redemptive possibility in universal humanism, Takeuchi squarely placed the burden of post-war reclamation on modernity, and its most crystallized embodiment in the nation.

Clearly, this is a conflictual agenda, because both the models of the nation and modernity are drawn from 'the West', even as 'the West' has to be negated. In Tagore's articulation of this predicament, we find substantially different negotiations of modernity and the West, as we shall analyse shortly. Likewise, there is a different openness to the transformative principles of the past, which is a fundamental resource for the creation of non-Western modernity (or modernities, as we would prefer to pluralize the word today, at times with the emphasis on 'alternative' modernities). In addition, Tagore's understanding of the transformative power of the past is hinged on a fundamentally redemptionist notion of the transcendental self. Tellingly, even while Gora discovers himself through a recognition of 'nothing', there is no reason to believe that the society surrounding him is likely to change in any substantial way.[30] For Takeuchi, as indeed, for revolutionary writers like Lu Hsun, this transcendental self is no substitute for political action and the resurgence of society at large.

Underlying these fundamental differences between Tagore's and Takeuchi's grasp of 'nothing' is their antithetical relationship to the nation. While Takeuchi saw in the nation a collective agency for social and political reconstruction in Asia, the poet envisioned in the triumph of the nation the very destruction of world civilization. Nationalism, for Tagore, particularly after the writing of *Gora*, could never be the solution for the humiliation of a defeated people, whether this defeat was viewed in terms of colonization or war. Indeed, if his Gora had transformed himself into a reformed nationalist, following up on his realization of 'nothing', this would have been a total betrayal of the poet's ideals.

AGAINST NATIONALISM

Between the writing of *Gora* and his highly controversial lectures against *Nationalism* in Japan in 1916, Tagore had consolidated his universal humanist position not with the acumen of a political theorist, but with all the ambivalence and metaphoric richness of a poet. 'I am only a poet,' as he vainly attempted to reassure his audiences, inevitably after provoking them with his views on politics, which he expressed with a singular lack of diplomacy and what would be called 'political correctness' today. Tagore's political incorrectness could be profound, bordering at times on dangerous risk-taking. He spoke his mind far too freely for the comfort of ideologues, but this poetic license is precisely why his views on unresolved matters like nationalism continue to be of unusual interest. Even in the context of today's seemingly evolved political theory, where there is more sympathy than ever before for the task of deconstructing the nation, if not writing it out of history altogether, Tagore's anti-nationalism continues to bewilder, if not outrage his most respectful critics, in addition to his more sceptical devotees.

Part of the problem could be that Tagore's almost pathological opposition to the nation is relentless, bordering at times on hysteria:

a hysteria that is embodied in the *excess* of language that spills into shifting registers of revulsion and fear directed at the monstrous, almost vampire-like mechanisms of the nation. Tagore is obsessed by the predatory power of the nation, which is evoked with a rhetoric that is almost more lurid than the most strident anti-globalization discourse of our times. For example, we are warned how 'our life-blood' is being drained by the 'economic dragons'[31] of Western nations, while India itself is being reduced to 'predigested morsels of food', consumed by the 'monster commercial organizations of the world' (96). Along with the terror of being cannibalized, Tagore plays on the manufacture of fear, as he evokes 'nations fearing each other like prowling wild beasts of the night-time; shutting their doors of hospitality, combining only for purpose of aggression or defence; hiding in their holes, their trade secrets, state secrets, secrets of their armaments' (40). Continuing his diatribe, Tagore builds the emotional pitch of his argument with rhetorical questions that seethe with indignation: 'Are we to bend our knees to this spirit of nationalism, which is sowing broadcast over all the world seeds of fear, greed, suspicion, unashamed lies of its diplomacy, and unctuous lies of its profession of peace and goodwill and the universal brotherhood of Man?' (40).

In more acerbic references that punctuate his overburdened rhetoric, the mechanization of the nation is compared to the anonymity and tastelessness of 'tinned food' (54), to the 'applied science' of a 'hydraulic press' (56), and to the numbing effect of 'anaesthetics' (73). As opposed to the living rhythms of the hand-loom, nationalism capitulates to the soul-denying efficiency of the power-loom (57). Even the comfort of 'walk[ing] barefooted upon ground strewn with gravel', where 'our feet come gradually to adjust themselves to the caprices of the inhospitable earth', is contrasted with the discomfort of wearing shoes, which represent the closed and pinched world of 'the government by the Nation', where all instinct is regulated by decorum (61).

While these concrete and highly suggestive images indicate Tagore's ingenuity in making his anti-nationalism palpable and deeply human, it would be inaccurate to restrict his position within the limits of poetic rhetoric. Certainly, for all his occasionally political *faux pas*, notably his colossal misreading of Mussolini as a great personality, Tagore was sufficiently canny to realize the limits of what could be named or opposed in terms of the realpolitik. However, this discretion did not stop the poet from lashing out with muted rage against the imperialist designs of Japan as a nation. Without specifically naming Korea, whose oppression under Japanese rule from 1910 onwards was becoming increasingly well known, Tagore inserted into his lecture a memorable passage that is the very antithesis of Okakura's defence of Japanese imperialism in relation to Korea, which I had addressed in the earlier section. Indeed, this passage must have been profoundly disturbing for his Japanese audience, or at least for those who understood the English language. Like almost all such passages in Tagore's anti-nationalist polemic, it remains a prophetic warning for the contemporary warmongers of our times:

Never think for a moment that the hurt you inflict upon other races will not infect you, or that the enmities you sow around your homes will be a wall of protection to you for all time to come... [T]o perpetuate the humiliation of defeated nations by exhibiting trophies won from war, and using these in schools in order to breed in children's minds contempt for others, is imitating the West where she has a festering sore, whose swelling is a swelling of disease eating into its vitality.   [67]

Tellingly, while the metaphor of disease is specifically linked to nationalism and the modernity of 'the West', the basic assumption is that, for all Japan's perversions, the nation that causes Tagore so much concern is the Nation of the West. 'We', in the 'non-West', constitute a 'No-Nation'.

Within these polarities, it is easy to fall into the trap of what has been theorized as the 'illegitimacy of nationalism'[32] in order to uphold an anti-state, anti-modern, anti-secularist agenda, on the lines of Ashis Nandy's civilizational critique which he has extended to his reading of Tagore. 'Illegitimacy,' I would argue, is perhaps too euphemistic a term for Tagore's deep abhorrence of the idea of nationalism. However, the rejection of nationalism does not mean that Tagore's affiliations to the imaginary of the nation, at civic and creative levels, should be summarily dismissed, or collapsed into his critique of nationalism at the level of the state and government. This is the first discrimination that informs the discussion on Tagore's anti-nationalism in the following pages.

Yet another discrimination that needs to be kept in mind is that while Tagore rejects the idea of nationalism, he does not in the process unequivocally endorse civilization. Certainly, there is an affirmation of civilization in Tagore's critique of nationalism, but it is layered and circumspect, if not deeply self-questioning and open to doubt. Civilization, like any other term in Tagore's lexicon, is not to be branded as offering some kind of panacea for the world's problems; it is to be questioned within the spectrum of its contradictory interpretations.

The third discrimination that needs to be emphasized is that Tagore's hostility towards nationalism does not result in his rejection of modernity altogether, which is another source of ambivalence that frustrates anti-modernist communitarian critics. In the following pages, I will attempt to heighten these three discriminations so that Tagore's anti-nationalism does not get reduced to a merely polemical position. Nor, I would emphasize, should we try to hitch it to ongoing critiques of nationalism in the age of globalization, without recognizing its specific nuances and confusions within the context of his times.

With these qualifications, let us work towards a reflexive reading of Tagore's concept of civilization, which I will try to argue is deeply fissured, at once mirroring and responding to the split between what he called the Nation of the West and the Spirit of the West. This articulation becomes all the more complex because the entire thrust of Tagore's civilizing mission cannot be separated outside of Asia, which in turn is inextricably linked to the Orient.

REORIENTING THE ORIENT

Before beginning to read Tagore's dyadic understanding of civilization, it would be useful to address the Saidian legacy of *Orientalism* (1978), which is bound to haunt almost any framing of the Orient today. It is by now well established that the seminal influence of Said's text rests on an incomplete project, which demands new negotiations at two primary levels: first, the production of and reception to the Orient in and through non-Western cultures and histories outside of the Middle East, which was Said's specific locus of investigation; and second, the problematization of the exchange of Orientalist intellectual production within Asia itself through the creation of multiple orients, those determined at some level by the Orient produced in the West, but also sustained through other trajectories in the non-West.

In order to destabilize the dominant modes of the Orient, I would emphasize the need for a different understanding of the asymmetries in the axes of power and exchange, outside the predetermined routes mapped on a specifically East–West trajectory. What the subject of this book involuntarily opens through its reading of Tagore and Okakura is the relatively uninvestigated East–East trajectories of exchange, now theoretically recognized as 'inter-Asian'. That 'the West' is always a presence in such trajectories can be regarded as a given, but its implicit mediation cannot prevent non-Western trajectories from proliferating in ways that have yet to be adequately inscribed in dominant readings of Orientalism.

Pushing the existing priorities in dominant postcolonial discourse, it is also necessary to deflect the over-represented processes of self-Orientalization vis-à-vis the Orient produced in 'the West' through mimicry, parody, or internalized fantasies, which can produce strategies of resistance. Certainly, there is an element of self-Orientalization in the ways in which both Tagore and Okakura presented themselves to Western audiences in their highly choreographed performances as seers from the East. We will examine this performativity later in the next section of this book dealing with cosmopolitanism. Now, the problem concerns the more difficult destabilization of the epistemology of the Orient, which has been singularized for far too long.

Within the cultural geography of Asia, the Orient, I would argue, is not merely replicated, it is also produced, reproduced, transported, mythologized, and shared across different locations. While there may be apparent overlaps between the 'Orient produced in Europe' and 'the orients produced in Asia', they are not quite the same in their raison d'être, despite broad epistemological similarities. The imbalances of power between these constructions are not merely reverse images of each other; rather, they operate with different deceptions, vulnerabilities, and hopes, at times with imagined affiliations, which are systematically betrayed.

In highlighting these priorities, I am merely inflecting the agenda initiated by Stefan Tanaka in his critical reading of Said through Japan's construction of the Orient—or more specifically, *toyo*, which gradually came to mean 'that which was not the Occident' in the aftermath of the Meiji Restoration.[33] Tanaka correctly emphasizes Said's overly determined dominance of the Occident over the Orient as some kind of 'one-way relationship': a dominance that needs to be supplemented by other reciprocities of relationship in which the Orient can talk back to the Occident in several tongues, or else incorporate the Occident in 'a voice of its own'.[34] A more complex position, insufficiently highlighted by Said, is the dependence of the subject on its object in Orientalist discourse, which Tanaka elaborates with great detail in the way *toyoshi* (Japanese oriental history) not merely 'objectified *shina* [China], defined it, authorized a particular view of it, taught it, and managed it',[35] but, in the process of defining itself in terms of this object, became a 'captive to its own discourse'.[36]

Neither Tagore nor Okakura, it should be emphasized, were directly implicated in the academic institutionalization of Orientalism, which has significantly different historical temporalities in the contexts of India and Japan. While in India Orientalism can be traced back to the late eighteenth century with the inauguration of the Asiatic Society of Bengal in 1784 catalysed by William Jones, whose translation of *Shakuntala* in 1789 can be said to have sparked the origin of the Orient in European consciousness, Japan's Oriental studies (*toyoshi*) was institutionalized in the immediate aftermath of the Russo-Japanese War in 1904–5 with the formation of the Ajia Gakkai (Asia Society) in 1905.[37] In the context of these disparate temporalities, it becomes possible to hypothesize Tagore's relative distance from the somewhat moribund discourse of Orientalism in Bengal, which by the turn of the twentieth century had lost its interventionist immediacy. Okakura's writings, however, were coterminious with the formation of Japanese Oriental studies, which perhaps accounts at yet another level for the embattled nature of his discourse.

At one level, Japan was orientalized, if it existed at all, within the framework of European world-history. However, even as it attempted to construct its own *toyo* (Orient), based on 'cultural difference' rather than 'inherent backwardness' (as exemplified in the West's Orient),[38] it was unable to fully level its relationship with the West because it continued to be dependent, if not subservient, to other cultures in Asia, notably China, for its self-definition.[39] As we have examined in the earlier section on Asia, Okakura's attempts to seek Asian affinities were constantly ruptured by his assertions of Japan's cultural superiority; so much so that his Orient inadvertently challenged the more metaphysical possibilities of a truly harmonious One Asia. As Tanaka emphasizes, there is a clear indication of a toyo in Okakura's assertion of Japan as 'the new Asiatic power. Not only to return to our past ideals, but also to feel and revivify the dormant life of the old Asiatic unity, becomes our mission'.[40] The only difference from the more formal historians and ideologues of toyo is that while they attempted to 'extract from the past the datum for a positivistic history', Okakura was more interested in regaining 'a lost beauty of Asia', to counter 'negative and conflictual Western influences'.[41]

Tagore's idiom in retrieving this 'lost beauty' on his own terms was cast in a similarly diffused language outside of the determinations of history. From his lectures on *Nationalism*, we learn how the Asia of his dreams is set in a timeless zone, in the prehistory of 'those days, when the whole of eastern Asia from Burma to Japan was united with India in the closest tie of friendship, the only natural tie which can exist between nations. There was a living communication of hearts...' (23). Likewise, Okakura waxes eloquent about 'the ancient intercourse which flowed from the Yangtse-kiang to the Ganges, and rolled back from Baghdad to the Long Walls'.[42] This is Orientalist utopianism in its most rhapsodic register, devoid of any attempt to historicize the relatively limited exchanges across Asia during the first millennium, activated by pilgrims and Buddhist scholars. The 'natural ties' envisioned by Tagore and the 'ancient intercourse' invoked by Okakura are more imagined than real, constituting a primordial fellowship and genealogy without which it would have been impossible for them to invent an 'Asia' outside the Orientalist strictures of the West.

The invention of 'Asia' is further amplified in the discourse of a more ardent Orientalist from China, Liang Chi Chao (1873–1929), the president of the Beijing Lecture Association who had invited Tagore to China in 1924. In his panegyric to the Indian poet, Liang romanticized the reunion of India and China in the context of fraternity. At different points in the address, India was invoked as 'our nearest and dearest brother'; China was described as the 'little brother' to India's 'very good elder brother'; and, at one point, the countries even become 'twin brothers'.[43] The final image of Liang's address was cast in an elegiac mode, as both India and China confront 'a thousand years of separation':

Both of us bear lines of sorrow on our face, our hair is grey with age, we stare with a blank and vacant look as if we are just awakened from a dream, but, as we gaze on each other, what recollection and fond memories of our early youth rise in our mind,—of those days, when we shared our joys and sorrows together.[44]

One can understand why the revolutionary writer Lu Xun was so profoundly irked by what he described as the 'magical spell' (moli) that Tagore seemed to have cast on his reactionary Chinese hosts. The poet's visit was so 'perfumed' with hagiography that it 'fumigated' his fans 'with literary and metaphysical flavour'.[45] But even within the limits of hagiography, where Liang essentialized himself and Tagore as the very embodiments of China and India, what was he specifically addressing in terms of Asia's 'lost youth'?

Interestingly, the primary metaphor used by Liang Chi Chao to evoke the affinities of India and China is cast in the language of fraternity rather than parenthood. India is not the 'father' or the 'mother' of China, but the 'brother'. This is a totally different trope from what Stefan Tanaka has emphasized in the context of Japan's orientalist discourse, drawing on David Lowenthal's *The Past is a Foreign*

Country: 'Even as non-Western countries must deal with their own past—their "parent"—they must also grapple with the West, another "parent". The problem is that although the West is also a parent, it has a quite different past and, moreover, one that has relegated its own non-Western past to antiquity.'[46] Apparently oblivious of this rather complicated framework of reference, Liang Chi Chao adopted a different line of asserting respectful affection towards an older sibling rather than obedience to two conflicting sets of parents. In this invocation of the language of fraternity rather than parenthood, there is some evidence here for the more vexed political slogan that continues to haunt Indo-Chinese dialogue even today in the aftermath of war and border disputes: '*Hindi-Chini bhai bhai*' (*bhai*, 'brother').

In the process of asserting the ancient fraternity of India and China, Liang also provided some rare historical facts in which he catalogued the specific numbers of Indian and Chinese monks and Buddhist scholars who had crossed their respective national borders:

From the tenth year of Han Yung Tsin in the fifth year of Tang Chen Yuan (AD 67–780), roughly during eight hundred years, the Hindu scholars who came to China numbered twenty-four, to which may be added thirteen from Kashmir (which in Tang times was not recognized as part of India). ...Our scholars who went to India to study, during the period from the western Tsin to the Tang dynasties (AD 265–790) number 187, the names of 105 of whom we can ascertain.[47]

In addition to the tantalizing reference to Kashmir's autonomy, Liang is providing documentary evidence that would seem to contradict his evocation of India and China as being in some form of continuous dialogue in the first millennium. Even so, that dialogue, suggesting an intrinsic 'unity' of mutual interests and concerns, had to be posited as an essential fact or else it would not have been possible for Liang to assume that 'We Were One'.

If 'we were/are one', then what happened to our alleged ' oneness'? Here one has to credit Okakura with some candour, as he acknowledges that the contemporary situation in Asia is marked by 'the absence of communication and interchange', which had resulted in 'a standing barrier to the formulation of the fundamental principles of our common civilization'.[48] If only Okakura could have sustained this candour, he would not have attempted to prove the illusory dogma that 'We are One'. However, under the pressure of his self-imposed 'ideals of Asia', Okakura is compelled to blame the rupture of Asia partially on the brutality of the Mongol invasion, long before the incursions of colonization and imperialism. Tagore is far less specific about the cause of the rupture in his lectures on *Nationalism* and metaphorizes it in a more apocalyptic register: 'Then fell the darkness of the night upon all the lands of the East' (18). It is against this continuing darkness that Tagore makes his specific plea to Japan: '[I]n your voice Asia shall answer the questions that Europe has submitted to the conference of Man' (23).

This is a staggering statement, I would submit, that demands some analysis. Evidently there is an abdication of voice here at two levels: Not only does Tagore assume Japan's right, if not responsibility, to represent Asia, he also accepts that the questions to which Japan will respond have already been submitted by Europe to the conference of Man. It would appear that defeated nations have no voice whatsoever, except in lectures where their presumption to berate the developed world risks being duly mocked. From '*your* voice', the Land of the Rising Sun is formally told to 'remember that *she* has the mission of the East to fulfil. She *must* infuse the sap of a fuller humanity into the heart of modern civilization' (30, my emphases). Peremptory in its impulse, the mission has all the ardour of a redemptionist Orientalist project, in which Japan is encouraged to save modern civilization with humanity.

CRISIS IN 'CIVILIZATION'

Before proceeding further, it is perhaps useful to ask how the word 'civilization' is being used by the protagonists of this narrative. Once again, when it comes to critical reflection on the terms of his discourse, Okakura exudes such a surfeit of confidence and cultivated eloquence that he totally negates the value of self-reflexivity. At no point does he reveal any discomfort with the dominant usage of *bunmei* (civilization) in the late Meiji period. A neologism, bunmei replaced the Chinese notion of *ka*, by substituting its focus on 'order and propriety', 'harmony and hierarchy' with the dynamics of 'progress' based in pragmatic notions of 'production'.[49] While at first bunmei was inevitably prefixed with the adjectives 'new' or 'Japanese', the word (and concept) got 'gradually naturalized'.[50] As Carol Gluck clarifies, 'By the end of the period, "civilization" appeared as an indigenous fact of social life... By the 1900s even those displeased with the effects of bunmei were not free to dismiss the notion, any more than they could—or would—roll up the railroad tracks that were the material epitome of its achievement.'[51]

Okakura fully embraced this materialist notion of civilization despite his occasional potshots at the crudity of the modern era and his affirmation of a rather vague spirituality in art. At best he permitted himself a certain irony about the mixed benefits of civilization, as he wittily commented in his best-selling *The Book of Tea* (1906): 'The average Westerner...was wont to regard Japan as barbarous while she was indulging in the gentle arts of peace; he calls her civilized since she began to commit wholesale slaughter on the Manchurian fields. ...Fain would we remain barbarians, if our claim to civilization were to be based on the gruesome glory of war.'[52] And yet, that is precisely what *The Book of Tea* succeeds in doing: it celebrates the cultivation of tea-culture not as some kind of archaic ritual or exotic equivalent of 'afternoon tea', but as a militant code and embodiment of 'national resistance, manly self-control and virile self-sacrifice'.[53] These were precisely the 'civilized' virtues hailed by the Boston Brahmins who patronized Okakura's art. As Christopher Benfey has deftly expressed it, Okakura was arguing that 'one could be an aesthete and a soldier, Oscar Wilde and Teddy Roosevelt, that the way of tea and the way of the samurai were one'.[54] For all his individual eccentricities, Okakura was a product of bunmei; so much so that he never attempted to redefine civilization because he was far too comfortable enjoying its benefits.

This was not the case with Tagore who, literally, till the very last year of his life, when he was eighty years old, was still struggling to find an adequate way of translating 'civilization' into Bengali. His very last writing, significantly entitled *Sabhyatar Sankat* (Crisis in Civilization, 1941) is, at one level, an acknowledgement of the crisis in language. Acknowledging the instability of the word in Bengali usage, Tagore reluctantly invokes the Sanskrit word '*sadachar*', which was used by Manu to designate 'proper conduct', and more broadly, the 'conduct prescribed by the tradition of the race'.[55] Within the obvious geographical, racial, and sectarian limits of such a formulation, Tagore emphasizes how the 'pharisaic formalism' of 'proper conduct' soon degenerated into 'socialized tyranny'.[56]

Rejecting sadachar, Tagore uses the more contemporary Bengali word for 'civilization', *sabhyata*, in the very title of his essay, a word that approximates the associations of materiality, progress, Westernization, enlightenment, and modernity denoted in the Japanese word bunmei. Even so, this word barely conveys the layers of meaning that Tagore was extrapolating from *his* envisioning of 'civilization' at the very moment of its crisis during the Second World War. *Ekei ki bole sabhyata?* (Is this Civilization?) is the audacious title of Michael Madhusadan Dutt's empathetic satire on the excesses and pretensions of the Young Bengal movement, which consciously provoked the pieties of Hindu orthodoxy and social custom. While this movement had lost its edge by the time Tagore was born, and arguably he would never have supported its flamboyant radical gestures,[57] the title of Madhusadan's play can be reworked ironically in the context of Tagore's continuing struggle to define civilization. *Sabhyata* — Is this 'Civilization'? Perhaps not, one could argue, in the larger context of Tagore's metaphysical and moral ideals.

The closest that Tagore ever came to elaborating on 'civilization' in English was during his lecture tour in China, where he used the multivalence of *dharma* to counter the limits of progress. In a pithy statement in a particularly vivid talk on 'Culture and Civilization', Tagore claimed: 'That which drives is called the principle of progress, that which sustains we call *dharma*; and this word *dharma* I believe should be translated as civilization.'[58] Dharma is what 'holds' us together, leading to 'our best welfare'.[59] At the heart of Tagore's civilizational ideal was 'some guiding moral force which we have evolved in our society for the object of attaining perfection.'[60] However, this moral force was not some doctrinaire principle upholding the rule of law; it was more like a 'creative ideal that binds its members in a rhythm of relationship'; a relationship that is 'beautiful and not merely utilitarian'.[61]

If this appears to be an excessively idealized and normative understanding of civilization, one should emphasize Tagore's more down-to-earth descriptions of its actual practice in the context of hospitality. He narrates at least two stories in this context that get to the heart of the matter. One is set in war-torn Afghanistan where some British airmen have been compelled to make a forced landing in the midst of a Mahsud village. Even as the area is being bombed, 'five or six old women...brandishing dangerous looking knives' escort the airmen into a cave, where they are royally fed by the maliks (chieftains), and finally escorted to safety, disguised as Mahsuds. This is a charming story, from which Tagore draws a very temperate insight into civilization: 'The Mahsud may have many faults for which he should be held accountable; but that, which has imparted for him more value to hospitality than to revenge, may not be called progress, but is certainly civilization.'[62]

Likewise, in another anecdote, dealing with the trials of driving back to Calcutta from a rural area in a car that periodically breaks down, Tagore points out the discrepancy between rural hospitality and urban greed. While the villagers cannot think of accepting money in exchange for the water they provide for the car, the suburbanites have no difficulty in selling the water, even though it is more readily available in their area.

Having provided some background on the multiple connotations of the word 'civilization', we can now analyse how Tagore uses it to frame his argument against nationalism. The most obvious strategy adopted by Tagore was to demarcate different sets of values relating to Eastern and Western civilization, which are separated and distinguished with conflicting attributes. 'Eastern civilization has been pursuing its own path..., which [is] not political but social, not predatory and mechanically efficient but spiritual and based upon all the varied and deeper relations of humanity.'[63] In contrast, 'the political, mechanical, and commercial character of modern civilization was threatening to devour Asia's spiritual civilization'.[64] The rhetoric is laden with oppositions, as indeed, the word 'civilization' is constantly being qualified and inflected, as if it cannot be trusted on its own terms. Therefore, 'Western civilization' is also substituted by 'political civilization' and 'modern civilization', while 'Eastern civilization' is also identified as 'social civilization', 'spiritual civilization', and 'civilization of human relationship'.

To risk a somewhat schematic analysis, the West, for Tagore, is a two-sided Janus-like phenomenon as it oscillates between the Nation of the West and the Spirit of the West. This Spirit of the West is what makes Western civilization desirable to the East. But the Nation intervenes as an unconditional, non-negotiable negative factor; rather like a 'dam' that 'check[s] the free flow of Western civilization into the country of the No-Nation' (59). Civilizational ties with the West can therefore be reconciled only through a severance of the Nation, or else, through a separation of 'spirit' and 'nation', which have to be kept apart. In contrast, Tagore valorizes the Spirit of the East but he is unable (by his own formulation) to accept the Nation of the East. For countries like India, which is a No-Nation, the problem of relating Spirit to Nation does not arise. What then about highly developed nations like Japan where, arguably, in the Meiji period itself, the Spirit of the East and the Nation of the East were regarded by its leading ideologues as virtually a single entity?

Tagore could not deal with this question, among other abstruse components of Japanese polity, and it is therefore not surprising that his lectures on nationalism in Japan in 1916 were highly controversial. We shall examine a few Japanese reactions to these lectures at a later point in the discussion, but let us now substantiate further the depth of Tagore's anti-nationalism. In my view, we would be dishonouring his critique by attempting to soften it, or by seeking a 'good nationalism' in opposition to a 'bad nationalism'. Certainly, Tagore would not attempt Takeuchi Yoshimi's strategy of 'drawing a genuine nationalism' from out of 'ultra-nationalism', a logic that Karatani Kojin has correctly described as extremely 'risky' in the neo-religious attempt to draw 'revolution from within counter-revolution'; passing through 'evil' in search of 'salvation'.[65] Such a strategy would, in all probability, have been considered duplicitous by Tagore, who unfailingly rejected the ethics of adopting bad means to realize ostensibly good ends.

Apart from avoiding the discriminations of nationalism between 'good' and 'evil', 'exclusionary' and 'inclusive', Tagore did not seek any alternative ground to nationalism in patriotism. In contrast, even the most rabid anti-national postmodern critics of our times have attempted to inflect their critique of the state by acknowledging the nebulous structure of feelings contained in patriotism. This is the site where the civic affiliations of 'imagined communities' are almost divested of ethnic closures and opened to hybrid mixtures of more than one sense of national belongingness. Today, in 'diasporic public spheres', there are new articulations of multiple patriotisms as opposed to monopatriotism. In Tagore, one finds no such illusions of neo-liberal pluralism.[66]

Likewise, in more traditional readings of Indian pluralism, there have been attempts to provide a more universalist understanding of patriotism on the lines of *bharatchinta* or *swadeshchinta*, literally 'thinking about or concern with India or one's own country'.[67] This form of patriotism is endorsed by none other than Ashis Nandy in his critique of 'the illegitimacy of nationalism' on the grounds that it conveys 'the idea of patriotism without nationalism', contributing to 'a self-definition transcending the geographical barriers of India'.[68] At some level we have already encountered the possibilities of such patriotism in Gora's recantation of nationalism, but very tellingly, Tagore leaves his state of transformation unnamed in social and political terms. Certainly, in his own writings on nationalism, Tagore made no attempt to soften his anti-nationalist criticism by imagining patriotism as a communitarian or universalizing alternative. Even when one of his patriotic songs became the Indian national anthem, when he adopted what could be described as an obligatory patriotism, he satisfied none of his critics. As Nandy is compelled to acknowledge, '[H]is version of patriotism rejected the violence propagated by terrorists and revolutionaries; it rejected the concept of a single-ethnic Hindu *rashtra* [state] as anti-India, and even anti-Hindu; and it dismissed the idea of the nation-state as being the main actor in Indian political life'.[69]

In the context of such summary rejections and dismissals, it is doubtful whether Tagore can be said to endorse patriotism at all. Singularly avoiding any ambivalence in the articulation of his position, he criticizes patriotism with as much vehemence as he rails against nationalism, at times using the words synonymously with no attempt to inflect their difference. Far from humanizing nationalism, patriotism, for Tagore, serves to intensify its destructive propensities: 'The Nation, with all its paraphernalia of power and prosperity, its flags and pious hymns, its blasphemous prayers in the churches, and the literary mock thunders of its patriotic bragging, cannot hide the fact that the Nation is the greatest evil for the Nation' (65). In this oddly tautological construction, the 'paraphernalia' of the first Nation would seem to be the bogus patriotic apparatus for the political Nation, but it is not just 'blood and thunder' but the 'greatest evil'.

Against this profound distrust of patriotism, one is compelled to question how Tagore is remembered today as the only composer of two national anthems in the world, thereby challenging the assumptions of monolithic loyalty to any one nation.[70] 'Amar sonar Bangla', that extraordinarily lyrical invocation of Bengal as motherland, is Tagore's posthumous gift to the nation of Bangladesh, which coexists with the more robust Indian anthem Jana Gana Mana. Indeed, Tagore has left behind a legacy of the most deeply internalized patriotic songs in Bengal, which cannot be separated from their national content, even as he was scrupulously vigilant in negotiating their secular idiom, as in the case of Bande Mataram.[71] Ideologically, the poet may have distanced himself from the politics of swadeshi, but the songs of that time remain to haunt Bengal's culture of resistance even to this day.

In this context, is it possible to conceive of Tagore, the Gurudev of Bharatbarsha, as an anti-nationalist? For all his fierce rejection of the idea of nationalism, is it possible to deny his national aura, which Gandhi in his typically forthright manner confirmed by hailing Tagore as an 'ardent nationalist' in his obituary written on the poet's death?[72] Perhaps we will never fully resolve these questions within the limitations of the existing languages of nationalism available to us in political theory, and in the increasingly strident critiques of nationalism pervading subalternist and communitarian discourse.

Instead of attempting to resolve the contradiction of Tagore's profoundly national anti-nationalism, we would be better off viewing it as a provocation that can trouble us to find new ways of re-imagining the 'national' in opposition to 'nationalism'.[73] Ashis Nandy comes close to affirming 'a "national" ideology that would transcend nationalism',[74] but he is ultimately unable to fully accept this as a viable ground, and remains entrapped in a vague attempt to separate nationalism from anti-imperialism and patriotism. He is on stronger ground when he posits a 'politics of the self', but is unable to elaborate on how this 'self' can respond to the lived history of the nation, as opposed to the historiography and politics of the nation–state. What is missing here is the role of the imagination in transforming the nation through the self. Indeed, is it possible to 'imagine' the nation differently not through the trajectories of print-capitalism, as outlined by Benedict Anderson in his now widely circulated theory, but through a different grounding of the imagination altogether in the creative and social affinities of the self? Or is this quasi-literary and discursive attempt to find new grounds for the 'national' ultimately entrapped in Third World utopianism?

We shall return to this question later while dealing with Tagore's envisioning of a poet's 'history' and the misunderstandings surrounding his position. Let us now proceed to contextualize the reception to Tagore's lectures on nationalism in Japan itself within the larger context of how he was often misunderstood in his own times.

GROUNDS FOR MISUNDERSTANDING

Tagore's poetic inflections of politics and history contributed to the misunderstandings surrounding him as a public intellectual. In 1916, in the midst of the First World War, when Japan had already joined the club of the most developed nations in the West, it was bewildering, if not humiliating, for Tagore's Japanese audience to confront his critical onslaught on the idea of nationalism. After being welcomed as the 'son of the East', the first Asian writer to win the Nobel Prize, Tagore failed to live up to his media-hyped 'Asian' credentials. In questioning the modern developments of the Japanese nation, his verdict was bleak: the nation that had appeared to be a model for the rest of Asia was potentially doomed in its own right.

The critical reception to Tagore in Japan has been thoroughly documented by Stephen Hay (1970), so I will not elaborate on it at length here. Suffice it to say that Tagore's old-worldly 'resignationism' was subjected to ridicule, notably by Japan's most influential and powerful official scholar, Inoue Tetsujiro, who was among the first to deride Tagore's voice as 'the song of a ruined country'.[75] Known primarily for his official interpretation of the 1890 Imperial Rescript on Education, which had sold four million copies all over Japan, Inoue took Tagore to task for his apparent hostility to science and total indifference to practical matters relating to society, nation, and state. 'As the people of a rising nation,' he declared, 'I think we should make every effort to exclude the Indian tendency toward pessimism and dispiritedness.'[76] It is significant how the attack on Tagore was inevitably mediated by a larger contempt for the defeated nation of India. Even as his poetic powers were acknowledged, he himself remained the 'beautiful flower of a ruined country'.[77]

The opposition to Tagore extended to his spiritual allies, temperamentally linked through creative and humanist enterprises. Even those artists and intellectuals, who had reason to question the emerging 'culturalism' (bunkashugi) of the early Taisho period, marked by the values of autonomy, individualism, and growing cosmopolitanism, found Tagore's refusal to deal with the benefits of materiality incomprehensible. The utopian leader of the Shirakaba-ha, or the White Birch school of writers, Mushanokoji Saneatsu, for instance, was dismayed by Tagore's lack of realism: '[H]e doesn't even mention the possible use of material civilization for the benefit of all mankind... Of course I hate bad civilization, but I want the strength to raise bad civilization to good civilization. I find nothing in Tagore's writings about this strength.'[78] Clearly, the very idea of civilization is in dispute here: for all his Tolstoyan missionary zeal in rejuvenating rural Japan through the 'new village movement', Mushanokoji could not free himself from the material bases of bunmei. Nor was he alert to Tagore's very wry qualifications, which were perhaps less evident in his philosophical lectures than in his parting words from Japan, when he compared material civilization to a 'sharp razor': 'Use [it], but do not be used by it.'[79]

The Bengali critic Sisir Kumar Das, among other Tagore scholars, has rejected Stephen Hay's thesis that Tagore's prophetic aura and pontification contributed largely towards his being misunderstood, not just in Japan but also in China, where the opposition to the poet was even fiercer and predetermined. Indeed, there could be some substance in the poet's accusation that 'these people [Chinese communists and radical groups] are *determined* to misunderstand me.[80] From Das's meticulous research, we learn how members of the Communist Party and the Communist Youth League in China were extremely wary of how Tagore could be 'used' by his conservative and reactionary hosts, and in the process, 'mislead' the youth. 'We, therefore have no option but to oppose him,'[81] was the general consensus, to which Zhou Zeren, the brother of Lu Xun, provided an extremely nuanced perspective in retrospect: 'The [Oppose Tagore Movement] followers think they are scientific thinkers and Westernizers, but they lack the spirit of scepticism and toleration. Actually they are still the kind of Orientals who persecute heretics. If Eastern civilization contains poisons of the worst kind, then this sort of authoritarian fanaticism is one.'[82]

Against this reasoned critique, one could build an argument that the Communists had very legitimate grounds to oppose the feudalism and patriarchy of ancient Chinese civilization, which Tagore seemed to endorse through his refusal to engage with China's lack of development. An excerpt from one of the Chinese manifestos captures some of the rage felt by Tagore's not-so-intimate enemies:

Our agriculture, which hardly feeds our peasants, our industry, which is strictly household industry, our carts and our boats, which go only a few miles a day, our monosyllabic language and our ideographic writing, our printing, which has remained at the stage of carved wood-blocks, our streets, which are latrines, and our deplorably dirty kitchens, have made us lose our reputation. And here Mr Tagore comes to reproach us for our *excess* of material civilization! How can we fail to protest against him?[83]

Most definitely, this was not the social and economic context that Tagore had confronted in Japan in 1916, eight years before his trip to China. These staggering rifts in development across Asian countries become only too evident when one recalls some of the basic features of the Japanese economy.

Already by the first two decades (1868–87) of the Meiji period, through 'centralization, conscription, tax reform, the movement for parliamentary government, and the drafting of a constitution', the capitalist economy of Japan was already in the process of taking shape, with a growing infrastructure of 'railroads, communications, financial institutions'.[84] A national compulsory education system at the primary level had already been established. Print-capitalism was burgeoning, with newspapers, magazines, pamphlets, pornography, and popular novels circulating beyond the confines of cities into the provinces. As early as 1900 the magazine *Taiyo* had a monthly circulation of 300,000, and by 1913, the year that Tagore won the Nobel Prize following which his writings were liberally translated into Japanese, Japan was producing around 27,000 book titles a year, the highest in the world after Germany.[85] This was the beginning of the Taisho period (1913–25), when the material priorities of civilization (bunmei) were being replaced by the individualist avocations of culture (*bunka*). Simultaneously, as Harry Harootunian has mapped the transition between the Meiji and Taisho eras, the goals of public culture and social service were being substituted by the more autonomous desires of the private sphere, with the Meiji ideal of *shugyo* (education) being gradually overpowered by the Taisho avocation of *kyoyo* (cultivation).[86] It was precisely this period of privatization that saw the rise of mass culture and consumption, typified by department stores, movie theatres, bars, and other sources of entertainment and pleasure, which were later condemned under the stigma of 'Americanization'.

Perhaps the effervescence of Taisho culture had not yet fully established itself by the time Tagore visited Japan, but its signs were already in place. Clearly, they did not represent the 'Old Japan' sentimentalized by the poet in his lectures, who was hopelessly out of sync with the times, which were aggressive and competitive, distanced from the transcendental and spiritual priorities of pan-Asian idealists like Okakura. At no level was the shift in priority more significant, yet barely perceptible, than in the attitude to beauty. Here there is a subtle schism that can be traced between the affirmation of traditional Japanese aesthetics in Tagore's lectures, and his more circumspect response to bunkashugi representing the Taisho era.

In his lectures on nationalism, Tagore had valorized the 'genius of Japan' in terms of 'the vision of beauty in nature and the power of realizing it in [one's] life' (32). It was this ubiquity of beauty, extending from 'the language of lines and the music of colours' to the 'commonest utensils of everyday life' (31), which Tagore had communicated to his painter–nephew, Abanindranath, in a famous letter:

The more I travel and see Japan, the more I feel that all of you should have come with me. Sitting in your south verandah you will never realize how much contact with the living art of Japan we need to revitalize the art of our country. The winds of art have not blown in our country and art has no vital links with our social life — it is something superficial that may or may not be there — so you can never draw full sustenance from its soil. If you come here just once, you will know how this whole nation is nurtured by its art; their whole life speaks through this art. [87]

This rapturous affirmation of the transformation of art in everyday life is sharply contrasted with the art sequestered in the 'south verandah' of the Bengal school, tucked away in the ancestral home of the Tagores in Jorasanko, Calcutta. Tagore is clearly indicating his impatience with the élitist aesthetics of coterie art in favour of a more socially dynamic creative energy animating society at large.

Even so, this is just one side of the picture. Even as Tagore affirmed the beauty of functionality in Japanese public culture, and the grace of its 'natural sensibility', he was also aware that this beauty was in the process of petrifying, if ever so slightly. In a deeply insightful letter to his friend and confidant, the British painter William Rothenstein, who had introduced him to Yeats, Tagore reveals some astonishing insights into Taisho culture, even though he does not specifically contextualize his critique within the cultural politics of the times:

The genius [of the Japanese] has taken the course of the definite—they revel in the rhythm of proportion in lines and movements. But music is lacking in them and the deeper currents of poetry which deal with the ineffable. They have acquired a perfect sense of the form at some cost of the spirit. Their nature is solely aesthetic and not spiritual. Therefore it has been easier for them to make their ideals almost universal in their peoples. For these ideals are more in the sense of the decorum and deftness of mind and fingers than in the sense of the infinite in man.[88]

This rarely quoted critique needs to be far more inscribed in the art history of the Bengal school in order to deflect the hagiography surrounding the Japanese sense of beauty. Indeed, it needs to be set alongside Tagore's own valorization of the beauty of Old Japan which, for him, was entirely linked to Okakura's sensibility and neo-traditionalist experiments in Japanese art (*nihonga*). While the specific implications of Tagore's critique of Taisho culture in terms of art practice lie outside the framework of this book, I have consciously called attention to it in order to supplement the critique of modernization represented in his lecture on nationalism. Tagore does not specifically reflect on the impact of modernization on beauty, but its negative consequences are apparent in his anguish relating to the rigidities of national culture and the negation of freedom.

DISCRIMINATING THE MODERN

Against this backdrop of Taisho culture, it becomes easier to understand why Tagore's anti-materialist views must have bordered on 'non-sense' for most of his Japanese audience. Steeped in the commercialism and growing consumerism of the Taisho cultural economy, they had reason to be provoked. If Tagore had lambasted the modern unequivocally, his position might have been more easily comprehended, even if it would have been rejected. However, almost perversely, Tagore complicates an easy critique through the sheer complexity of his position on modernism vis-à-vis modernization. While this discrimination in *Nationalism* is all too brief in Tagore's cryptic articulation, it is among his most suggestive interventions which challenges us even today.

What is tantalizing is not so much what Tagore says, as what he leaves suspended for future deliberation. First of all, he describes modernism as 'freedom of mind, not slavery of taste'; 'independence of thought and action, not tutelage under European schoolmasters'; 'science, but not its wrong application to life' (34). This modernism, which would suggest an attitude and temperament rather than a set of properties, has to be differentiated from the literary and artistic movement of Modernism in Europe in the early twentieth century, to which Tagore had an ambivalent position, as revealed in his much later essay *Adhunik Kabya* (Modern Poetry), written in 1932.[89] However, if there is one commonality between Tagore's position on modernism in *Nationalism* and in the later essay, it is his insistence that it knows no temporal or spatial boundaries. Refusing to periodize or to essentialize its salient features, Tagore chooses to differentiate modernism from modernization, which he does not specifically define in *Nationalism*, but which suggests a process of incorporating through imitation the materials, objects and technologies of Europe into the structures of everyday life in Asia. If there is one principle that Tagore rejected outright both in the aesthetic and social realms of life—and, in this regard, his position was totally compatible with that of Okakura—it was his resistance to the idea of imitation. 'It hampers our true nature; it is always in our way,' as Tagore explains in his lecture. Then, breaking any illusion of equanimity, he adds: 'It is like dressing our skeleton with another man's skin' (20).

Modernism is, at some level, linked to being 'true to nature', while modernization is what disrupts this process of self-realization through the act of imitation. Though Tagore does not theorize this discrimination, he implies that there can be no fixed causality between modernism and modernization. In other words, one cannot assume that modernization leads to modernism, any more so than secularization leads to secularism or the formation of secular identities, as we know from our own experience today in the Indian subcontinent. The relationship between modernism and modernization can be disjunctive, interruptive, full of reversals, but it is not resolutely unilinear. From Tagore's formulation, it is possible to deduce that modernization can be detached entirely from the state of modernism, which is a challenging proposition. More unequivocally, there is a clear indication in the poet's critique that modernism cannot be assumed as the prerogative of Europe. It can exist anywhere, ostensibly in anyone, in any community, but in an independent state of mind.

Ironically, while Tagore's discourse on modernism was largely rejected by his Japanese audience in 1916, it almost seemed to be endorsed during the famous conference on 'overcoming the modern' (*kindai no chokoku*) held in Kyoto in July 1942. In this caucus of distinguished Japanese intellectuals and scholars from the Kyoto School of Philosophy (Kyoto Gakuha), the Literary Society (Bungaku-kai), and the Japanese Romantic group (Nihon Romanha), there was a concerted, though eventually unsuccessful and disingenuous attempt, to reverse the modernism of the Showa period, based on the commercialism and consumerism of the Taisho period, and the civilization and enlightenment discourse of the Meiji period. Immersed within, and yet apparently oblivious to, the intensified militarism of Japan, the intellectuals at the Kyoto conference chose to agonize about the spiritual and cultural implications of their modern legacy, barely six months after the bombing of Pearl Harbour and the imperialist assertion of Japan's power across Southeast Asia.

Envisioning a new world order, or more precisely, an Asian order under Japan's assumed leadership, the intellectuals in Kyoto failed to disentangle their own self-hatred, unavoidably nurtured through their intellectual and philosophical links with the West, from their xenophobia linked to their implicit defence of the war. In different registers of disillusionment, they castigated the deadening effects of Western rationality and the compartmentalization of knowledge, which seemed to have demeaned the authentic and intrinsically civilizational ideals of an earlier, more mythic Japan, committed to the timeless essences of beauty and spirituality. With a surfeit of metaphorical epithets, the delegates built their condemnation of modernity around categories like 'a time without belief', 'subjective nothingness', the dissolution of the 'self', the 'sickness' and 'contagion' of Westernization, and the 'excess of historical consciousness', which seemed to stifle 'intellectual creativity and cultural originality'.[90]

Indeed, at a rhetorical level, many of these categories would appear to have some resemblance to Tagore's lament for the disappearance of moral values and beauty through the onslaught of materialism. Even so, it would be rashly inaccurate to imagine that the intellectuals of the Kyoto conference were genuinely serious about a 'renewed belief in gods', still less a 'return to "Oriental religious" practice',[91] or that they were ready to singularly reject the technologies of modernization on which they were only too dependent. Such was their apparent rejection of contemporaneity that it extended to the allegedly demoniac pleasure derived from Hollywood, which was a particular target of moral condemnation in their general diatribe against the Americanization of Japanese society. In contrast to the decadence of Hollywood, the documentaries of Leni Riefenstahl were acknowledged as a significant alternative,[92] insofar as they countered the 'valueless mediocrity, shallowness and triviality' of Americanization.[93]

Yet, for all the loathing directed against the cultural effects of Americanization, the participants of the conference were not entirely ready to sever their links from its very source of patronage in industrial and social capital. Harry Harootunian gets to the point when he emphasizes that the symposium 'never got around to directly constructing a critique of capitalism as a political and economic system'.[94] Entrapped within the privileges of its own lacerating self-critique, it failed to grapple with the central contradiction of its discourse, namely, that 'Modernity was already an overcoming, and any attempt to imagine an overcoming of an overcoming could lead only to a reaffirmation of the very processes of modernity that induced people to think about eventfulness and change'.[95]

One needs to stress at this point that, for all its inner contradictions that were never fully worked out in the language of the social sciences, Tagore's critique of the modern era was not entrapped within the conflicting logic of 'overcoming modernity' precisely because he was in a position to differentiate between 'modernism' and 'modernization'. For all the severity of his critique, he was confident that it was possible to be modern through a moral and ethical affirmation of the self. What Tagore opposed was the cult of modernity, and its arrogant assumption that there is nothing to be learned from the past.

In contrast, Okakura's position on modernity straddled the positions adopted by Tagore and the delegates of the Kyoto conference, insofar as it worked through a spectrum of compromises. While sharing Tagore's aversion towards imitation, Okakura had a somewhat more pragmatic approach in defining the modern in relation to modernization. In his lecture presented at the World's Fair in St Louis in September 1904, Okakura had clarified that 'the word "modernization" means the occidentalization of the world'[96] — a fact that he did not seem to judge or to endorse or to condemn, but simply to accept as an incontrovertible fact. Against modernization, Okakura did attempt to uphold the modern in his attempt to be 'true to self', which was the motto of his neo-traditionalist school Nihon Bijutsuin. Inevitably, this understanding of the modern was almost totally mediated by art, and more specifically, painting. Within this realm, the 'democratic indifference of the market' and the 'cold-blooded touch of the machine'[97] were marked as sources of opposition, but they were never entirely rejected on the ethical and moral grounds of Tagore's critique of modernization.

In the long run, Okakura seemed to align himself in an uneasy alliance with market forces: on the one hand, he derided the 'menace' of 'modern industrialism' in which beauty had been substituted by 'cheapness',[98] but, on the other hand, he competed in the world art market like a savvy professional, perfectly at ease with the technologies of international travel, trade, business, and diplomacy. Ideationally, however, he held on to the notion that modernization is an external force imposed by the West, while modernism is achieved from within. Unlike Tagore, Okakura never really elaborated on this interiority, which remained problematically nebulous in his writings, if not overtly aestheticized.

Aligning himself with 'conservatives' rather than 'progressives', Okakura, in the course of his lecture in St Louis on 'Modern Problems in Painting', had attempted to clarify his own position:

To [the conservatives] Western society is not necessarily the paragon which all mankind should imitate. They believe in the homogeneity of civilization, but that true homogeneity must be the result of a realization from within, not an accumulation of outside matter.[99]

Then, characteristically, Okakura shifted this seeming endorsement of a spiritualized aesthetics into a militant register:

To them [the conservatives, and, by implication, himself], Japanese paintings are by no means the simple weapons to which they are likened, but a potent machine to carry on a special kind of aesthetic warfare.[100]

One is compelled to ask whether this 'potent machine' is not a product of the modernization that Okakura ostensibly derides. More chillingly, is it not the modernization of war?

At no point in Okakura's oeuvre was there a conscious dismantling of the aesthetics of war, and in this context it would be impossible to imagine him affirming, along with Tagore, that 'in a little flower, there is a living power hidden in beauty which is more potent than a Maxim gun'.[101] For Okakura, the flower and the Maxim gun could be interrelated conceptually within the rigour of a militant aesthetic. For Tagore, on the other hand, beauty and war embodied two totally antithetical realms of nature and mechanization. There could be no negotiation of their coexistence, even as Tagore almost flaunted the language of non-violence in his defiance of omnipotent power: 'I believe that in the bird's notes nature expresses herself with a force which is greater than that revealed in the deafening roar of the cannonade.'

Here one has no other choice but to recall Gandhi's famous riposte to Tagore in one of their many critical exchanges. While Tagore had idealized the image of the bird in 'The Call of Truth' by emphasizing that its songs emblematize the call of 'universal humanity', transcending the 'search for food', Gandhi, in an unforgettable response, had told the poet in plain terms: 'But I have had the pain of watching birds who for want of strength could not be coaxed even into a flutter of their wings. The human bird under the Indian sky gets up weaker than when he pretended to retire. For millions it is an eternal vigil or an eternal trance. It is an indescribably painful state which has to be experienced to be realized.'[102] I do believe that Gandhi has the last word in this particular debate.

HOMAGE TO THE WEST

Apart from the complexities relating to Tagore's differentiation between modernism and modernization, there is yet another area of misunderstanding that must have bothered Tagore's critics in Japan in 1916: the poet's unstinted homage to Europe. This 'homage' should be differentiated from acknowledging a 'debt' to Europe, on the lines of contemporary subaltern critics, who have dutifully acknowledged that they would never have been able to *think* without grasping the fundamental *grammar* of primary concepts relating to state and civil society, derived from Europe's master texts.[103] Tagore's praise for Europe extended far beyond 'grammar' to its very ethics and civic values relating to the 'love of justice' (27), 'disinterested love of freedom' (27), 'liberty of conscience, liberty in thought and action, liberty in the ideals of art and literature' (44), and so on.

Elsewhere, in his lecture on *Nationalism in the West*, which he delivered in almost twenty cities on a whirlwind lecture tour in the United States following his trip to Japan, Tagore almost seemed to contradict his distrust of the law, suggested in his earlier writings. On this US tour, he acknowledged that 'The protection of [English] law is not only a boon, but it is a valuable lesson to us.... We are realizing through it that there is a universal standard of justice to which all men, irrespective of their caste and colour, have their equal claim' (57). Such statements seem to verify E.P. Thompson's view that Tagore's 'anti-politics' was not devoid of a profound faith in civil society, a category that the poet never specifically invoked, but to which he alluded in his constant search for a society based on mutual trust and respect for the individual, based on autonomous social relationships, free of statist strictures and repressive laws.[104]

Arguably, Thompson conflates Tagore's reading of samaj with 'society', and more specifically, 'civil society': distinctions that tend to get lost when drawing selectively on Tagore's statements in which 'society' appears to be unconditionally endorsed. 'Society as such has no ulterior purpose. It is an end in itself. It is a spontaneous self-expression of man as a social being' (51). From such affirmations, it becomes possible to deduce, as Thompson does, that Tagore is 'envisioning something distinct from and of stronger and more personal texture than political or economic structures', but the moot point is whether this denotes a 'clear conception of civil society'.[105] Perhaps, as I have attempted to suggest in my earlier reading of samaj, it is relatively easier to clarify what Tagore is *against* in terms of the existing political and economic structures, but it is a great deal more difficult to assert what he is *for* in the existing language of contemporary political discourse.

Despite his critique of materiality in the West, Tagore does inscribe his homage to Europe through gracious acknowledgments of its civic, social, and legal institutions. In words that would affront any nationalist in any cultural context, Tagore even had the nerve to spell out the extent to which his homage to Europe could extend: '[W]e have to recognize that the history of India does not belong to one particular race but to a process of creation to which various races of the world contributed.... [W]e neither have the right nor the power to exclude this people [the English] from the building of the destiny of India' (55). What seems like an almost totally uncritical, if not Orientalist submission to the civilizing mission of the West, however, should be immediately qualified by the fact that the larger history Tagore has in mind is the 'history of Man' and not just that of India (56).

It would be rash, I believe, to read deference in either Tagore's homage to the West or his allegiance to a larger Orientalist redemptionist project. On the contrary, there is an incredible self-confidence here and not just moral fervour in the way he implicates his critique of the Nation of the West so thoroughly in the *love* he upheld for the Spirit of Western civilization. This embedding of love within a critique of the West is the absolute antithesis of contemporary readings of Occidentalism, premised on *hate*. I refer to Ian Buruma and Avishai Margalit's description of Occidentalism as 'the dehumanizing picture of the West painted by its enemies'—more specifically, the 'loathing' of the 'Western world', and of America and Israel in particular, by the likes of the Al Qaeda and militant Islamists.[106]

This is not the place to enter into a detailed discussion of this narrow reading of Occidentalism, which completely eliminates any perspective on how the West has been a source of love and enlightenment for thinkers like Tagore and his mentor Rammohan Roy, among other Oriental scholars and seekers. Suffice it to say that Buruma and Margalit's liberal argument is heightened by their very attempt to 'understand' Westoxification and anti-Semitism within the political, historical, religious, and cultural contexts of the Middle East, which is also the implicit target of attack in their book. They make a strong case for understanding, and not merely demonizing the enemy. In this regard, they take pains to emphasize the fact that 'Occidentalism cannot be reduced to a Middle Eastern sickness',[107] and that 'Islam cannot be reduced to a death cult'.[108] All this sounds eminently reasonable, but the very excess of civility leads Buruma and Margalit to affirm that Occidentalism, like all other modern isms, including capitalism and Marxism, has its roots in Europe, even though it can exist anywhere. What seems like a gracious acknowledgement in shifting the grounds of blaming the source of Occidentalism transpires to be a strategy in deepening the critique against the 'enemy'.

So, for instance, anti-Americanism can be traced to Hitler's repugnance of the cult of mechanization in America; the critique of godlessness and rootless cosmopolitanism embodied in the sinful metropolitan city can be found in Wagner's demonization of Venusberg; the cult of heroic suicide as represented by the Japanese *kamikaze* or Tokkotai (Special Attack Forces) was reinforced through their readings of Nietzsche, Hegel, Fichte, and Kant; and even Russian Slavophilia authenticated through German Romanticism can be said to have left a dubious legacy in its commemoration of the 'soul' against Western materialism. At no point is there any attempt on the part of Buruma and Margalit to suggest that there could be multiple readings of categories like 'soul', or 'godlessness', or 'mechanization', or 'sacrifice', or that they could mean significantly different things to different communities and to individual thinkers like Tagore, who, indeed, has used these very categories to articulate his understanding of universal humanism. With an almost myopic precision, Buruma and Margalit brand these categories as 'occidentalist' and, in the process, divest them of their multivalent ethical and spiritual implications.

While, at one level, it could be argued that Buruma and Margalit offer a refreshingly anti-Romantic reading of Occidentalism, the non-reflexive tenor of their critique is also disturbingly smug. Indeed, it would almost seem as if there are no indigenous grounds for hating the West except for those embedded in the concepts and tropes that have been transferred to non-Western cultures through the trajectories of Western enlightenment. Even at the level of hatred, the non-West is denied its grounds of resistance. It is almost incapable of thinking for itself. This is a condescending position, that enables Buruma and Margalit to adopt an implicitly superior moral ground, if not a redemptionist position that 'without understanding those who hate the West, we cannot hope to stop them from destroying humanity'.[109] One would be tempted to deepen the dialectic here by suggesting that an understanding of those who hate the Arab world, notably Zionists, could also contribute towards world peace. However, such an argument merely reinforces Buruma and Margalit's Manichaean vision of the world, which they presume to condemn in others: those who hate and those who don't; those who can save the world and those who can't.

At one level, the presumptuous premise in attempting to 'stop humanity from destroying itself', echoes Tagore's profound and unquestionably romantic humanitarianism voiced in his 'Crisis in Civilization'. The difference is that while Tagore's faith in Man across borders and differences is rooted in love, the rescue mission of Buruma and Margalit is premised on understanding hate. Far from avoiding a demonization of 'their' enemies, the overall thrust of this critique of Occidentalism seems to echo the vicious premise endorsed by Samuel Huntington that 'unless we hate what we are not, we cannot love what we are'.[110] A more ruthless anti-Tagorean position would be hard to find.

To return to Tagore, what makes his love for the Spirit of the West so resolute is his refusal to surrender the right to criticize its limitations and failures. What he demonstrates is the fundamental ambiguity that you can love and critique the West at the same time, which is somewhat different from Buruma and Margalit's position on Muhammad Iqbal, for instance, when they acknowledge that he was a 'critic of the West', though not an Occidentalist.[111] The point is that criticism can coexist with love; it is not simply an alibi for not dehumanizing the West, which is, at best, a negative attribute.

Tagore's position becomes all the more complex because even as he would acknowledge the right of the West to shape the historical destiny of India, he would also affirm the equal right of India, among other Asian nations, to shape the destiny of the West, if not the future of the universe at large. His self-confidence in this regard is matched by political audacity, which is particularly marked in the conclusion to *Nationalism*: 'We should actively try to adapt the world powers to guide our history to its own perfect end' (99). This is very different from saying that we want to be part of world history, that ultimate abstraction, most powerfully enunciated by Hegel, in which only the most powerful European nation–states could claim an exclusive membership, not least because they have evolved not just a culture or society but a state. It is precisely this pinnacle of achievement that Tagore rejects in order to evolve 'our history to its own perfect end'.

'OUR HISTORY'

What could Tagore have meant by 'our history'? This question leads us to some ongoing debates in postcolonial circles, where the process of differentiating colonial and national historiography from subaltern history ('a history from below') is now being further questioned through new discriminations. Indeed, has subaltern historiography itself failed to recognize the creative dynamics of another kind of 'history'; a history that dare not speak its name, a poet's history?

The current controversy that engages with this question focuses on a relatively unknown recorded conversation and transcribed text between Tagore and the modern Bengali writer Buddhadev Bose which has, at least in one of its incarnations, been entitled *Sahitye Aitihasikata* (Historicality in Literature, 1941). However, long before this conversation took place in the last year of Tagore's life, when he was too weak to write—hence, the oral mode of transmission—the poet had in a much earlier phase of his career reflected on *Bharatbarsher Itihas* (1902).[112] This title could be translated simply as 'India's History', but as we have already discussed in the course of this narrative, 'Bharatbarsha' has a much wider and more expansive resonance than 'India'.

In this early essay, Tagore gets to the core of the matter by identifying—and, at some level, ridiculing—the academic history that is learned by rote in order to pass examinations. This is the history that thrives on listing invasions and successions of different dynasties, fratricidal battles and the tensions between cliques, which have nothing to do with 'us' and our deeply imbricated relationship with Bharatbarsha, which has been nurtured over centuries through cultural traditions and practices. This lived history, which deals with our immersion, if not dwelling, in the primordial home of Bharatbarsha, the very heart of India, would seem to be out of bounds for academic historians. In order to research this deeply embedded history, Tagore is clear that one has to relinquish the assumption that history has to be the same for all peoples. Indeed, historiography (the representation of history) cannot be assumed to have the same forms in different cultures. Those who assume this sameness are Western-trained historians who turn to the archives in search of facts relating to dynasties and chronicles of war. When they do not find what they are looking for in the absence of documentary authentication, they become exasperated and declare: 'Where there is no politics, there cannot be history.'[113] With sly humour, Tagore adds, 'These people are looking for aubergines in paddy-fields and when they do not find what they are looking for, they declare paddy as being unworthy of harvest. The wise man knows that the same harvest cannot be reaped from all fields.'[114]

While this early essay indicates the poet's impatience with the hegemonic control of history by academics, he makes no attempt to claim an independent history as such. He is more preoccupied with outlining philosophical ideals relating to India's heterogeneous, conflictual unity, in which differences are reconciled without being legislated into uniformity or homogenized into sameness. It is the complexities relating to India's unity (as opposed to Europe's specious notion of 'equality') and the specifically Indian connotations of reconciling *prema* and *karma* to dharma, that are among his central concerns in the essay. Once again, dharma is invoked in a civilizational context, sharply differentiated from the European notion of 'religion', which has asserted itself through the fragmentation of the sacred and the profane. Rejecting this fragmentation of human life into separate domains, Tagore represents his position with vivid eloquence: 'Just as the life of the hand, the life of the feet, the life of the head, the life of the belly, are not separated from each other, so also does India refuse to fragment religions into various domains: the religion of faith and that of actual behaviour; the religion of Sunday and that of the other six days in the week; the religion of the Church and that of the household.'[115] Against this highly textured reading of the indivisibility of dharma within the social and political domains of life, history (as written by academic historians) is at best a sequestered task in determining what is non-essential in human life and society. The poet has more vital matters to ponder, emerging from the creative intuitions of his poetry and relationship to the world.

In *Sahitye Aitihasikata*, the penultimate article in Tagore's oeuvre published in the Centenary Edition of his collected works, the poet appears to have somewhat different stakes in the larger debate relating to history. At least, this is the position articulated by the doyen of Subaltern Studies, Ranajit Guha, who in an astonishing reflection on 'history at the limit of world-history', has, in the spirit of an 'auto-critique', called attention to Tagore's rich discrimination of 'historicality' from the over-inscribed, state-oriented priorities of 'historiography'.[116] Indeed, it is nothing short of a brave theoretical intervention for Guha to translate *aitihasikata* as 'historicality'. In the very choice of this rather arcane word, there is an obvious discrimination being made in relation to 'history', 'historiography', and 'historicity'.[117] Through the inscription of 'historicality' within his own seminal contributions to the Subaltern Studies project on peasant insurgency and dominance without hegemony, among other critical issues, Guha is settling scores as much with himself as with the master narrators of world history who have shaped his thinking.

Taking on Hegel with all the respectful discomfort of a dissenting disciple, Guha calls attention to the dogma embedded in the world-historical axiom: 'No state, no history' (10), which has led to the fetishization of the state in contemporary readings of the political. Pushing his search for 'a creative engagement with the past as a story of man's being in the everyday world' (6), Guha strays into the world of the Mahabharata, more often than territorialized by scholars of ancient history. Here he dwells on *itihasa*, and the shaping of its narrative through 'the retelling of what has been told many times', and the subsequent 're-perception'/'re-audition' of the narrative which remains forever indefinite and open (68). Without valorizing this site as an authentic source of history-telling, Guha elaborates on the 'complicity of Orientalism in hitching *itihasa* to World-history' (51), and thereby, he creates multiple frames for building his argument around the need to review history as it has been written in the past and revised in the more recent present.

Finally, almost in the nature of a secular pilgrimage, Guha turns to Tagore's *Sahitye Aitihasikata* (Historicality in Literature) in his search for a history freed of 'statist blinkers' (94). Dare one also add subalternist blinkers? Defying academic protocol, Tagore's essay, which is a transcribed compilation of fragmented thoughts, converges around images from his childhood. Dew glistening on top of a coconut grove at sunrise, a mass of clouds gathering in the sky above his ancestral home, and a cow licking the back of a foal: these are the central sources of his evidence on which he bases his reflections on 'history' itself. Drawing on this repository of images, Tagore traces his own evolution as a poet by claiming the lived experience of everyday life transformed within the individual 'I'. It is through the mediation of his inner soul (*antaratma*) that a mysterious 'history' unfolds. And instead of apologizing about the *limitations* of this history—its subjectivity, insignificance, transience, and the quirks of memory—Tagore has no difficulty in using these seeming limitations to indicate the *limits* of historiography. In place of the history exclusively restricted to the public sphere, he offers the lessons of *sedinkar itihas*, the 'history of that day', which resonates with insights into the details of everyday life that most historians do not see.

Briefly, this is the gist of Guha's reading of Buddhadev Bose's transcription of Tagore's thoughts, into which Guha has inserted some post-subaltern thinking on the value of rethinking the 'facticity of being' in opposition to 'the factuality of historiographical representation' (79). Referring to the inner reservoir of Tagore's images drawn from childhood as 'a sort of prehistory' embodying experiences 'coiled in the incipience of sheer possibility', Guha guides his own argument of 'historicality' away from actuality in favour of a 'tendency that does not know where it is going' (78–9). If there is a political unconscious at work in Guha's text, it is surely Heidegger, whose construction of 'being' is invoked without being problematized. Emphasizing that even historicality demands facts, especially when it involves 'writing about one's own being', as Tagore does, Guha is compelled to embrace Heidegger's transformation of factuality into facticity in the philosopher's own words: 'The concept of facticity implies that an "innerworldly" being has being-in-the world in such a way that it can understand itself as bound up in its "destiny" with the being of those beings which it encounters within its own world' (79). This would include the beings of dawn, dew, sunrise, clouds, and the animal world, which Tagore imbibes in his own being.

Moving beyond Heidegger's philosophical mediation, Guha turns to creativity, and by allusion, to the 'opening of the eyes' by which moments of being in everyday life are transfigured within the lived history of poets such as Tagore. Perhaps somewhat too reductively, Guha links this poetic 'seeing' to Henri Lefebvre's *Critique of Everyday Life*, where the concreteness of the quotidian is revealed, and in the process, divested of 'whimsical interpretations' and 'empty abstractions' (94). Once again, more emphatically than in his passing references to Heidegger, there is no reading of Lefebvre as such, but it is almost as if Guha needs to insert some contemporary theoretical evidence to vindicate his thesis that it is possible to rescue 'historicality' from its larger 'containment in World-history' (6).

Needless to say, Guha's implicit, and to my mind, courageous attempt to acknowledge the limits of history, has not gone down well either with diehard subalternists or with literary theorists. While the former would like him to stick to his guns, as it were, and retain the rigour of subaltern analysis in more explicit political terms, the latter sees some kind of a presumption in the assumption that Tagore would want to appropriate the role of the historian. At least, this would appear to be one of the premises underlying an indignant reading of 'subalternist misrepresentations',[118] where Guha (and indirectly, the leading authority of Tagore studies in Bengal, Sankho Ghosh) are taken to task for undermining the messy publishing history surrounding *Sahitye Aitihasikata*.

Instead of being an 'authorized transcript', as claimed by Guha on the basis of Ghosh's learned opinion of the 'Bangla original' (95), this text went through many changes. A second part was added to it, and Tagore consciously attempted to suppress the publication of the first part on grounds that its 'deliberate exaggeration' was a consequence of 'much bitterness' that had accumulated in him.[119] This bitterness, according to the historian Nepal Majumdar, was not directed against the enterprise of history as such, but against those critics who had taken issue with the poet's alleged indifference to 'social realism' from a historical/materialist (*aitihasik bastubaad*) perspective.[120] However, even as these controversies surrounding Tagore's text should have been acknowledged by Guha, if only to complicate his somewhat too seamless endorsement of Tagore's historicality, the poet's distress with his own text—and subsequent self-censorship—is revealing. If his position relating to history had not been so volatile, he might not have attempted to cover it up. The very camouflage suggests that the written text mattered to him, and that the complexities of its thought were not fully rendered by the transcript and subsequent rewrite of his verbal utterance.

Far from confirming the overly literal position that literature operates with a significantly different relationship to the world from history, is the poet not pushing this premise somewhat further in suggesting that there is another 'history' worth recording? Tagore, I would suggest, is entering areas where historians fear to tread and, in this critical sense, he is *trespassing*. At one level, this is his poetic license, which enables him to say, without arrogance, 'In his own field of creativity, Rabindranath has been entirely alone and tied to no public by history' (97). Arguably, this field of creativity could cover social and political realities relating to the trials and tribulations of everyday life. These are as much subject to the imaginary processes of creative solitude, as more ostensibly private states of mind.[121] What is significant here is Tagore's claim to a highly personalized history, instead of the mere defence that poetry is not expected to serve as an accomplice to history's instrumentality. As opposed to the self-critique of 'exaggeration' that he had brought on himself, Tagore is crossing borders here, if ever so tentatively. Tellingly, he is not saying what has been a leitmotif throughout his career, 'I am merely a poet'. Tagore is not seeking refuge in poetry; he is using his considerable self-knowledge as a poet to claim another way of seeing history.

Needless to say, this does not make him a 'historian': why would he want to be one? However, the ambivalence of his position does lend itself to being appropriated in the larger interest of rescuing history from its limits, and limitations. Perhaps, Guha's alleged 'misinterpretation' is more of a strategic appropriation of Tagore's position than either he or his critics would care to admit. As for Tagore, I am reminded of a moment during his visit to China, when he dared to betray his role as an apolitical poet by calling attention to the fact that he was more like 'contraband'.[122] 'Smuggled on to the wrong shore of time,' Tagore lamented the fact that he was destined to be mistrusted on both sides of the border—on the one side, as an iconoclast; on the other side, as a reactionary conservative. Once again, targeted by his Chinese critics for writing poetry that appeared too ethereal to deal with the trials of everyday life, Tagore affirmed proudly that his songs had entered the hearts and minds of people. 'This too is the work of a revolutionist,' he had emphasized.[123] An oddly peculiar word, 'revolutionist', the poet's way of inflecting the more mundane 'revolutionary'.

From this example, one realizes that even as Tagore knew his limits as a poet, he was not going to accept the definitions of others, particularly in relation to his own capacity to transgress the limits of available categories. If Tagore felt the need to withdraw his 'exaggerated' statements on history recorded in *Sahitye Aitihasikata*, it is because he feared, to my mind, the pain of being misunderstood. He was too old to fight this particular battle in cold print, where he knew that it would have to be fought against the grain of historical materialism, around which there was a growing caucus of social realists. In the withdrawal of his article, and the very obvious panic in his vacillations regarding its publication, I do believe that we have signs of a Poet's History that was suppressed. In its silencing, we have lost an articulation that could have counterpointed the Poet's Religion, but, in the remnants of what was not entirely silenced, there are signs of 'historicality in literature' that await retrieval and reconstruction. Ranajit Guha's reading is a formative attempt in this direction.

COUNTERING TAGORE

Not surprisingly, it has been more or less trashed by Partha Chatterjee in a cursory dismissal of Guha's valorization of Tagore's sense of being in everyday life. This forms part of his larger critique against Tagore's reading of history, state, and nation in an article entitled *Rabindrik nation ki?* (2003), which could be translated as 'What is Tagore's nation?', though the possibly ironic inflection of 'Rabindrik' is not easily conveyed in this literal translation. The argumentative thrust of this essay has been followed up by Chatterjee in a more elaborate essay entitled *Rabindrik nation prasange aro du-char katha* ('A few more words on Tagore's nation', 2004).[124] Tellingly, Tagore was conspicuous by his absence in Chatterjee's now canonical study of *Nationalist Thought and the Colonial World* (1986). In critical hindsight, it is evident that Tagore could not fit within the Gramscian trajectories of Chatterjee's mapping of nationalist thought, which was determined all too precisely by the 'point of departure', the 'point of manoeuvre', and the 'point of arrival', with each of these historical moments problematized in the figures of Bankimchandra Chattopadhyay, Mahatma Gandhi, and Jawaharlal Nehru, respectively. Tagore's dissenting position on nationalism was summarily left out of the discussion, with the exception of some passing references and a solitary footnote. Is it possible to assume from this exclusion that Tagore could not be subsumed within the parameters of a nationalist discourse, 'derivative' or otherwise? Also that he posed some form of interruption, if not threat, to Chatterjee's stabilizing master narrative on the Indian nation–state?

In *Rabindrik nation ki?* Chatterjee does not attempt to make amends for his earlier exclusion of Tagore, still less to provide a self-reflexive critique on his own gaps in reading nationalism in the Indian context. At best, in a few brisk pages, he summarizes the key moments in Tagore's understanding of nationalism, beginning suggestively with his reading of Renan in *Nation Ki?*, (What is the Nation?, 1901), where Tagore acknowledges that the nation is a 'living concept' (*sajib satta*) which cannot be reduced to the sum of its components relating to race, language, economics, religion, geography, among other quantifiable elements.[125] With acute prescience, almost anticipating the evolution of new political entities like the European Union, Tagore had emphasized the impermanence of the nation, prophesying that just as it was created in the course of history, it could well disappear in time.

From this philosophical reflection, Tagore's views on the nation gradually hardened from the idealization of samaj in the swadeshi period, through the failure of the swadeshi movement, into his withdrawal from the ethos of nationalism. At the peak of his disenchantment, he attempted to define the nation in the language of the social sciences as 'the political and economic union of a people, in that aspect which a whole population assumes when organized for a mechanical purpose'.[126] Chatterjee seizes on this 'mechanical purpose' and highlights Tagore's anti-machine phobia and aversion to technology against which he affirmed the 'natural' bonds and ties of society. While the poet had at one point grudgingly acknowledged some need for the 'importation' of modern state machinery, particularly in order to administer society outside of the immediacies of rural communities, he had ultimately settled for the dictum that Bharatbarsha cannot be run by machines alone — a qualification that has already been addressed in my discussion of *Swadeshi Swaraj*.

Making no attempt to disguise his impatience with Tagore's élitist imaginary that fails to account for the needs of ordinary people, including professionals like himself, Chatterjee positions himself somewhat too bluntly as a dealer in 'ordinary prose' (*sadharan godya*), who thoroughly distrusts the 'magic of insight' (*antardrishtir jadubol*).[127] In order to confront the politics of power in direct ways, he argues that it is necessary to negotiate the so-called mechanization of state institutions which, contrary to Tagore's belief, are essential for the daily functioning of modern society, as well as for the democratization of 'public opinion' (*janamat*) and the 'consent of the people' (*janasadharaner sammati*) from which the poet seemed to have distanced himself altogether.[128] In fact, Chatterjee openly questions whether the poet would have favoured the establishment of democracy in the twentieth century on a worldwide basis.

In the sequel to *Rabindrik nation ki?*, Chatterjee develops this position even more categorically by contextualizing his argument within the emergent institutional processes of democracy in India of the 1920s. Adopting a public intellectual stance, Chatterjee reiterates that Rabindranath had distanced himself from the emergent social welfare systems of his time relating to the production of khadi, national schools, flood and famine relief organizations, which provided the foundations for social projects relating to health care and the primary school system, corresponding to the mass education and literacy movements of our times. These organizations of the 1920s developed at precisely the same time that the Congress party had succeeded in decentralizing its power to the remotest *taluka*s and villages, where anybody could participate in the elections regardless of barriers relating to caste, religion, and gender. Rather than responding to this groundswell and expansion of democratic organizations, Tagore chose to see the institutionalization of power purely in the context of an almost demoniac mechanization that killed individual freedom. Chatterjee minces no words in stating that one of the big questions of the twentieth century is to figure out how to bring about massive social welfare through power structures—a question that was of no concern whatsoever to Rabindranath.[129]

Rejecting the poet's upholding of individual freedom over and above the mechanization underlying the organizational structures of democracy, Chatterjee makes a strong defence for the need to uphold democracy without whitewashing its connections with war, pollution, or the influx of refugees, among other problems. Democracy, it would seem, is a messy business, and we have no other option but to dirty our fingers while dealing with it. To imagine in this regard that 'the good in democracy can be upheld while politicians can be cursed for what is bad in democracy' is to submit to the worst kind of dualism. If democracy has to be supported, then it needs to be embraced in its entirety, both in its good and bad aspects. While Rabindranath did not succumb to the duplicity of selectively endorsing a 'good' democracy against a 'bad' democracy, just as he avoided differentiating between different kinds of nationalism, he seemed to deny democracy in its entirety by exclusively protesting against its bad aspects and failing to accept the viability of fully organized democratic structures.[130]

Countering the romanticization of Tagore through an embrace of critical realism, Chatterjee punctures the pervasive illusions surrounding the apparently simple lives of ordinary people. The truth is that ordinary people in today's world do not live 'simple' lives. Rather, they are compelled to be 'strategic' as they engage in the most intricate negotiations of survival with the state, the civic administration, development systems, the market economy, and NGOs. In this ongoing struggle to negotiate the public domain, there is no place for a romantic retreat into Tagore's dreamworld, even as Chatterjee acknowledges that it provides the possibilities of momentary peace. Although this qualification appears to be a somewhat more graceful, if grudging, inflection of his earlier position, the point is that Chatterjee does not yield any ground in acknowledging that there could be other ways of imagining society outside of the existing terms and strictures of his political discourse.

While it is true that there is a demonization of the nation–state as a colossal soul-denying machine in Tagore's discourse, it is reductive to essentialize this reading independently of Tagore's embrace of civil liberties and political rights in his arguably anti-political and universalist defence of civil society, as posited by E.P. Thompson. More critically, in his envisioning of a samaj that does not as yet exist — in this critical sense, Tagore's Samaj and Gandhi's Swaraj are emphatically utopian constructions — there is another society in the making grounded in the primacy and ethics of *atmashakti* (self-reliance), which has the potential to be translated into another imaginary of the political. Indeed, this imaginary could yet enable us to extricate ourselves from the *bhulbhulaiya*, the labyrinthine inner traps of the present system, in which we are entrapped, as Chatterjee has the candour to acknowledge. Perhaps, it could be argued that some element of utopianism is a necessary counterpoint to the disillusioned endorsement of critical realism, but such is Chatterjee's vigorous scepticism of utopian thinking that he prefers to work through the realities of disillusionment rather than to accept a politics of hope based on the intransigent dreams of the unknown.

In a more subalternist register, Chatterjee undermines 'world citizenship' (*visva nagarikatta*) and 'world humanism' (*visva manabata*),[131] categories attributed to Tagore's universality, on the grounds that they can only begin to make sense if the journey of labour can supplement the journey of capital worldwide. However, at no point in Chatterjee's critique is there any attempt to differentiate the 'universal' from the 'global', or to realize its humanizing and transformative potential in the shaping of a different language, indeed, a different epistemology of the nation. Chatterjee would seem to reject all alternatives that do not stand up to the rigour of his rationalist criteria. While he acknowledges that there may be a place for creativity in the expression of a person's individual life-force (*pranshakti*), its enigmas have no place in the immediacies and practicalities of the political state system. To imagine that we are not embedded in this system by drawing our inspiration from the creative freedom of Tagore is to subject ourselves to the worst kind of euphoria. Adopting a non-theoretical, almost activist, idiom, Chatterjee directs his sarcasm towards the members of his own bhadralok class:

In everyday life, we follow traffic rules, pay taxes, vote or don't vote, make our children sit for exams, abuse the useless government and bribe-taking politicians, and within ourselves, we say, 'All these things are merely external, but in the depths of our minds, we know that we haven't played into the system.' The dream is beautiful.[132]

Against the critical realism of this reading, it is not entirely surprising that Ranajit Guha's attempt to stretch history outside the limits of world history by blurring the lines between history and literature, does not warrant analysis in Chatterjee's reading. In contrast to his overly determined presentist politics, I would suggest that Guha's arguably futurist position is valuable for the way it pushes the existing limits of writing, and imagining, history. By disentangling historicality from historiography, he stimulates us to inflect our own limited vocabularies and perspectives in attempting to disimbricate the 'national' from the totally discredited discourse of 'nationalism' — a disimbrication that, as I have indicated earlier, is a necessary manoeuver in the political culture of our times.

I would argue that in today's communalized climate of Hindutva in the Indian subcontinent, where we cannot afford the luxury of post-nationalism, we may have no other option but to re-imagine the national in ways that can actively resist the growing dominance of a virulently intolerant state. This resistance could take the form of a renationalization of the state, as recommended by Samir Amin, through an incorporation of new alliances of grass-root people's movements which, arguably, were never part of the national imaginary in the first place.[133] Tagore does not provide us with any answers in this direction: his aversion to mass movements and symbols is well known. The Gandhian cult of the *charkha*, for instance, was intrinsically tyrannical for him in its subordination of individual creativity to monotonous routine.

Not unfairly, Chatterjee alleges that Tagore does not provide us with answers to the questions that most concern us today. One could, however, also suggest that the poet's enduring significance could lie in the fact that he compels us to reformulate the existing questions. Indeed, Tagore's greatest value could be that he makes life difficult for us. He makes it harder for us to think by denying us easy alternatives and glib solutions. Instead of branding him somewhat condescendingly as a 'shamefaced' (*lojjito*) nationalist,[134] I would say that he is a profoundly anti-nationalist nationalitarian, whose universality cannot be collapsed into political internationalism, still less into globalism. Tagore defies dominant categories, and in this regard we have to be prepared to accept that if he rejected the 'fierce self-idolatory of nation-worship' (48), he was equally scathing about 'the colourless vagueness of cosmopolitanism' (48) as a valid alternative. Indeed, cosmopolitanism, contrary to its theoretical retrieval in postcolonial thinking, may not be a viable answer to counter the nationalist underpinnings of either Hindutva or New Asianism. However, before assuming that point, it would be useful to reflect on the adequacy of the word 'cosmopolitanism' to describe the universal avocations of both Tagore and Okakura, who will re-enter the narrative at this point.

3

Cosmopolitanism

ASIAN COSMOPOLITANS?

Both Tagore and Okakura were world travellers. Superstars in their own right, if not Asian celebrities, Tagore was a Nobel Prize winner while Okakura was one of the biggest players in the international art market at the turn of the last century. While Tagore had no compunctions whatsoever in charging '$700 a scold'[1] for each of his public lectures, at least in the first lap of his success as a world poet when he pontificated on the evils of nationalism, Okakura was a strikingly familiar, if somewhat exotic, presence in the rarefied and affluent world surrounding the Museum of Fine Arts, Boston. While at one level these were distinct worlds — the worlds of the poet and that of the curator — there were considerable overlaps in their circuits through larger global connections with rich donors, dealers, agents, diplomats, connoisseurs, disciples, and fans.

One such cosmopolitan character, for example, who cuts across the worlds of Bengal and Boston, the Ramakrishna Mission and the Museum of Fine Arts, Boston, is a rather colourful traveller called Ole Bull, a close friend of Josephine MacLeod, who in turn was one of Sister Nivedita's most trusted correspondents. Contrary to the Spanish-sounding ring of her name, Ole Bull was a Bostonian married to a Norwegian violinist, whose house on Brattle Street in Cambridge, Massachusetts, was used by Okakura to display the paintings of

Yokoyama Taikan, Hishida Shunso, and other representatives of the Nihon Bijutsuin school. This is one instance of what could be described as global cosmopolitanism, in which the seemingly distinct worlds of spirituality and art intersected across Asia and the United States, bringing together an élite coterie of world travellers, connoisseurs, and spiritual seekers.

While both Tagore and Okakura presented themselves to rapt audiences as representatives of 'India' and 'Japan', particularly in the way they dressed, they also seemed to transcend their specific national origins as seers of the world who happened to speak exquisite English, notwithstanding their graceful denials to the contrary. Unquestionably, both Tagore and Okakura were master performers in their own right, whether they were lecturing in universities or world fairs, or addressing dignitaries, prime ministers, or bureaucrats in a committee meeting. In their grinding schedules, which had a harrowing effect on their health, they nonetheless maintained an almost iconic sense of detachment, rising above the topicalities of their professional commitments and social engagements.

At a physical level, they were riveting. One could cite numerous examples of how Tagore was almost an object of *darshan* for his spectators; even those critics who were caustic about his writing had no other option but to praise his otherworldly beauty, not least his carefully combed beard. As the great Japanese novelist Soseki Natsume once acknowledged, 'I suppose from those pictures [in the newspapers] that he is more splendid in his appearance than many Japanese'.[2] Likewise, Okakura was an object of adoration, particularly by women in the most select circle of Boston Brahmins, including ageing opera singers and rich heiresses like Isabella Gardner, who designed entire events around Okakura's performative presence in her neo-Venetian mansion Fenway Court. In short, one could elaborate on many such vignettes relating to the worldliness and socialization of Tagore and Okakura among the glitterati, royalty, and an epic cast of characters who have been splendidly evoked by Christopher Benfey in his entertaining narrative on 'Gilded Age misfits' and 'Japanese eccentrics'.[3]

In the company of 'misfits' and 'eccentrics' at the turn of the century, it is almost impossible not to label Tagore and Okakura as cosmopolitan, without feeling any need to add the obligatory postmodern prefixes of 'vernacular' or 'discrepant'.[4] Even so, it is my submission that 'cosmopolitanism' does not quite account for the specific contradictions and tensions shared by these peripatetic men, though Okakura seems to lend himself more easily to the flamboyance of Euro-American metropolitan worldliness than Tagore. Certainly, neither of them attempted to describe their world travel under the sign of cosmopolitanism, though, arguably, both of them had entered what Okakura once described as the 'time-devouring locomotion' of the West, as opposed to the deeper 'travel culture of the pilgrimage and the wandering monk'.[5] Indeed, even within Asia, and more specifically in Japan in the late Meiji period, 'locomotion' had entered with a vengeance, not just with the expansion of the railways but with the emergence of tourism, conducted by agencies such as Thomas Cook.

However, for neither Tagore nor Okakura was global travel equated with the crudities of tourism, or with the more expansive embrace of a cosmopolitan existence. As I have already indicated, Tagore dismissed the ostensibly counter-nationalist mode of cosmopolitanism as 'colourless vagueness', and Okakura had little to say on the subject beyond its allusions to 'Westernization'. Neither of them ever claimed their identities as 'cosmopolitans', which is not to deny the possibility of an implicit, unnamed cosmopolitanism fuelling their mission in propagating the 'ideals of the East' to the Western world. In today's theoretical retrieval and re-reading of cosmopolitanism in postcolonial studies, Tagore and Okakura are particularly vulnerable to being marked in ways that they might not have imagined. It would be useful at this point to provide a brief overview of how the idea of cosmopolitanism is being pushed against the grain of its earlier prerogatives and assumptions of exclusivity.

Reclaiming Cosmopolitanism

Against the onslaught of new nationalisms and the upsurge of xenophobia in increasingly deceptive and virulent ways, a need to reclaim cosmopolitanism in the age of globalization has emerged in different disciplines and from a spectrum of philosophical directions. Mediated through multiculturalism and diasporic studies, there is a clear shift away from the classical origins of cosmopolitanism in Stoic philosophy and its Eurocentrist legacy affirming 'citizens of the world' who constituted, and are still imagined to consitute, 'one worldwide community of human beings'.[6] Despite some continuing philosophical adherence to such dated and unilateral constructions, there is a more robust questioning, whether apparent universals such as cosmopolitanism can ever be extricated from the vested interests of specific national and transnational contexts. It is now more widely accepted that all universals are grounded in the particularities of the history in which they are imbricated, and from which constructions of the universal are invented, more often than not to perpetuate the vested interests and consumerist needs of specific constitutencies. Far from being 'detached' free-floating citizens of the world, today's cosmopolitans are 'rooted' in agendas where national and global forces intersect, in a mutating *cosmopolitical* field of economic, social, and political forces.[7]

Even as the privileges of cosmopolitanism are being steadily exposed and rejected, it is striking that this has not led to a systematic disenchantment with, if not rejection of, the word altogether. Tellingly, there has been no attempt to strategically 'freeze' the European history of cosmopolitanism as a term in order to name, and in the process, define, other modes of migrant culture and identity-formation in specifically non-Western contexts.[8] On the contrary, cosmopolitanism is being annexed to these other experiences, even as their vastly different historical, political, and economic differences are being highlighted. Far from being regarded as a residual category that cannot begin to account for the turbulent causes of migration and statelessness in a globalized world, cosmopolitanism is being claimed to define precisely these states of chaos. Almost like a new imperialist category for the erstwhile oppressed of the world, now seeking new futures in conditions of neo-slavery, its territory is expanding rather than shrinking, its affiliations to different kinds of travel-culture are widening, even as its identifying markers are becoming increasingly more diffused.

In the course of this extremely paradoxical theoretical terrain, some interventions have been useful: for example, the need to focus on more *situated* modes of cosmopolitanism. Following Bruce Robbins's eminently sensible proposition, 'No one actually is or even can be a cosmopolitan in the sense of belonging nowhere', or, for that matter, 'belonging everywhere', as Donna Harraway has put it in another context. Such 'cultural relativism' would not be 'desirable', even if it were 'conceivable'.[9] Likewise, moving away from the overly philosophical and normative premises of cosmopolitanism as some kind of ideal state of mind, the tendency today is to examine cosmopolitanism as a series of disjunctive *practices* and *processes* of 'thinking and feeling beyond the nation'.[10] This prioritization of the 'beyond' bears some resemblance to the theoretical manoeuver of pushing history beyond the limits of world history, insofar as the most ardent advocates of cosmopolitanism would seem to jettison the idea of 'the world' altogether in favour of different reinventions of the cosmopolis. So vehement is the embrace of heterogeneous spaces that it is assumed that cosmopolitanism's 'conceptual content and pragmatic character' are best left 'unspecified', because 'specifying cosmopolitanism positively and definitely is an uncosmopolitan thing to do.'[11] The archness of this position is really a classic instance of postmodern evasion.

Defining 'cosmopolitans' (as opposed to 'cosmopolitanism') has been subject to even greater scepticism, if not disdain. It would be difficult, for instance, to think of many postcolonial theorists subscribing to Julia Kristeva's somewhat precious assertion, 'I am a cosmopolitan', because this position would seem to work against the more viable theoretical proposition of seeing cosmopolitanism less as a 'fully assumable identity' than as an 'advocated ideal'.[12] In fact, there is an equally strong resistance towards establishing the normativity of any one cosmopolitan ideal. Rather, the thrust has been towards seeking differentiated states of cosmopolitanism in all their rawness and conflictual cohabitation. Within the imperatives of such an approach, the tendency today is not so much to claim one's own cosmopolitanism as an identity or ideal, but to graft its emergent, almost always beneficent, possibilities on to others, in a larger acceptance of the disjunctive flow of capital.

In a neo-liberal context, one catalytic agency for the creation of new cosmopolitanisms is the circulation of an increasingly globalized cultural capital, which impacts with randomness in different parts of the world, independently of its national origins and affiliations to particular groups or classes of people. Inevitably, this capital becomes accessible to those individuals inhabiting an apparently free-floating diaspora who are in a position, economically and intellectually, to appropriate it as cultures of choice. For those cultural dissidents not formally part of any diaspora, but living in exile in their own countries, the cultural capital from other locations can enable them to redefine their identities against the grain of national culture.

Disputing the notion that there are fixed cultural identities shaped by entities like 'the West' and 'Asia', Naoki Sakai calls attention to the diverse and hybrid ways in which new identities can be shaped through cultural and social practices that are neither strictly Asian nor Western. Divested of primordial considerations relating to birth, or culture, or nationality, the new identities and practices can assume the form of intriguing 'oxymorons':

[A] Chinese with superb taste in classical European music, a black American with upper middle class mannerisms, a poor white American whose faith seems utterly incompatible with the secularised sense of 'modern' and 'Western' religiosity... [A]n Indonesian preoccupied with Chinese ethics, a white French male, who is superhumanly meticulous and patient with his rather 'Asiatic' handwork in the fine details of his 'traditional' craftsmanship, and so forth.[13]

Independently of Sakai's theoretical framing of such identities against the narrow, sectarian ethnicity of 'we Asians', it strikes me that these 'oxymorons' greatly resemble the eccentrics and misfits alluded to earlier in the more assertively cosmopolitan acquisition of cultural capital at the turn of the last century. Without intending to engage in the discourse of cosmopolitanism, Sakai inadvertently perpetuates its most tenacious tropes. In his prioritization of striking individuals, iconoclastic taste, diverse exposures to interculturality, and professional skills, all of which are components of an undeniably privileged appropriation of cultural capital, this intervention would seem to perpetuate an older enlightened reading of cosmopolitanism, albeit in a global diasporic context.

The difficulty with Sakai's position is that it assumes an unproblematized readiness to embrace the cultures of the world, and in this sense, he simply reiterates the liberal premise of Ulf Hannerz's much-cited reading of cosmopolitanism as 'an orientation, a willingness to engage with the Other...an intellectual and aesthetic stance of openness toward divergent cultural experiences'.[14] Responding to this excessively optimistic stance, Ackbar Abbas has correctly pointed out that while a sense of 'openness' may be 'sustainable' in metropolitan centres where 'movement and travel are undertaken with ease and where the encounter with other cultures is a matter of free choice, negotiated on favourable grounds', the situation is different when these favourable conditions of travel and access to other cultures are simply not available, as in conditions of colonial rule where 'divergent cultural experiences' are forced on the subjects of a colonized state.[15] This is a critical point that is all too often overlooked in liberal readings of interculturalism, where the valorization of 'cultures of choice' does not sufficiently negotiate their coercive imposition.

Tellingly, Abbas does not pursue the critical question whether cosmopolitanism could be another form of cultural imperialism. Instead, he falls back on a rather chic culturalist endorsement of 'arbitrage', where the global economic strategy of using electronic technologies across arbitrary time-zones and market systems to maximize profits can be reinterpreted to refer to the 'everyday strategies for negotiating the disequilibria and dislocations that globalism has created'.[16] Ostensibly, this form of cosmopolitanism is directed specifically towards those 'less privileged men and women' who are 'placed or displaced in the transnational space of the city', and who are trying to 'make sense of its spatial and temporal contradictions'.[17] To what extent they would be able to make sense of Abbas's rereading of the cosmopolitan not as a 'universalist arbiter of value, but as an arbitrageur/arbitrageuse',[18] is an open question.

Indeed, the reclamation of cosmopolitanism raises more questions than it answers, specifically about the theoretical desires of global postcolonial intellectuals in figuring out their own, perhaps insufficiently acknowledged need to settle scores with the privileges of their own cosmopolitan locations. In this context, the assumption that 'silenced and marginalized voices are bringing themselves into the conversation of cosmopolitan projects',[19] rather than waiting to be included, needs to be questioned outside the discursive terrain that legislates such assertions of voluntarist rather than coercive inclusion. Who is including whom in the domain of the cosmopolitan, and for what reasons? The difficulties deepen as the ostensibly open membership of cosmopolitanism attempts to embrace the subaltern.

THE SUBALTERN 'COSMOPOLITAN'

In his influential reflection on 'travelling cultures', a precursor to his magisterial remapping of 'routes', James Clifford, for instance, has attempted to infiltrate the protocols of the white cosmopolitan club of anthropologists by opening its doors to include non-European servants, helpers, companions, guides, native informants, translators: indeed, all those marginalized individuals who may have serviced the narratives of cosmopolitanism, but who remained on the periphery, rendered invisible under different conditions of coercion, humiliation, economic exploitation, if not political oppression.[20] 'They too are cosmopolitan,' would seem to be Clifford's pitch for de-nativizing the notorious hierarchies and power play of his colonial discipline, in which he has, arguably, succeeded in nativizing his own colleagues.[21] One is bound to question whether such gestures of democratization are not somewhat specious in the absence of any dialogue or empirical evidence to suggest that the erstwhile 'natives' would like to be considered 'cosmopolitan' (at least on Clifford's terms). Indeed, whether it is possible for them to imagine any identity other than that marked by their country of origin, religion, community, class, and economic subordination. This doesn't mean that they cannot imagine a better future for themselves. Only the future is not cosmopolitan.

To inflect the somewhat deterministic ring of that last statement, let me insert into the narrative an extraordinary, if somewhat chilling, description of one such subaltern: a Japanese landscape gardener working in the ancestral house of the Tagores at Jorasanko in Calcutta. At one level, it is obvious that the insertion of the gardener is strategic insofar as his presence highlights the élitist, if not aristocratic, milieu that Tagore and Okakura shared. Indeed, it is impossible to separate their 'cosmopolitanism', however one chooses to qualify the affiliation, from the privileges of class and caste. If the gardener is allowed to enter their world, he does so within the protocols of courtesy and deference available to him, indicating the larger disparities and rifts in the global cosmopolitical field of travel, employment, and multiple identities. Tagore, Okakura, and the Japanese gardener are all world travellers, but they travel in significantly different ways and for different purposes.

While the gardener remains unnamed, he is vividly captured in a description provided by Abanindranath Tagore, the leader of the Bengal school of painting, who observes Okakura absorbed in deep conversation with the painter Nandalal Bose. Then, there is a shift in Abanindranath's focus, as the gardener makes his entrance:

The man came up to the door, hesitated, peeped in, but didn't venture to announce himself. He would not come in even when I asked him to. He was standing near the door, rubbing his hands in awkward silence when Okakura's glance fell on him and he raised his right forefinger as a sign of recognition of his presence and permission for him to enter. The man at once knelt down and entered [sic] his presence walking on his knees, his head moving up and down in unison with his movement. Okakura spoke a few words in his own language and the interview was at an end. The exit was in the same fashion as the entrance.[22]

I quote this passage at length because it provides a terrifying glimpse into the perpetuation of Japanese feudal codes within the aristocratic milieu of an enlightened Bengali bhadralok family. There would appear to be no disjunction between these contexts, even though Abanindranath does question the gardener at a later point about the 'reason for this abject behaviour' (85). To this the gardener responds (ostensibly in Bengali, though Abanindranath does not specify the language in which he speaks): 'Oh, Sir, he is considered as a divine person in our country.' (85).

Clearly, we are revisiting the old problem of whether the subaltern can speak, and if indeed he does speak (as in this particular case), in whose narrative and language is his voice inscribed? The incident with the unnamed gardener is just one vignette in Abanindranath's memoir, which builds on the elegiac *rasa* (flavour) of Okakura's last visit to India in 1912, which culminates in a trip to the temple of Jagannath in Puri, where Okakura (as a foreigner) is denied entrance. 'Even the Viceroy Curzon,' we are told by Abanindranath, 'the man who was accustomed to have his own way in everything, had to put up with their refusal' (86). (Abanindranath's reference to Curzon, I should add, is not so distant as it appears, when one considers that it was in the 'grand imperial spectacle' of this infamous viceroy's durbar in 1903 that his paintings first received 'nationwide publicity').[23] Following the reference to Curzon, there is an almost miraculous transformation in the narrative: 'The Lion Gate was flung open...the keepers stood at attention and my friend had a right royal reception inside the enclosure' (86). Yet another extension of Okakura's quasi-divine status, alluded to earlier by the Japanese gardener. Only here the attendants are transfixed, as it were, standing to attention, not genuflecting on their knees. After paying his obeisance to Lord Jagannath, presumably on his knees, Okakura then moves on to Konarak, where he goes into 'ecstasy over the ruins there' (86). Abanindranath just basks in the glory of his 'bliss' (86).

Like many memorable memoirs, there is a little catch at the end of the piece. Abanindranath inserts a somewhat self-serving reference to the 'neo-Bengali school composed of Nandalal and others', of which he was the widely acknowledged, though increasingly distanced guru. On his first visit to India, in 1902, Okakura 'had seen nothing of the kind' [i.e. no such 'neo-Bengali' paintings]. This observation is followed by a quote from Okakura: 'And if I come back after another ten years, I am sure I shall see some worthwhile achievements' (86). Then follows the final paragraph:

But he never came back. As for me, I too am waiting to see something worthwhile. Perhaps I will have to come back for that. Who knows?   [86]

This gratuitous personal inscription at the end of the piece is Abanindranath's signature, which subtly shifts the reader's attention away from Okakura to his own role in the 'neo-Bengali' school, where something 'worthwhile' has yet to be achieved. In the process of weighing the legacy of this school, the Japanese gardener is forgotten.

How could one begin to retrieve his history? On the one hand, it could be argued that the gardener, like Okakura, had travelled across the seas from Japan to India. However, unlike our jet-setting traveller, who merely flitted in and out of the subcontinent, the gardener would seem to have become a more permanent resident in India; a foreign labourer with expertise in the rather exotic field of landscape gardening. In short, a subaltern with 'specialized skills'; the kind who would, in all probability, fall into a specific visa category today. For all our speculations, we know almost nothing about this man, who enters and exits Abanindranath's description like a supernumerary in a social play. Clearly, if he had to speak about his observations in the Tagore household, we would get an unprecedented perspective on Bengal's most illustrious and enlightened family. Indeed, how enlightened were they in their dealings with servants? An enormous amount of literature exists in Bengali on Tagore's relationships with servants, who wielded 'authority' through all kinds of strategies, in which the child Rabindranath was both knowing and complicit.[24] While the Japanese gardener would seem to be a later addition to the Tagore household, his observations on 'the family' could surely have deepened our critical insights into the interplay of the landlord–servant relationship, attesting to the 'discrepant' cosmopolitanisms at work within the seemingly homogenized framework of aristocratic bhadralok culture.

Having acknowledged this point, I am not sure whether the gardener in question would necessarily uphold a cosmopolitan identity, on the basis of his migrant status. What we can more accurately assume is that he is thrust within a cosmopolitical field of conflicting national and global forces, which he has entered ostensibly by choice. However, his possibilities of exit (did he ever return to

Japan?) are, hypothetically, far more determined by the economic realities of his savings, family responsibilities, and his particular hopes for the future. None of these can be readily assumed. In this sense, his condition is symptomatic of migrant workers in the age of globalization living and working outside their homelands, who may not have severed their ties entirely with 'home', but who have not yet fully accepted the state of belonging to their country of domicile. As for 'belonging to the world' at large, this is a cosmopolitan myth that may need to be rejected as an ahistorical, overprivileged reading of metropolitan migrancy, which all too often tends to be universalized in liberal diasporic circles for the human condition itself.[25]

NEGOTIATING PRIVILEGE

Having provided some kind of empirical counter to the different ways in which cosmopolitanism is being reclaimed today at a theoretical level, we can now proceed to complicate how Tagore and Okakura negotiated their unquestionably privileged world. Privilege in itself cannot be regarded as the *sine qua non* of cosmopolitan identity, even though it can facilitate certain modes of socialization across national borders and constituencies. Through their incessant travel as celebrities, both Tagore and Okakura were exposed to some of the leading personalities and artistic movements of the world. Clearly, this 'world' was catalysed for them by the global movement of capital, mediated through art and educational institutions, lecture tours, exhibitions, book publications, catalogues, auctions, and the buying and selling of art objects. None of this activity would have been possible in Tagore and Okakura's time without private funding, and the five-star conveniences that invariably accompany élite patronage.

Okakura, as we have already hinted, was surrounded by some fabulously rich Bostonians, many of whom he befriended while they were residing in Japan and building their own collections of Japanese art. William Bigelow, in particular, was his most ardent benefactor, who not only funded the creation of the Nihon Bijutsuin, but who facilitated Okakura's career in the Museum of Fine Arts, Boston, through an important letter of recommendation. In the museum itself, Okakura succeeded in getting more money through the creation of funds, such as the Special Chinese and Japanese Fund, which was built by Bigelow and the extended family of Edward Jackson Holmes, who was, at several points in time, the director and president of the Museum. So close were the connections between Okakura and his patrons that he affectionately nicknamed Mrs Holmes his 'Jewel Bunny'. By 1905, when Okakura was appointed as an Advisor to the Museum, he had funds amounting to $15,775: at one level, 'a small sum given the prices for Japanese art in the West at the time but a substantial one for Boston when compared with the $1,153 available to the Museum's Painting Department that year'.[26] So confident was Okakura during his frequent purchasing trips to Japan and China that he could send a telegram to the museum authorities with emphatic demands for more money, at times expressed in monosyllabic messages: 'More.'[27]

In contrast to this funding game, which in today's art world would be considered essential for the survival of any institution, Tagore was more of a reluctant tactician in his association with funding agencies. More often than not, they sought him out, because they realized his cultural capital on which they could rely to make profits. Indeed, there were competing agencies that indirectly facilitated Tagore's first trip to Japan in 1916 en route to the United States where he was scheduled to deliver a series of lectures. First he received an offer of $10,000 with an additional $3,000 for travel expenses from an agent in New York called Keedick.[28] When the demand for forty lectures proved to be daunting, the poet switched his allegiance to a counter offer that he received from the impresario James Pond of J.B. Pond Lyceum Bureau. In the background of these deals were publishing companies like Macmillan that cashed in on quick publications of Tagore's translations, independently of their accuracy or artistic merit.

It is true that Tagore's marketability somewhat decreased as the years passed, in direct response to his politically incorrect gestures in condemning nationalism and returning his knighthood following the Jallianwala Bagh massacre in Amritsar, which were unfavourably represented in the international press. Besides, even among his most ardent literary admirers, notably Yeats, there was a considerable distancing from their earlier endorsement of *Gitanjali*'s genius. Shoddy translations of the poet's work contributed towards diminishing his aura, but the phenomenon of Tagore prevailed, transcending the actual assessments of his worth as a poet. Elevated to some kind of honorary world-citizen, he could always be relied upon to draw a crowd, and in the process, to feed the credentials of his international sponsors.

The significant difference with Okakura, however, is that while Tagore might have known how to elicit funds, he was hopeless at generating new income or in making lucrative investments. Almost all his money earned abroad was used to support his school in Santiniketan, and in sustaining experiments in agriculture, community development, and banking in Sriniketan. In contrast, Okakura's negotiation of capital was almost entirely tied up with getting the best possible deal for his employers at the Museum of Fine Arts, Boston. It is true that Okakura too had his own utopian retreat in the idyllic surroundings of Izura in Japan, where his painters were forming one of the first independent artistic colonies. However, by and large, he kept these worlds apart, and, arguably, his real professional base was in the United States, not in Japan.

This brings us to a critical issue relating to the politics of location vis-à-vis the larger ethos of universality. Tagore has been accused of catering to the West by building his image of the 'world poet' (*visva kobi*) according to its demands. As the writer Amit Chaudhuri has expressed it strongly, this was a 'harmful falsification, symptomatic of a time when western humanism presumed the translatability of all cultures into one another's terms, and the existence of a generalized "human" sensibility; in short, it required the Tagore it invented'.[29] Arguably, this reading does not take into account that the poet had his own views on universal humanism, which did not simply play into dominant Western assumptions of humanity, still less into notions of cosmopolitanism. Indeed, even as these assumptions were severely challenged by the brutality of the Second World War, the poet's 'faith in Man' deepened, even as it risked appearing to be totally redundant even to those intellectuals who opposed the war. Whatever the reading of Tagore's universal humanism and its opportunistic relationship to the 'world poet' image, the point is that it was constantly nurtured by his creativity and work in Santiniketan. This was his 'home' in relation to 'the world', even as this 'home' accommodated the universe, as the motto of Visva-Bharati reveals: 'where the whole world finds its home in one nest'. It would be unthinkable to imagine that this 'nest' could have existed anywhere in 'the West', as, for example, in Boston.

For Okakura, America, or more precisely, the Museum of Fine Arts, Boston, was not exactly his 'nest', but it was a kind of 'halfway house' between the East and West.[30] Unlike Tagore, who travelled relentlessly outside of India, at times for months on end, but who always returned to his 'nest' — in that sense, he was a nomad who, for all his migrations, returned to a base on a seasonal basis — Okakura was a great deal more pragmatic in strategizing his career through a series of relocations. Indeed, he can be said to be a forerunner in setting the contemporary academic trend of negotiating a 'six-month contract' with his American employers, as he divided his time between the United States and Asia. Japan was less and less the 'home' to which he retreated as he immersed himself in the activities relating to the Museum between 1904 until his premature death in 1913. Boston, in short, was his professional base, where he fashioned his cosmopolitan persona as a curator and art dealer, perfectly at ease with the speculations of the art market. The degree to which Okakura was 'at home' in Boston, we shall discuss later in this section. Now let us substantiate the materialist underpinnings of his cosmopolitan enterprise.

CULTURAL PROPERTY, OR LOOT?

For all his nationalism and reverence for Japanese art, Okakura justified his position in Boston on what I am compelled to describe as dubious grounds. While acknowledging that there was a 'loss' in the fact that some of the treasures of Japanese art were no longer in Japan, he attempted to justify this loss in a diplomatic way, by referring to 'Japan' in the third person:

Perhaps Japan may console herself for the loss of her treasures in the thought that this expensive outlay was a necessary factor in creating the universal appreciation and respect which the West has come to entertain nowadays towards Eastern art. Certainly, it has stimulated Japan herself into a recognition of the sense of duty to these, her ancestral landmarks of civilization.[31]

This statement becomes all the more outrageous in the context of the sheer scale of the American acquisitions of Japanese art, particularly in the 1880s. In Okakura's own estimate, we have some staggering figures of the sheer quantity of art exported from Japan to the US:

The magnificent gift of Dr Bigelow [to the Museum of Fine Arts] comprises 59,838 objects in all, covering the whole range of Far Eastern Art. The Chinese and Japanese paintings alone number 3,634; of prints there are 20,000 and of drawings 25,000. The Fenollosa Collection consists of 1,099 paintings; these were bought and bequeathed to the Museum by Dr Charles Goddard Weld, together with nearly a thousand objects collected by Dr Weld himself. The Morse Collection of Japanese pottery includes upward of five thousand pieces.[32]

When confronted with these figures, it becomes almost impossible not to question the euphemism suggested by the word 'gift', or the more archaic 'bequeathing' of paintings and art objects to the Museum. In a more political reading, this massive collection is nothing short of loot.

Predicably, it is justified on eminently pragmatic political grounds. Bigelow, Fenollosa, Morse and others happened to be in the right place at the right time, when, in the immediate turmoil of the Meiji Restoration, with the repercussions of civil war, there was little or no protection for traditional art. Feudal families, which had lost their status, sold their art treasures for a song, while Buddhist temple complexes, faced by the ideological challenge of Shintoism, were denied patronage, if not burned to the ground. In this maelstrom of violence and political uncertainty, traditional cultural artefacts were expendable, which is precisely on what the American scholars and collectors capitalized.

In a generous interpretation, one could say that they salvaged what could have been destroyed forever. However, the real ethical issue is that a scholar like Fenollosa was making these purchases at precisely the time when he was appointed by the Japanese government to play an active role in surveying, and thereby protecting, national treasures at shrines, temples, and in the collections of the imperial household. Tellingly, Okakura, his erstwhile student and interpreter, was his accomplice on these missions to 'save' traditional Japanese art from extinction. Even so, in critical retrospect, it would seem that the ultimate beneficiary of this rescue mission was the Museum of Fine Arts, Boston, which is today regarded as one of the most impressive collections of Japanese and Chinese art in the world.

By the time Okakura had joined the museum, the Japanese government had already become extremely vigilant about the export of its national treasures. Consequently, it was possible for Okakura to self-righteously endorse the government's position: 'Practically no temple-treasures are now permitted to go out of the country; and no piece of importation on sale can be acquired by foreigners except by keen competition with the native purchasers.'[33] This did not stop Okakura from looking elsewhere for the best possible bargains of original and finely crafted traditional art. For all his sensitivity towards the 'ghastly spectacle of [the] auction room',[34] to which the treasures of Chinese royal families were subjected, he had no qualms whatsoever in pursuing aggressive business tactics in China itself. In a sophisticated sales pitch presented to the leading committee members of the museum, he had called their attention to the 'vast opportunities in China', emphasizing that 'the Buddhist temples are falling to pieces'. In this crisis, the museum could cash in on 'obtain[ing] things for the mere cost of transportation'.[35]

Who is Okakura servicing at this point? Asia or the United States? Significantly, unlike China and Japan, India had not yet been prioritized in the Asian collection of the Museum of Fine Arts, Boston. This inclusion would come in due course following Okakura's death when Ananda Coomaraswamy assumed leadership in curating Asia for the museum with his own distinctive brand of authority and impeccable scholarship. If Okakura had lived through the 1930s, one wonders how he would have reacted to that extraordinary curatorial coup in 1936, involving a collaboration between the Japanese government, Harvard University, and the Museum of Fine Arts, Boston, on a major exhibition of art treasures from Japan. These treasures included masterworks from the Imperial Household, which in normal circumstances could not have left Japan, in addition to items belonging to the Showa emperor Hirohito. The art historian Mimi Yiengpruksawan has documented this moment with considerable precision and political insight:

It seems remarkable that the Japanese government, in times of worsening relations with the United States (Pearl Harbor was less than five years away), sent an exhibition of its National Treasures across the Pacific. Certainly it speaks to confidence in the ability of art to best represent the essence and character—for some, the superiority—of a people. More realistically it amounted to a strategy for negotiating and defusing American power. On these grounds it might be said that the nineteenth-century partnership between Japanese and American art historians that began with Okakura and Fenollosa became in the twentieth century, if I might borrow from John W. Dower, a tight embrace.[36]

Indeed, Okakura's earlier endorsement of art as 'aesthetic warfare' would seem to be confirmed by the exhibition of 1936. Had he been alive, he would in all probability have been appointed the curator of this exhibition; the man trusted by both parties, the Japanese government and his friends at Harvard and the Museum of Fine Arts, Boston. How Okakura would have played the role of the mediator in the context of imminent war is anyone's guess, but my own conjecture is that he would have distinguished himself as an intercultural ambassador.

Looking back on Okakura's relatively short, but productive, stint in building and authenticating the Japanese and Chinese collection in Boston, and recontextualizing that moment today within global museological practices, what is striking is not so much the difference between these historical moments, but their uncanny similarities. Ultimately, what connects these moments is the logic of capital in which curatorial practices across the century, for all their apparent changes, continue to derive their legitimacy. Thus, in 1999–2000, we have yet another astonishing curatorial coup with the Museum of Fine Arts, Boston, collaborating with its sister organization, Nagoya/ Boston Museum of Fine Arts, on an exhibition dealing exclusively with Okakura's connection with the museum in Boston. While the American director of the museum praised the exhibition on grounds that it 'serve[d] as an exquisite representation of the relationship that has been cultivated between the MFA and Japan for over 100 years', his Japanese counterpart described the collaboration as 'a joyous opportunity to contribute to renewed cultural exchange between Japan and the United States of America'.[37]

An exchange of diplomatic niceties, one could argue, but has anything changed? While it would, perhaps, have been too radical a curatorial gesture for the exhibition to acknowledge the dubious ethics and aggressive marketing that enabled the Boston collection to be built in the first place, one would at least want the legacy to be problematized in broader historical and political terms. This problematization is however singularly missing in the exhibition, whose lavish catalogue authenticates the pristine beauty of art objects, outdoing Okakura in the precision of its catalogue entries, but basically retaining his aesthetic priorities and conceptual criteria. In this emphatic celebration of beauty, there is no rupture whatsoever in suggesting that the Museum of Fine Arts, Boston, is 'returning' Japanese art to Japan. On the contrary, it is re-establishing its ownership rights, and in the process reducing Nagoya, an admittedly undistinguished industrialized city in Japan, to a cultural outpost. Okakura's cultural politics, I would argue, has not come full circle. Rather, the circle is simply enlarging to authenticate itself.

COSMOPOLITICS OF DRESS AND LANGUAGE

This critique of the politics of museology seems to have taken us far away from the global stakes of cosmopolitanism, but the reality is that they facilitate each other's operations. Okakura, it could be argued, played his cards very shrewdly but, in doing so, he merely followed the rules of the game. At one level, for all his 'native' flamboyance, he was a highly circumspect interventionist, who politicized his expertise to make a niche for himself in an almost exclusively white circle of Boston Brahmins. He appeared to infiltrate their ranks on his own terms. Today the terms themselves seem ambiguous, if not self-contradictory.

There is, for instance, the famous piece of advice he gave his son that one should only wear traditional Japanese dress, so long as one speaks perfect English: 'Never wear Japanese costume if you talk broken English.'[38] The provocation is priceless. Does one risk nativizing oneself only if one has the capacity to talk back? Imagine the shock of those Yankees who apparently accosted the kimono-clad Okakura and his friends on the street and teased them by asking, 'What sort of a 'nese are you? Are you Chinese, or Japanese, or Javanese?' To that Okakura responded with a sharp repartee: 'We are Japanese gentlemen. But what kind of a 'key are you? Are you a Yankee, or a donkey, or a monkey?'[39] While applauding this wit, one is tempted to question here the price of nativized cosmopolitanism. Is this a reaction to enforced acculturation? What does it mean to retain one's foreignness in order to assert a larger sense of belonging to the world? At what point does this foreignness become a trap? Or conversely, at what point does this attempt at belonging to the world cease to be relevant?

It would be useful to ask how these questions apply to Tagore, if at all. His choice of attire, for example, came out of a deeply personal critical introspection, in direct response to the politics of culture at home. Tagore, one could say, choreographed his appearance, not only for the Western audience, but for his own sense of personhood, and the dignity, self-respect, and grace attached to it. Like his poetry, this attire was a distinctive invention; a highly subjective sartorial signature in which he could distinguish himself, and yet feel at ease. Rejecting the Gandhian choice of khadi to affirm swadeshi politics, Tagore arrived at a more complex form of hybridizing a Hindu–Muslim sartorial style through his use of the *chapkan*, a loose overcoat worn over the *jubba* (tunic). Emphasizing the different varieties of chapkan, Tagore believed that in his particular selection 'one does not only see Muslim inventiveness but also the creation and freedom of the

Hindus.'[40] The dhoti, in comparison, was too Hindu in its associations, apart from not being practical in everyday life. Unlike Gandhi, who purified khadi to such a degree that he derided foreign cloth as 'filthy', 'defiling', and even 'untouchable',[41] Tagore had no such phobia and opted for a variety of handloom materials in a subtle spectrum of earth colours, thereby fashioning his own appearance as a contemporary Indian seer.

At no point did Tagore subscribe to Okakura's position that nativism is best affirmed in counterpoint with the English language. Here one needs to review the problematic of English, which is the language that enabled both Tagore and Okakura to communicate with each other, and with audiences outside of their respective homes. While Okakura wrote almost exclusively in English once he published *The Ideals of the East*, and in that sense, his cosmopolitanism is unthinkable outside of the globality of English as the language of trade, business, museology, and the art market, Tagore never abandoned his mother tongue. Indeed, the possibility of that thought is almost sacrilegious, given his prolific and radical contributions to the Bengali language in the largest range of genres that any writer in the world has ever attempted from songs, poems, short stories, novels, novellas, plays, dance-dramas, essays, and lectures to the most inspired scribbles decorating his images and sketches, which could be described as a sub-genre in their own right. In addition, at the risk of emphasizing the obvious, one should call attention to Tagore's seminal contributions to Bengali linguistics, beginning with his Bengali primer *Sahaj Path* (Easy Reading), through the more technical considerations of etymology and morphology in *Shabdatattwa* (Linguistics, 1909), into his classic on *Banglabhasha-Parichay* (Introduction to Bengali Language, 1938). It is, indeed, a humbling thought that the poet at the very peak of his career, and just a few years before his death, should have felt compelled to write an 'introduction' to the language in which he was hailed as a genius.

If Bengali was the very source of Tagore's creative sustenance, he nonetheless used the English language at a predominantly functional level, not only for his international professional assignments, but also for his interventions in the Indian national scenario. In multilingual

India, where there was no consensus on the 'one nation, one language' consensus adopted by other colonized countries like Indonesia, English remained the predominant language of public discourse, legal controversies, official protests against government policy, letters to the editor, and national debates, notably Tagore's heated exchanges with Gandhi, which could not have happened in Gujarati, Bengali or Hindi. All this political business was conducted in English, though in a significantly different metaphorical and emotional register from Tagore's prolific political writings in Bengali.

I should emphasize at this point that it is somewhat reductive to equate English with internationalist and nationalist politics, and Bengali with the more private and enigmatic dimensions of the poet's life. Arguably, some of the most intimate revelations of the poet relating to his restlessness and inner frustrations were conveyed in letters written to his dearest friends and confidants, almost all of whom were English: the painter William Rothenstein, the social reformer Leonard Elmhirst who did pioneering work in Sriniketan, and his closest associates at Santiniketan, W.W. Pearson and C.F. Andrews. Notwithstanding these intimate exchanges, the point is that Tagore never wrote his most memorable poetry or songs in English. Rabindrasangeet, in particular, is inextricably linked to the rhythms, sounds, colours, and textures of a distinctively musical Bengali, which, at some level, remains 'untranslatable'.[42]

In distinct contrast to Tagore's veneration for the mother-tongue, Okakura's ease with the English language needs to be seen in relation to his 'inferiority complex' towards the Japanese language. According to Fred Notehelfer, Okakura never wielded Japanese with as much rhetorical eloquence as he used the English language, albeit in a mannered and archaic mode. As for his 'poor' calligraphy, it appears that 'only the adoption of a highly eccentric style allowed him to cover what remained a fundamental cultural weakness'.[43] These limitations in Okakura's expertise are generally attributed at a biographical level to the fact that his early education was conducted almost entirely in English. It appears that when he was eight years old, his father took him to Tokyo only to discover that his son could not read any of the street signs in Japanese. Young Kakuzo was promptly placed in a temple school where he began to learn Japanese and the Chinese classics, while his lessons in English continued in the afternoon with American missionaries.[44]

There is no such split in the youth of Rabindranath, who was, by our contemporary standards, a dropout from school. His education of the mind and the senses was nurtured through his precocious reading of the classics and mythology, devotional erotic poetry and philosophy. English is very much Tagore's acquired language in which he developed an uncanny facility, even though he was extremely reluctant to acknowledge this gift. So unswerving, I would argue, is his faith in the 'original' language, that he had a poor opinion of the task of translation; an opinion that bordered on condescension, if not outright impatience and contempt. In this sense, he was very different from his more cosmopolitan friend Okakura, who was at home in many languages, even though he wrote almost exclusively in English for at least the last twelve years of his life. However, for pleasure and the sheer *joie de vivre* of entertaining his foreign friends, he enjoyed translating Oriental exotica, inscriptions, names, epithets, and esoteric texts, despite some grandiloquent reservations: 'Translation is always a treason, and as a Ming author observes, can at its best be only the reverse side of a brocade—all the threads are there, but not the subtlety of colour or design.'[45] Tagore would take it further; for him, translation bordered on impossibility, so why bother with it?

There is one startling story that gets to the core of the matter, not just at the level of translation, but in relating language to cosmopolitanism. The story revolves around one of Tagore's most beloved female companions, the sophisticated and vivacious Argentinian author, Victoria Ocampo (1890–1979), who is remembered today as the editor of the international literary magazine *Sur* (South), a title that was apparently selected by the pre-eminent philosopher and critic José Ortega y Gasset. Apart from Jorge Luis Borges, *Sur* published a glittering range of writers from across Europe and the United States, including Thomas Mann, Henry Miller, T.S. Eliot, Paul Claudel, Nathalie Sarraute, Martin Heidegger, Ezra Pound, Evelyn Waugh, and André Breton.[46] All these luminaries were translated into Spanish, testifying to the multilingualism of *Sur*'s cosmopolis. Fluent in English, Ocampo had read Tagore in Spanish in the translations of Juan Ramon Jimenez and his wife Zenobia Camprubi, though she preferred Gide's translations in French.

Ocampo first enters Tagore's life as his gracious hostess in Argentina, where she took care of him while he was convalescing from an illness at a villa in San Isidro in 1924. Six years later, in May 1930, when the poet was discovering himself as a painter, Ocampo was instrumental in rallying support for his first art exhibition in Paris at the Galerie Pigalle. From these European and Latin American references, we get some sense of Ocampo as an aristocratic, multilingual world-traveller, a cosmopolitan in the most vibrant and uncomplicated sense of the word. While she knew very little about India, she loved Tagore as a friend, though the precise nature of this love has been a source of controversy among Bengali critics.[47]

To return to the dynamics of cosmopolitanism and language, which had precipitated the introduction of Victoria Ocampo in this narrative, let me turn to one episode in the Tagore–Ocampo relationship.[48] While convalescing in the panoramic surroundings of San Isidro, it appears that Tagore wrote a poem *Kankal* (A Skeleton), one among many poems that finally were collected in a volume entitled *Purabi* (Easterner), dedicated to Ocampo. Inspired by the sight of some bleached bones of an animal on the pampas, Tagore composed the poem and then read it aloud in Bengali to Ocampo, whereupon he improvised an oral translation of the poem into English. When he eventually did the written translation, however, Ocampo 'could not suppress her disappointment: he had omitted the most valuable part of the poem' (258). This was not untypical of Rabindranath, who could leave out entire sections in translations of his novels and plays. Indeed, it sometimes feels as if he is consciously mutilating his own text. When Ocampo accused the poet of leaving things out, it is said that 'he thought *that* would not interest Westerners' (258). From Ocampo's report, we learn of her spontaneous reaction: 'The blood rose to my cheeks as if I had been slapped' (258).

It is true that the poet did make amends by translating the poem more caringly. However, the point that needs to be made here is that

Tagore, for all the warmth that he derived from his foreign friends, was almost sanguine about the fact that, at some fundamental levels, they would never be able to understand his inner world as a poet. More precisely, they would never be in a position to grasp the subtleties of his Bengali, and he was not overly concerned about caring to translate the difference. A more uncosmopolitan attitude would be hard to find. One can understand why Ocampo felt as if she had been 'slapped'. More than any other fact, it seems to me that Tagore's fundamental disbelief in being able to make others think and feel the immediacies of his mother tongue Bengali, is what circumscribes his 'world poet' image. It is the very opposite of today's Third World celebrities like Salman Rushdie and Arundhati Roy, whose global cosmopolitanism is, at one level, directly attributed to the fact that they are in a position to make 'other worlds' accessible in English. While Tagore remains largely inaccessible to this day, this limitation can also be regarded as a sign of his specific richness and complexity as a poet, which demands nothing less than a labour of love to read him in Bengali, or through a close interlingual reading of existing translations.

If I had to be pushed into defining Tagore's sense of being in the world, I would be compelled to evoke it in terms of universality rather than cosmopolitanism. While both these terms share some common ground, I would agree with Bruce Robbins that 'cosmopolitanism is not as philosophically ambitious as the word *universalism*',[49] circumscribed as it is by sociality, worldliness, and the flows of cultural capital in the global economy. Even as Tagore was compelled to work through the cosmopolitan demands of surviving as a celebrity, not without some strategic use of its economic benefits, he evolved his own philosophy that enabled him, even in the depths of his awareness of the 'crisis in civilization', to envision 'a day when Man will retrace his path of conquest, despite all barriers, to win back his lost human heritage'.[50] Against the moral and spiritual fibre of Tagore's 'faith in Man', I would tend to agree with Fred Notehelfer that, in the final analysis, Okakura 'could not break through to universalism', though I do not share his somewhat too categorical view that Okakura's universalism could have been achieved if he could have affirmed that

Rabindranath Tagore: The Swadeshi Portrait
1905/6. Photo: Sukumar Ray.

◄   The Young 'Samurai': Okakura Tenshin.

▲ Tagore at the villa of Okakura Tenshin, 1916. Photo: K. Maekawa.

◄ A cup of tea: Tagore in Japan, 1916. Photo: K. Maekawa.

▼ Tagore relaxing in the Japanese countryside, 1929.

◀ Draft of an
original portrait of
Okakura Tenshin,
1922, painted by
Kanzan Shimomura,
on the 25th memo-
rial exhibition of the
Nihon Bijutsuin.

◀ Okakura wearing the uniform of the Tokyo School of Fine Arts, seated on his horse Wakakusa ('Fresh Grass'), 1892.

▶ Okakura in his avatar as a fisherman, celebrating the energies of nature and the universe, embodied in the Tao cap.

▲ Priyambada Devi Banerjee. Photo: J.Kapp & Co. Calcutta, from the
collection of Pulinbihari Sen.

▲ Surendranath Tagore.

◄ Okakura in a hooded robe.

▲ Tagore and Okakura's family, August 1916. From left to right: Okakura's wife Motoko, his younger sister Choko, his grandson Koshiro, his eldest son Kazuo, and Kazuo's wife Takako.

'the goal of mankind everywhere was the subjugation of raw military power by culture'.[51] Perhaps, universalism cannot be dictated in these terms because, in essence, it is not merely the assertion of an agenda, or a mere reaction to nationalism or imperialism or militarism. Indeed, if Tagore's example is anything to go by, his universalism emerges and is constantly being renewed not out of any fixed ideological conviction, but out of his immersion in the particularities of a creative process through which moments of being in everyday life are at once embodied, illuminated, and transcended.

There is no better way to illustrate the tangibility of Tagore's sense of the universal than to evoke one such moment, which has been suggestively captured in an illumination of 'creative unity'.[52] The person who reveals this unity to Tagore is an 'ascetic woman' called Sarva-khepi by the local villagers: 'the woman who is mad about all things'. Sarva-khepi fixes her 'star-like eyes' upon Tagore and startles him with a question:

'When are you coming to meet me underneath the trees?' Evidently she pitied me who lived (according to her) prisoned behind walls, banished away from the great meeting-place of the All, where she had her dwelling. Just at that moment my gardener came with his basket, and when the woman understood that the flowers in the vase on my table were going to be thrown away, to make place for the fresh ones, she looked pained and said to me, 'You are always engaged reading and writing; you do not see.' Then she took the discarded flowers in her palms, kissed them and touched them with her forehead, and reverently murmured to herself, 'Beloved of my heart.' I felt that this woman, in her direct vision of the infinite personality in the heart of all things, truly represented the spirit of India.[53]

This is an extraordinary passage, which illuminates the universal through gesture and poetry more suggestively than through any reference to the Upanishads or to some weighty philosophical reflection on the 'sense of beauty' (*soundaryabodh*).[54] In such reflections, where Tagore linked beauty to normative notions of beneficence and truth, intrinsically restrained and temperate in their opposition to any possibility of excess, there is, to my mind at least, less beauty than that which is evoked in the sheer *unpredictability* of Sarva-khepi's gesture. Tellingly, though her background is not clarified, she is associated with the Baul singers, whose capacity to reveal the infinite through the most direct utterance had 'stirred' Tagore's mind. It is from this source of 'folk religion', which asserts 'not only that God is *for* each of us, but also that God is *in* each of us',[55] that Tagore affirms the 'spirit of India'; a spirit that transcends the national boundaries of space and time to embrace the universe. This spirit is palpable because it is neither explicated nor moralized in the theoretical language of beauty or aesthetics. It exists in its own right, at once tangible and immediate, in its direct illumination of the universe.

THE COSMOPOLITAN IN EXILE

Against Tagore's idealized affirmation of universalism, Okakura, it could be argued, spread himself too thin at far too many levels. In the process, like many élite cosmopolitans of our times, caught within the webs of careerism and frenetic travel, he succumbed to the all-too-familiar global predicament of a quick burnout. No critical reading of Okakura would be fair, however, if it did not acknowledge the pathos of his complicity in the role-playing demanded of his cosmopolitan world. In Okakura's letters, we have some candid, and sad, admissions about his life in Boston, from which I would like to quote at length:

Boston is sad and dreary, I am consoling myself with my work.[56]

I have few friends. I go out very little into Society though the people here are very kind and solicitous about me. I make a brave attempt and go to their dinner-parties and come back bored and miserable. With best intentions they expect you to entertain them. Who am I, a weary spirit, to bring them laughter? I have a quiet apartment where two Japanese artists help me in keeping house and cook native dishes. I spend my evenings reading, dreaming and sometimes coining bad verses.[57]

[My well-wishers] do not know that I am wearing a mask of bravery and self-reliance in order to confront the world, that underneath it is a timid cowardly creature trembling at every commotion. It is fear which makes me proud.[58]

This self-critique is hardly representative of the proud pan-Asianist who, just ten years earlier, was declaiming that 'Asia is one'. Indeed, it is not a particularly reassuring portrait of a global cosmopolitan, who yearns for a quiet evening at home in the company of his own countrymen, eating 'native dishes'. Instead of the strategic Okakura, outperforming all his colleagues at the Museum, and the ruthless art-dealer, there is a 'timid cowardly creature'.

In his last months in Boston, Okakura had a surprise visitor, his friend Rabindranath whom he hadn't seen since 1902. The poet was busy giving far too many lectures, and was passing through Boston. On 4 February 1913, Okakura wrote:

Babu Rabindra came yesterday with his son and his charming daughter-in-law. I am hoping to make their short stay here as little of a bore as possible though of course being a stranger myself I cannot do much.[59]

This is hardly the statement one would expect from a man about town closely connected to the flamboyant heiress Isabella Gardner, who in turn was in touch with the *crème de la crème* of Boston society, including veteran writers like Henry James and a young T.S. Eliot. However, the sheer smartness of this society, for Okakura, was clearly no compensation for its boredom—an accusation that is, in essence, a deeply cosmopolitan charge. Cosmopolitans are known to hate boredom, but the peculiarity here is that Okakura is criticizing the boredom of one of the most ostensibly cosmopolitan cities in the world, accommodating institutions such as the Museum of Fine Arts, Boston, and Harvard University.

Even more telling is Okakura's reference to himself as a 'stranger', which in postcolonial terms surely carries the weight of *déjà vu*. How do we evaluate the self-description of a 'stranger' in exile? Inevitably, one is alerted to that canonical statement, originally attributed to a twelfth-century medieval monk, rediscovered by Erich Auerbach in his post-war requiem for Western civilization in *Mimesis* (written in Istanbul between 1942–5 and first published in 1946), and later appropriated by Edward Said to constitute one of the most frequently quoted epigraphs for postcolonial exile:

The person who finds his homeland sweet is still a tender beginner; he to whom every soil is as his native one is already strong; but he is perfect to whom the entire world is a foreign place. The tender soul has fixed his love on one spot in the world; the strong person has extended his love to all places; the perfect man has extinguished his.[60]

Within the hierarchy of these injunctions, it is unlikely that Okakura ever qualified for, or aspired to, the pinnacle of detachment to be found in the exile's estrangement from the 'entire world'. His escape-route was always to return to the Orient, and more specifically, to his home in Izura. 'An Oriental at home, at one with the Orient?': perhaps not quite so rapturously, as Okakura had once affirmed the state of being Oriental in *The Awakening of the East*. It could be argued that Okakura remained something of a stranger even in the midst of his family and disciples in Izura, though he never derided their familial care. In Boston, however, he was becoming, less ambiguously, a stranger to himself.

A few weeks after Tagore had arrived in Boston, he left to pursue his commitments elsewhere. This was the year in which he would win the Nobel Prize, but that was months away. On 3 March 1913, Okakura wrote:

It is snowing here still and I long for the sunshine and flowers of the Orient. Your uncle has left for Chicago and I feel a sudden loneliness.[61]

This statement has all the ingredients of a haiku. It conveys its own *rasa*, or more precisely, *hana* (flower), in the *suddenness* of the loneliness.

We shall leave Okakura in this unsettled state and ask a question that should have been raised earlier: To whom is he writing these letters? Letters which seem to humanize him, no longer promoting Asia or the world of Japanese art, but talking about the simple things of everyday life, like the weather, food, home, meeting a few friends. Okakura is writing to his most intimate confidant in the last months of his life, a Bengali widow and poet, Priyambada Devi Banerjee, whom he had fortuitously met on his second trip to India in 1912. This was a rushed and somewhat perfunctory trip, when Indian art was no longer on his agenda. Besides, Tagore was away in Europe, because *his* globetrotting days had accelerated by this time. It was during this trip to India, which so very easily might not have happened given Okakura's gruelling schedule, that he and Priyambada met each other in the home of Surendranath Tagore over a cup of tea. What developed was more than a platonic intimacy, which grew long-distance through an exchange of love letters, from Calcutta to Boston, and then to Izura and back.

Along with these love letters, there was also an opera in the making, Okakura's last creative experiment, enigmatically entitled *The White Fox*, which he shared with Priyambada in the course of writing to her. It is with the libretto of this opera that I will begin the next section of this book, throwing out a few questions on love and friendship.

4

Friendship

The Intertexts of Love

With *The White Fox*, we are exposed to the retelling of a familiar Japanese legend, which forms part of the traditional repertoire of many narrative traditions, including Noh drama and the puppet tradition of Bunraku. The fox, which is generally feminized, as in Okakura's opera, has the supernatural capacity to assume a human form, generally the body of a beautiful woman who has been abducted or forcibly separated from her lover.[1] The tragedy of the fox is that while she can love like a woman, and even bear the hero a child, she has no other alternative but to return to her animal form when the real woman reappears. The fox, therefore, becomes a surrogate of love; a testament to the ephemeral existence of life itself.

When Yasuna, the hero in Okakura's opera, first catches sight of Kolha, the fox in her transfigured state, he imagines first that it is a 'phantasy' of his 'longing soul',[2] because he knows that his betrothed Kuzunoha has been abducted by the wizard knight Akeimon. Kolha, reflected in a pool of water, challenges his suspicion of phantasy:

> In this world of semblance,
> Who speaks so lightly of delusion?   [WF348]

Further questioned by Yasuna to confirm whether she is 'real', Kolha responds:

No more than thou!
Is not reality
But an illusion delayed?   [WF348]

While *The White Fox* was dedicated to Isabella Gardner, who served as
the mediator with the French composer Loeffler, who ultimately
failed to convince Okakura that he had to edit his libretto to two
acts, the real Muse of the opera is clearly Priyambada. In fact, at one
level, the libretto was directly inspired by her love letters to Okakura.
For all their formality and middle-class *bhadramahila* (educated Bengali
lady) protocol — Priyambada inscribed each of her letters under the
sign of 'Om' — they were almost undisguised revelations of 'longing'.

If there is one leitmotif in this Orientalized *Tristan and Isolde*, it is,
from Priyambada's side, the 'beauty of a longing', 'the unsatisfied
longing', the 'heart longing for the infinite sky', the longing of
'wander-thirst', and the longing in which the dead lover finds 'rest
and peace'.[3] Okakura had initiated this rhetoric with one of his early
letters in which he had voiced 'a longing for the Jade-flower — the
ambrosia of the Taoists'. Is longing beautiful, as he questioned
rhetorically, and with all the confidence of a seasoned lover, precisely
'because of its being never fulfilled'?[4]

Within the unmitigated romanticism of longing shared by
Okakura and Priyambada, there was also an appropriation of
each other's words. Indeed, Okakura formally asked Priyambada's
permission to quote some lines from her poem 'The Unsatisfied
Longing', which he promptly placed not in the mouth of Kolha the
fox, but rather, in the voice of his male protagonist Yasuna. While
only the last lines in this passage are drawn from Priyambada, the
framing of the entire passage is Okakura's:

> Words are the widows of thought
> In black and white how coldly clad!
> My songs are a flimsy dyke
> To stem one moment the rushing tide
> Of love's fierce waters, uncontrolled.
> I cannot hold thee, dear, I cannot
> Bind thee in words or in rhymes enchain.

> I cannot hold thee, dear, I cannot
> Twine thee in my songs and call thee mine.   [WF360]

At this point in the libretto, Yasuna cannot fathom why Kolha seems so sad, though she knows that 'all being is evanescent' and 'all meeting must be parting' (WF356). In a subtle transgendering of Priyambada's inability to find an appropriate language of love, Okakura takes her indecision and makes it his own through Yasuna's voice.

In a follow-up to his first draft of the opera, Okakura added that in the line 'words are [the] widows of thought', he had specifically meant 'the written word' through which it is almost impossible to capture the 'quality' of the human voice.[5] In contrast, the spoken word provides a direct insight into the soul. Would it make a difference, Okakura asked, if his letters to Priyambada had been written in Japanese rather than in English? In Japanese, he might have addressed her 'in politer and less brutal' ways; he could have 'veil[ed] [his] thoughts better'. However, the very 'imperfection' of his English is what enabled him to be 'more frank'.[6]

In her response, Priyambada was compelled to agree: 'I do not know if writing to you in Bengali would improve matters much with me either, but alien speech is always a difficulty. Yet I am grateful to it because it has made our communication possible' (PB265). There is the strange beauty of making love—or more specifically, writing love—in a foreign tongue. Even after Okakura's death, Priyambada took pains to translate many of her poems from Bengali into English, and she continued to write to him in at least one of her notebooks, in chaste English. At the same time, while he was alive, Priyambada could not help making a point to her distant cosmopolitan lover: 'You are naughty, professing love for India, yet never tried to know her language' (PB265). Okakura requests a Bengali grammar book which Priyambada dutifully provides, but he holds on to calling his fox-heroine 'Kolha', the Bengali word for 'plantain', whereas Priyambada would prefer to rename her 'Shukla' ('pure white', in Sanskrit).

I could easily continue to elaborate on such trivial details, the patter of love-talk, but this would deflect the more important point that Tagore is an absent presence in this love affair. At a purely biographical level, he remains the indulgent critic, who encourages Priyambada's efforts at translation, while indicating that 'something was wanting' in her poems, which had not yet 'formed into crystals' (PB248). Priyambada, lesser poet that she is, accepts his criticism, but strikes back ever so slightly when the poet chides her for sticking to the monotony of her household duties. 'He is a man,' Priyambada states her position candidly, 'and cannot realize that a woman's life is limited by many things—mostly by her own nature that cannot alienate itself from those nearest her, she must first serve them before she can take her place in the wider life' (PB248–9). Okakura listens attentively, while encouraging Priyambada to write.

If there is a shadow of Tagore in the love affair between Okakura and Priyambada, it is revealed in the intertextual interstices of their love letters, when Okakura begins to Orientalize his Indian muse almost as an embodiment of Asia herself. When he finally gets Priyambada's photograph, for which he has hankered like any avid surfer on a dating network seeking desperately to attach a face to a particular voice, he is satisfied: 'It is a saintly presence indeed.'[7] Earlier, in a voice that unmistakably echoes one of Tagore's most heartbreakingly real heroines Chitrangada, who attempts to reassert her true self through the counterfeit of beauty by demanding recognition on her own terms, Priyambada remonstrates with her Japanese lover:

What made you think of me? Are you never afraid that I may be a mirage, a [c]himera, a will-o'the'wisp, an illusion only? I may [be] all these, yet who knows I may be a reality too. Please do not think of me as an impossible perfection—I am nothing of the kind. ...I am only a woman, a human being, and that I think is dignity enough, don't you agree with me?

[PB254]

Tagore is speaking through Priyambada here, because, like all bhadralok Bengalis in her generation and after, she has not merely internalized his language of love in its myriad registers; she is able to *think* the state of being in love on account of his distinctive contribution to the Bengali imaginary of 'modern love' in the age of swadeshi. Now love could be individuated and debated, women had as much of a say in claiming love as men; love could be betrayed at very banal levels, and great heroes like Gora would eventually be compelled to see women in their own right, instead of as repositories of Bharatbarsha.

Tagore was much too a discreet tactician to play the role of the go-between in the relationship between Priyambada and Okakura. Technically, he was a distant family member: his niece Indira Devi (sister of Okakura's closest Bengali friend Surendranath) was married to the essayist Pramatha Choudhuri, the brother of Priyambada's mother Prasannamayi Devi, an author in her own right. If this sounds like a hopelessly complicated web of family ties — a concrete instance of the *atmiyasambandhasthapan* ('establishment of the relationship of relatives') mentioned in my section on *Swadeshi Samaj*, Priyambada puts it more gracefully to Okakura: 'Though in reality there is no relationship...the Tagores are our best friends. I have known them since I was a little girl and look upon them as very near and dear relations' (PB278). Given the intimacy of their ties, it is not unlikely that Tagore was fully aware of what was going on between Priyambada and Okakura, whose letters were occasionally intercepted by some unknown voyeur in their respectable Bengali social milieu.[8] While Tagore chose to remain scrupulously absent in their actual relationship, his silence is more than compensated by his profuse songs, in which the longing of their relationship had already been prefigured.

While all these songs would fall into the category of *prem* (love), the motif of *biraha* (separation) does not quite convey the infinitesimal and tangential references in the songs, which encompass a diversity of *bhavas* (emotions), which are counterpointed and mixed. Ultimately, the meaning of these songs can resonate only in performance; in the tense interplay between the words and the melody. The words alone are mere signifiers of what remains incomplete: a longing if you will for the music that gives them body. Here is a rare example of an exquisitely translated song from the Rabindrasangeet canon (*Tobu mone rekho jodi dure jai chole*), which I would like to quote at length for its sheer resonance:

> Even so, remember me
> If I should move far away, even so

If the old love should be lost in the mazes of a new passion
Even so, remember me
And if although I am near
My presence, like shadow, is shrouded with doubt
Your eyes might cloud with tears.
And if one lovely night this game should end
Even so, remember me
If, on an autumn morn, the final blow should fall, even so
And if, remembering me, tears do not come
Tears do not glisten in the corners of your eyes
Even so, remember me.[9]

Steeped in literariness, Priyambada cannot be separated from the translation of Rabindransangeet's idiom into what she reads and writes on a daily basis. Destined to be unread in Bengali literary circles today, she nonetheless wrote her life out through the most infinitesimal details, invariably cast in the same Romantic rhetoric, relentlessly filling diaries and notebooks with poems, sketches, impressions, and translations that she was reluctant, if not afraid, to publish. Sequestered in an oppressive dreamworld, where the claustrophobia of Calcutta is evoked through the almost total elision, if not erasure of political reality, Priyambada almost exoticizes herself as a modern-day version of Shakuntala—a Shakuntala, of course, who is widowed and childless. The very name 'Priyambada' (literally, 'sweetness of voice') is inextricably linked to Kalidasa's heroine, Priyambada being one of Shakuntala's *sakhis* (playmates)—and, if this detail is not literal enough, the real Priyambada is closely attached to nature and flowers, and to a doe named Ina whom she feeds in her garden.

In this highly mannered state of 'naturalness', where the day passes with decorum and the regulation of household duties, interspersed with writing and reading French and translating the Upanishads, there is an almost wilful surrender to a dark, melancholic, universe, with 'steel-grey clouds' and a heavy atmosphere. It is an upper-middle-class Bengali version of Marguerite Duras's *India Song*, whose hermeticism is heightened through the occasional 'cry of Savanakhet'—the voice of a beggar-woman whose reality is ruthlessly (and beautifully) disembodied. At no point in Priyambada's world is her isolation more marked than when she refers to the poor of India:

Orissa has been overflooded and the poor are in great distress. In Bengal and in Orissa, they have neither been able to sow crops at the proper time, and in districts where they could do it, the young crops have been quite drowned. So a very hard year is menacing our helpless poor. I often think of them and feel sad.   [PB279]

The fact that Priyambada felt the need to share the condition of the poor in Orissa with Okakura is perhaps more enigmatic than what follows: 'The last three days I had to take to bed again—and lying down I only read. Do you know Oscar Wilde's *De Profundis?*' (PB279). This, I would infer, is cosmopolitan civility in its most unconscious register of sharing 'profound' thoughts in a spirit of distraction, if not cultivated casualness, which resolutely postpones any confrontation of the real.

Beyond *De Profundis*, there are other such literary references that bind Okakura and Priyambada more intimately. She is enthusiastic about Keats's *Ode to Melancholy*, but is less enamoured of Chekhov. Indeed, she misreads Chekhov with all the vehemence of an educated Bengali exposed (though not perhaps on a regular basis) to the historical narratives and social dramas of the modern Bengali stage, imagining that this 'modernity' is at the centre of the world of theatre, and all other modernities are at best provincial. Chekhov's plays, for Priyambada, are not 'dramas'. There are 'beautiful thoughts in them,' as she grudgingly acknowledges, 'but they have no shape. They are long drawn and drawling [sic], and lack the intenseness of feeling which make[s] situation[s] dramatic' (PB250).

If Priyambada had read Chekhov more closely, she might have realized that the 'drama of inaction' is the very essence of his genius, where the very formlessness of everyday life and banal conversation is choreographed into a fine art. Indeed, with more empathy to her own predicament, Priyambada might have discovered Chekhov's seagull in herself. Okakura, indeed, is almost an eerie manifestation of Trigorin, the professional writer who breaks hearts, moving from one affair to the next, and who, whimsically, enjoys fishing. That was one critical aspect of the character that Stanislavski could never get, much to the chagrin of Chekhov. The Russian guru of modern acting was too busy romanticizing Trigorin, without checking out his fishing tackle.

Okakura loved to fish, and among his most innovative designs was a boat that hybridized the shapes of an American yacht and a traditional Japanese fishing boat. Affectionately named Ryu-wo (Dragon King), this boat, according to Okakura, looked like a 'good sailor'. In one of his more robust letters, Okakura describes his love for the sea in an idiom that bears some resemblance to Hemingway's *The Old Man and the Sea*:

Many years before I loved to shoot and nowadays I indulge in fishing. ...I go almost every morning to fish, awaking at two or three in the morning and having my breakfast on the water, reading sometimes and playing with the romance of the sea till noon. My boatman is an old denizen of the sea, learned in the ways of the aquatic tribes, a philosopher, like all fishermen who [have] communed with the deep all their lives, a poet in nature because he has learned to read the sea, its mysteries and its dangers. We are great friends and I talk India to him. He is a worshipper of the Dragon-King—a Naga Rajah which we got from you. Perhaps you will like him.[10]

Indeed, Okakura himself is eminently 'likeable' in this relaxed persona as a fisherman; very different from his more cosmopolitan and scholarly avatars. One is also compelled to note the male vigour of his prose, so different from Rabindranath's ethereal recollections of writing short stories and poetry on his beloved houseboat *Padma*, while cruising the riverine culture of Bangladesh, notably the river Padma itself. The poet, one should acknowledge, had been a strong swimmer in his youth, but one cannot really see him fishing alongside Okakura in the rough waters surrounding the rocky reefs of Izura.

This brings us to a somewhat difficult nuance for which I have indirectly prepared the ground in the previous pages, concerning the masculinities of Tagore and Okakura, in their very different life-practices and relationships with women and other men. I will turn to this issue now and tease out a few problems leading to the elusive dynamics of masculinity in the context of my narrative.

Beyond Masculinity

The word 'masculinity' raises a host of questions as it plays into stereotypical associations of strength, vigour, reason, an absence of tears and sentiments, the stiff upper lip, among other Anglo-American constructions of what it meant to be a 'man', particularly at the end of the last century. Going by Okakura's own flamboyant samurai–scholar persona, along with his suave elegance as a global cosmopolitan, not to mention his numerous conquests of women worldwide, it would seem that we have all the trappings here of a Japanese stud, though not perhaps in the homoeroticized Mishima mode. Okakura's masculinity is however deceptive, because if we are to trust the reaction of his most affectionate female companion Isabella Gardner, we learn that he was 'so interesting, so deep, so spiritual, so feminine'.[11] Indeed, as Gardner acknowledges, Okakura was the first person from whom she learnt 'her first lesson seeking to love instead of to be loved'.[12] Arguably, these words come from a woman whose own 'masculine' traits, such as 'boldness', 'authority', 'self-confidence', as Christopher Benfey has put it, 'found a complement in Okakura's sensitivity'.[13] In an age of queer studies, when the attributes of 'femininity' and 'masculinity' have been put under severe scrutiny, it is almost obligatory to challenge these unproblematized equations by suggesting that even though Okakura brought out what would appear to be a distinctly butch element in Isabella Gardner, this does not necessarily mean that he masqueraded an Oriental male version of Asian femininity. Perhaps, his masculinity remained intact despite its aura of inscrutable otherness.

In contrast, Tagore's femininity has been more overtly marked, not merely in his graceful, ethereal persona but in his high-pitched voice and almost falsetto delivery of poetry and songs, which was often subject to ridicule. There is no evidence to suggest, however, that this teasing demoralized the poet in any way, whose own sense of being a 'man' was highly evolved, transcending the more banal attributes of masculinity. This self-confidence was not however evident in Tagore's youth, when he was clearly challenged by the rough and ready humour of male bonding and camaraderie. In a startling recollection towards the end of his life, Tagore remembers how much he disliked school not only because of 'the fetters of fixed rules', but also on account of the crudity of his male peers:

The topics that most of the boys relished were so dirty, so nasty, that I could never bear their company. I used to feel sick. Once in my life, I went to attend some lectures in a college. I went with some enthusiasm. But I wore my hair longer than was customary, and my voice was soft—so, as soon as I entered, the boys said,—'Oh, here comes our *Baiji*' (a dancing woman of bad repute). I at once realized that this wouldn't do for me... So I left and went no more.'[14]

The fact that the poet remembered this taunt over fifty years after it happened indicates that it continued to trouble him. This hurt however never resulted in abject humiliation; rather, it compelled Tagore to resist the public school tradition of English masculinity and its notorious tolerance for 'ragging', in addition to its derivations of all kinds of authoritarian behaviour, including the violence of the army and the nation–state.

Rejecting the colonial norms of masculinity, Tagore realized that to be a 'man' in the true sense of the word did not require a total submission to the socialization of masculinity, just as to be 'modern' did not necessitate a surrender to modernization. There could be other ways of defining the self. Even so, it would be inaccurate to assume that Tagore's quest for self-realization was some kind of mystical process, entirely separated from the upper-class, Brahmo-dominated bhadralok culture in which he lived. As much as he questioned its taboos and restrictions, he never quite betrayed or rejected its legitimacy. Indeed, it is almost impossible to imagine Tagore straying from the codes of propriety that dominated his society. For all his radical interventions in Bengali language and culture, he remained almost distressingly compliant in his tactical adherence to social customs, religious ceremonies, caste taboos, and arranged marriages for his daughters, as many of his biographers have pointed out.

Quite unlike Okakura, who flouted all the rules, particularly in the 1890s, with his flagrant alcoholism and openly public affair with a married woman, Tagore comes across as the very model of Victorian rectitude and self-restraint. A widower at a very early age—indeed, in the very year that Okakura visited India in 1902—Tagore lived a solitary life almost entirely divested of sexual intimacies and relationships, notwithstanding the joy he derived from the companionship of young girls and the rumours that continue to circulate around his alleged love for Victoria Ocampo. If in Okakura's life there is a pattern that can be discerned in his ceaseless attraction for highly individuated, though maternal, women, in Tagore's life the movement is towards an almost asexual disembodiment of passion altogether. Indeed, this disembodiment is apparent in the way the poet presented himself to the world, as he appeared to sublimate his worldliness into a seer-like mode of being, which almost seemed to demand an emasculation of the sensual and corporeal dimensions of life.

At the level of physical presence, it is striking how this erasure manifested itself in Tagore's concealment of the body under layers of clothing, so antithetical to Gandhi's highly politicized exposure of the body, which almost flaunted the image of the 'naked fakir'. In contrast, the image of a bare-chested Tagore is almost irreverent, because it works against the enormous protocol that continues to camouflage his person even to this day. At one level, this need to maintain a venerable and spiritualized image of the poet can be linked to the regulatory codes of bhadralok censorship concealing an unacknowledged 'sexual panic'[15] in the cultures of everyday life. At all costs, respectability has to prevail and protect any possible distortion of Bengal's most sacrosanct icon. However, at another level, it could be argued that the poet himself constructed this seer-like image, and, in doing so, he consciously depersonalized his manhood in deference to 'Man', the larger phenomenon he unfailingly invoked in his writing as the ultimate arbiter of humanity.

In contrast to Tagore's rather abstract notion of personhood, Gandhi consciously worked through his troubled masculine 'self', asserting his body as the site of confrontation, struggle, shame, and penance. Openly sharing his controversial experiments with sexuality in the public domain within his larger search for truth, the Father of the Nation was not afraid to acknowledge the problem he perceived in his continued erections. This kind of disclosure would be unthinkable for Tagore, whose apparent transcendence of all passion earned from Gandhi the reverent description of 'Gurudev', even though he was not the first to use the honorific title, as is often imagined. At one level, the 'gurufication' of Tagore is a paradox given that the passions were seethingly alive in Tagore's imagination, which could be highly capricious, provocative, if not downright erotic, as is revealed in some of his late stories which dealt candidly with adult sexuality. However, the point is that this engagement with the passions was mediated entirely through fiction of some kind, which he was eminently in a position to control and sublimate. In the 'myriad-mindedness' of the poet, one is compelled to ask, where is the man?

This question has been provoked, at one level, on reading what could be one of the most comprehensive biographies on Tagore in English that encompasses the prodigious diversities of the poet's multiple experiences and achievements.[16] Even so, in the course of reading this detailed inventory of his life, which refreshingly avoids the traps of hagiography and bowdlerization, the 'man' in all his corporeal density appears to be singularly missing. I do not attribute this problem to the biography itself, but to something that seems fundamental to Tagore's self-construction, which the biography arguably effaces. We get a glimpse of this self-construction in an astonishing moment recorded by Maitraye Devi in which she catches the poet off-guard as he sits in a state of repose in her home in Mungpu, a village in the Darjeeling district. 'I feel you do not belong to us,' she tells him directly, to which the poet responds in telling detail:

Since you say that, I will admit the truth; really you are no one to me. What you call love, I have never felt it towards anyone. I lived in a large family, there were any number of dear ones and today you who are strangers have become more to me than all my kinsfolk. But...true friends, relations, domestic life, wife and children, I have never grasped any of them tightly. Somewhere deep in me I am impersonal—aloof. If it had not been so, if I had allowed myself to become enmeshed, then I should have been ruined. ...In my mind, I am for ever alone, detached—from boyhood, and even from childhood, I was like that.[17]

There is something chilling about the matter-of-fact way in which Tagore can tell his hostess and friend that 'you are no one to me' and that he is, essentially, 'impersonal', 'alone', 'detached'. The poet is not attitudinizing here, or posing as a saint, or trying to impress. He is, in his own words, admitting the 'truth'. On listening to his words, so carefully transcribed by Maitraye Devi, one hears echoes of his more metaphysical distinctions between *choto ami* and *boro ami* (Small I and Big I), *eka ami* and *maha ami* (the Lonely Isolate I and the Comprehensive Great I), *amar ami* and *param ami* (My Own I and the Supreme I). When we try to pin down Tagore to the choto ami he eludes our grasp and seems to slip between our fingers. It is not that he isn't human or capable of cracking jokes or being ironic or affectionate, but at some point or the other, this 'I' ceases to matter and gets merged in his other selves, which risk being articulated only in the language of transcendence.

I have consciously inserted what might seem to be a total detour in the reading of masculinity, which also runs the risk of playing into Tagore's cult of the genius, which critics like Partha Chatterjee have justifiably condemned as humanist mystification.[18] However, without some reckoning of Tagore's discrimination of multiple selves, and his own self-representation in everyday life, we have no other ground on which to posit a critique of masculinity that does not simply succumb uncritically to the existing tropes on the subject. I will now attempt to complicate the argument further by engaging with homosociality and its more arresting formulation as 'male homosocial desire'.[19]

HOMOSOCIALITY IN CONTEXT

In her seminal intervention on the subject, Eve Kosofsky Sedgwick has prepared a ground for investigating homosociality, which is challenging to confront in the context of Tagore and Okakura, not least because she specifically emphasizes caution in treating her formulations 'as cross-cultural or (far more) as universal'.[20] Bearing this in mind, I would emphasize that the axiomatic foundations of Sedgwick's discourse provide extremely useful points of reference for reflecting on homosociality in non-Western contexts, not least because, at some stage, they lend themselves flexibly as points of departure:

'Homosocial' is a word occasionally used in history and the social sciences, where it describes social bonds between persons of the same sex; it is a neologism, obviously formed by analogy with 'homosexual', and just as obviously meant to be distinguished from 'homosexual'. In fact, it is applied to such activities as 'male bonding', which may, as in our [Anglo-American] society be characterized by intense homophobia, fear and hatred of homosexuality.[21]

At a normative level, this distinction between the 'homosocial' and the 'homosexual' is valid in the context of the 'social bonds' between Tagore and Okakura, in addition to their relations with other men with whom they socialized and did business. These bonds were not sexualized, which doesn't mean that there were no homosexuals in their coteries: this would be highly unlikely among Boston Brahmins in particular, particularly those fraternizing in the art world, where even an apparently stolid figure like William Bigelow has been acknowledged to be a 'shy homosexual'.[22] The point is that the distinctions between the 'homosocial' and the 'homosexual' were implicitly understood and socially intelligible, even though, as we shall examine later, these terms should not be segregated into watertight compartments. Nonetheless, it would be a truism to state that social intimacies between men across cultures are neither necessarily nor intrinsically sexual, though they may appear to be so in particular contexts and circumstances.

    A more challenging aspect of Sedgwick's preliminary position is the specific inscription of a possible homophobia in homosociality. This 'fear and hatred of homosexuality', which Sedgwick, at one point, marks as 'brutal'[23] in her society, is, arguably, a lot less marked in non-Western societies, which doesn't mean that it doesn't exist in these places. However, the 'homosexual' himself/herself has yet to be adequately recognized and inscribed, at least in the public and secular discourse of India—and I refer to contemporary India, not just the Bengal of Tagore's time.[24] Sedgwick's assumptions of the homosexual's apparently unitary construction and existence also needs to be contextualized, insofar as it precedes her later destabilizing interventions in the determination of 'queer' identities, which followed her research on homosociality. However, even at this early stage of her research, Sedgwick had indicated a more transgressive possibility in her reading of the homosocial:

To draw the 'homosocial' back into the orbit of 'desire', of the potentially erotic, then, is to hypothesize the potential unbrokenness of a continuum between homosocial and homosexual — a continuum whose visibility, for men, in our [Anglo-American] society, is radically disrupted.[25]

While it is impossible to do justice to the sheer sweep and density of this statement within the limits of this particular narrative — and I will not even begin to engage with Sedgwick's equally challenging proposition that 'the diacritical opposition between the "homosocial" and the "homosexual" seems to be much less thorough and dichotomous for women, in [Anglo-American] society, than for men'[26] — I will offer one particular reading drawn from Tagore's oeuvre where I do believe that the continuum between the 'homosocial' and the 'homosexual' can be said to exist, without being 'radically disrupted'.

In the earlier section on masculinity, I had emphasized that to acknowledge the 'man' in Tagore in a more corporeal sense, is to work against the grain of his canonization. Without capitulating to this canonization, even while acknowledging that breaking its taboos is fraught with risks of controversy, I would suggest that Tagore's etherealized masculinity remains elusive, but not necessarily in the context of self-censorship. At one level, it is possible to read Tagore's public persona as 'closeted' in the way he scrupulously resisted any attempt to probe his privacy as an individual, but this would be too literal a reading for his own capacities to open himself to the eyes of the world. What I offer here is just one glimpse of the poet's capacity to push the protocols of travel writing in his sensuous description of the bodies of other men.

Quite tellingly, though ostensibly for stylistic reasons, this very passage has been singled out by one of the most respected Bengali editors of Tagore's collected writings in English, the late Sisir Kumar Das. It is drawn from Tagore's travelogue *Japan Jatri* (A Visit to Japan), which was written on board the ship S.S. Tosamaru, en route to Japan in 1916. Amidst philosophical musings in his travelogue, the poet also reacts to storms and boredom, life on the deck, and conversations with passengers. If there is anything Tagore hated as a traveller, it was the sight of docks and quays, with all the cacophony relating to loading and unloading cargo. In this mechanization, he often found his most potent image to lambast 'modern civilization'.

However, when the S.S. Tosamaru docked in Hong Kong, and Tagore had prepared himself to stay on board, 'at the risk of being disturbed by the noise of the stevedores', he saw something wondrous:

The first thing that struck my eyes was the work of the Chinese laborers on the wharves. Each of them was naked except for a pair of blue trousers. Never have I seen such well-muscled frames before, nor such rhythmic labor! Their bodies seemed to explode with a vigor that was harnessed into rhythm as the muscles of their glistening backs rippled in sinewy waves.[27]

The passage becomes more reflexive and complex in its hermeneutics:

The work of men at full strength is very beautiful: every moment molds and disciplines their bodies to beautiful form. In such a manner, too, could the bodies of women be brought to form—but it is rarely that this interplay of strength and beauty is found in a woman. That evening I saw the Chinese crew of the ship next to ours bathing on the deck—the beauty of the human form is truly a heavenly one![28]

It is necessary to point out that this ecstatic piece of writing men's bodies was envisioned, originally, in Bengali. In my view, the fullness of this description, and the sheer ease and flow of the language, in which the perception and the reality are almost fused, is very rarely encountered in Tagore's English writings. Not that Tagore consciously censored his sensory responses when he was writing in English, even though he was almost always addressing rather solemn and formal gatherings with a predominance of men, where he was compelled to play the role of the philosopher or the prophet. In this Bengali travelogue, we have a perception of the joy that fuelled the poet's nomadic wanderings, and it is this inflection of *jouissance* that we need to hold on to, rather than to seek a specific hermeneutics of his sexuality or masculinity.

Certainly, it would be rash to read a 'homosexual gaze' in the passage quoted above, though there is a perceptible homoeroticity that pervades the description of men bathing in public. One should also note how the observation of the Chinese labourers leads the poet to reflect more politically on China itself, specifically its potentiality of 'strength...increasing in freedom and joy'.[29] To these observations, Tagore adds a statement with startling contemporary resonance: 'As China's strength grows, America becomes afraid of her and, since she cannot be outworked, tries to stop her by force.'[30] A little later, the poet shifts his gaze to life on the junks, where entire families, 'husband, wife and children are living and working together'.[31] Here the poet is compelled to think of the social desuetude and bankrupt patriarchy of his own country:

Seeing this picture of harmony and wholeness, I sigh. When shall I see this in India? There men spend three-fourths of their lives in self-deception. This form of life where men, women and children are working together is the highest form: one day it will win a great victory.[32]

As we can see from the references above, there are deep connections being made between nation and family, which have been sparked in an altogether unprecedented way by the illumination of men's bodies.

The homosociality of Tagore's universe in this particular passage, therefore, covers wide ground, the references to body, nation, and family mutating and combining in unexpected ways. More precisely, the 'homosexual', or, more specifically, the 'homoerotic' dimension of the poet's experience merges into the continuum of the 'homosocial'. Tellingly, these gradations do not seem to register for Tagore, who is far too immersed in the sheer flow of his prose. What would be more challenging, I believe, is to discern whether these distinctions between the 'homosocial', the 'homoerotic', and the 'homosexual' have any cognitive significance for those countless readers and editors like Sisir Kumar Das, who may have read the very same passage, without sensing or feeling the need to point out those specific shifts in energy that are absolutely vital for my understanding and pleasure of the text. In short, I do not, indeed, cannot, assume that my reading is unequivocal even within the seemingly homogeneous context of Indian homosociality, which still awaits a theory that it can call its own.

MODALITIES OF FRIENDSHIP

If homosociality awaits more heterogeneous and context-sensitive theorization, this could to a large extent be attributed to the critical fact that friendship, the most ubiquitous and familiar manifestation of same-sex intimacy, resists codification within the cultures of everyday life. Perhaps, this was not always the case in the classical and medieval periods, when there were, in the Indian context at least, strong rules of behaviour regulating social interaction, firmly rooted in the strictures of caste, community, and religion, which prohibited intimacies even through the most basic social practices of eating, touching, or living together. To a large extent, these strictures continue to determine friendship in our times, particularly in tradition-bound societies, with minimal access to urbanization, secularization, and migration across socio-economic and cultural contexts. However, within the specific context of my narrative, which converges around the friendship of Tagore and Okakura, we are compelled to think of friendship in a more 'modern' context determined by autonomy and voluntarism functioning outside the jurisdiction of any religious organization or the state.[33]

In this regard, it is a truism to observe that while there can be laws relating to sexuality, marriage, family, kinship, and all kinds of activities relating to business, education, trade, commerce, entertainment, and so on, it is almost impossible to imagine laws determining friendship. This is one area of life that continues to have deep human significance through the very commodification of social relations and the globalization of cultures precisely because it has another value that cannot be reduced to market relations and economic benefits. This embeddedness of friendship in the informal sectors of everyday life is what challenges pragmatic, statistical, social scientist analysis, precisely because it does not have an agenda or any specifiable raison d'être that can be spelt out in categorical terms. It is true that a sharing of ideology can be a meeting ground for comradeship, but it is not necessarily the condition for friendship, which can cut across the most seemingly irreconcilable political differences. For this reason, friendship matters precisely because it does not matter to 'the world' outside the private, fragile, and yet, resilient, domain of mutually negotiated personal relationships.

In what could be one of the most rigorous readings of friendship in the modern context, Allan Silver has indicated some basic conditions, which are well worth reiterating. Friendships are 'voluntary, unspecialized, informal and private'; unlike 'contractual relations', they are grounded in 'open-ended commitments without explicit provision for their termination'[34] (though, as we shall see later in this section, friendships can be broken on ethical grounds, but this 'breaking' is personally negotiated, not predetermined within a specific time-frame). Silver also emphasizes that 'friendships are diminished in moral quality if terms of exchange between friends are consciously or scrupulously monitored'; in other words, friendships are not likely to last if they rest on a purely utilitarian basis (what Aziz, in A Passage to India, abhors as a 'give-and-take' model of friendship, which is 'disgusting').[35] Perhaps, the most luminous aspect of friendship is that it is grounded in 'the uniquely irreplaceable qualities of partners — their "true" or "real" selves, defined and valued independently of their place in public systems of power, utility, and esteem'.[36]

In the Tagore–Okakura friendship, it is precisely this mutual affection and respect, bordering on their 'uniquely irreplaceable qualities' that sustained their love for each other. However, before elaborating on this axiomatic, yet deeply enigmatic, truth, let us work through different modalities of friendship: at home, abroad, in the state of war, in love. Let us begin with a few reflections on friendship-in-fiction.

In Tagore's great novels in particular, friendship is a dominant trope, if not the primary structuring principle of his narratives. Indeed, it is impossible to think of Gora without his deep and turbulent friendship with Binoy; or of the activist-turned spiritual seeker Sachis in *Chaturanga* (Quartet) without the more pragmatic and earth-bound Sribilas; or, of the swadeshi-questioning Nikhilesh in *Ghare Baire* (Home and the World) without the charlatan 'revolutionary' hero Sandip. Arguably, this last relationship is less marked as a friendship, because the men fall out with each other, ideologically and politically. Of course, Sandip is also cheating on Nikhilesh's wife, though not without her complicity. In spite of these obvious obstacles to their friendship, the men are inextricably linked through each other's political positions. While a detailed reading of these narratives lies outside the limits of this book, suffice it to say that Tagore's friends are contrapuntal foils for each other; they are different in themselves, and yet they complete each other.

To read homosexual undercurrents in their intense intimacies is to miss the point, not least because friendship itself in the Bengali context of homosociality can be, in certain contexts, akin to love. *Bhalobasha* is a profoundly multivalent word, which totally blurs the Anglo-Saxon propriety of 'liking' someone and 'loving' that particular individual. The indeterminacies of the word heighten the aporias of friendship in social practice. In the opening page of *Chaturanga* (Quartet), for instance, the narrator Sribilas openly acknowledges, 'When I saw Sachis I felt as though I saw into his inmost soul and I loved him at once'.[37] This is not, as can be easily mistaken in the Euro-American context, an instance of clear-cut homosexual affinity. It is more akin to the language of hero-worship, in which Sribilas's intensity of friendship inspires him to compare Sachis to a 'shooting-star' as he 'glows' from within.[38] More so, this hero-worship is just one side of the picture, because Sribilas is totally confused about his feelings, not least because his hero is an atheist.

Ideas complicate the passion that brings men together, and yet, their conflicting ideologies enhance their intimacy, even as the men are likely to drift apart. This, in essence, is the precarious ground on which Gora and Binoy formalize their bonds as friends, before their affiliations to traditional Hinduism and reformist Brahmoism lead to a total breakdown in their relationship. Arguably, the severance of this intimacy is made all the more violent because of their involvement with women, despite Gora's initial reluctance to accept his attraction for the opposite sex. In the early part of the novel, however, Tagore idealizes the friendship, at least from Binoy's point of view:

[F]riendship with Gora was part of Binoy's life; an existence that did not contain this friendship was unimaginable for him. Until now Binoy had known no other human being who was closer to him than Gora. He had read books with him, and argued with him, had even quarrelled, but he loved only Gora.[39]

Even as Gora reciprocates this love by declaring to Binoy that 'we two are one', he also challenges the idea of a mortal friendship in his devotion to the higher cause of patriotism:

We are fond of one another but a greater love will unite us more firmly. Until that love becomes a reality we shall have to suffer blows and conflict, opposition and separation, at every step. Then a day will come when we shall forget all our differences, forget even our friendship, and shall achieve an immense self-abandonment in which we shall stand together, immovable. That will be the ultimate achievement of our friendship.[40]

Clearly, this 'self-abandonment', which is capable of sacrificing worldly friendship, is not operating within the framework of 'modernity'. It is more like a primordial swadeshi-driven passion through which friendship has to pass, almost like an *agnipariksha*, a test of fire. Needless to say, Binoy is not ready to prove his credentials as a patriot on Gora's unconditional, demagogic grounds and, as the novel proceeds, he arrives at a point where he refuses to accept Gora's valorization of Bharatbarsha, arguing that 'there is something above both society and the individual, and that is dharma'.[41] For the nationalist Gora, this is far too abstract an argument, and he proceeds to affirm his 'emotional attachment' to Bharatbarsha that Binoy singularly 'lacks'. Refusing to judge Bharatbarsha, Gora embraces its most vile aspects relating to caste discrimination and ritualism. His last words to Binoy in this heated exchange have all the passion of a frenzied lover: 'If you want to set yourself apart from it [Bharatbarsha], you will have to set yourself apart from me.'[42]

Tellingly, when Gora sees through his own bigotry in the closing pages of the novel, he is still estranged from Binoy. It is Anandomoyi, Gora's foster mother, who is neither a practising Hindu nor a Brahmo but a freethinking individual, who is given the last line of this epic novel: 'Gora, let me send for Binoy.'[43] It is on this note of reconciliation that the novel ends, with the renewal of friendship serving as the grace note concluding a tempestuous raga.

FOREIGN FRIENDS

If the nation intervenes between friends belonging to the same country, it is even more potentially invasive and destructive in the relationship between friends of different nationalities. Tagore did not specifically respond to the magisterial Forsterian position that culminates *A Passage to India,* when Aziz and Fielding are, arguably, most intimately linked when they are compelled to stay apart.[44] The world is 'not yet' ready for any resolution of their bicultural and homosexually charged friendship. Even so, within the actual field of exploring friendships in real life, both Tagore and Okakura can be said to have relished the companionship and confidence of their foreign friends.

Most intimate of all friends for Tagore was C.F. Andrews (1871–1940), long-time supporter of the poet's vision in Santiniketan, who has often been criticized for his gurufication of the poet and his excessively moralistic, if not prissy attitude in protecting the poet from all controversy. In his final reflection on the 'Crisis in Civilization', it is telling that Tagore acknowledges losing almost all 'feeling of respect for the English race', which was salvaged by the 'rare blessing of having Andrews — a real Englishman, a real Christian and a true man'.[45] The praise is unstinted: 'I count such Englishmen as Andrews not only as my personal and intimate friends but as friends of the whole human race.'[46] While it is as yet difficult to fathom the depths of this friendship beyond the obvious hagiography that surrounds it, and the bitchiness of its critical backlash, one primary motif that profoundly moved Tagore about Andrews was his devotion to India. Those foreigners who made India their home, like Andrews, among many other missionaries, educationists, and social workers, were not merely respected by the poet. In his own words, their spirit of self-sacrifice, so blatantly at odds with the exploitation of the colonial administration, could only give rise 'in our mind to a feeling of love bordering upon awe'.[47]

These words are drawn from a tribute by Tagore to a relatively unknown stranger from Sweden called Hammargren. He is not a familiar figure in many biographies of Tagore, but he comes alive in the poet's moving evocation, which I would like to quote at length:

When I was young a stranger from Europe came to Bengal. He chose his lodging among the people of the country, shared with them their frugal diet, and freely offered them his service. He found employment in the houses of the rich, teaching them French and German, and the money thus earned he spent to help poor students in buying books.[48]

Tagore then proceeds to elaborate on the actual labour and sacrifice underlying Hammargren's love, as he spends hours 'walking in the mid-day heat of a tropical summer':

He was pitiless in his exaction from himself of his resources, in money, time, and strength, to the point of privation; and all this for the sake of a people who were obscure, to whom he was not born, yet whom he dearly loved...[49]

Almost in the mode of an intercultural fable, Hammargren becomes the intimate stranger who finds another home in a different culture:

Though he did not know our language, he took every occasion to frequent our meetings and ceremonies; yet he was always afraid of intrusion. ...At last, under the continual strain of work in an alien climate and surroundings, his health broke down. He died, and was cremated at our burning ground, according to his express desire.[50]

At one level, there is an obvious recognition in this passage of the *seva* (service) represented by this Swedish traveller, who could be regarded as a cosmopolitan, on the lines of the contemporary social worker, or caregiver, in the jargon of global activism today. Cynics would add that Hammargren was merely a forerunner of those numerous guilt-ridden do-gooders coming to India from abroad, thereby contributing to the Mother Theresa syndrome of grass-roots charity.

However, at a less cynical level, what is moving in the passage is not just the sacrifice of this young man, but the fact that Tagore himself is awed by his cultural work and compassion for the poor. This foreigner counters the colonial administration's contempt for Indians in general, and in that very fundamental sense, he is something of an anomaly: not quite a foreigner, yet not entirely 'one of us'. When dealing with Tagore's greatness as a poet and philosopher of universal humanism, it is sometimes easy to forget that he was a colonial subject. The kindness of strangers assumes a dimension of wonder for the colonized, and Tagore is no exception in this regard.

As for denizens of 'the unconquered race' like Okakura, on what grounds could they befriend the colonized? It is one thing for Okakura to befriend American benefactors like Fenollosa, Bigelow, Gardner, and other representatives of Boston Brahmin society, but what does it mean for him to befriend Tagore's nephew Surendranath, who is perhaps even a closer friend of Okakura's than Tagore himself? Here I think we find a very perceptible clue in Priyambada's notebook, when she writes that friendship circumvents all gender-related and national considerations: 'You think of her or of him as a friend, an epithet which by the dictates of unyielding grammar must always be of common gender. When thinking of [friends], you forget whether they are English, Indian, French or Chinese. They bear the magic name that is balm to every pain, benediction in every evil and consolation in every sorrow, they make you happy and you are content.'[51]

The apparent simplicity of that last statement is what makes friendship so theoretically complex, apart from being compelling and enduring across cultures. Of course, one may not share the implicit cosmopolitan privilege underlying Priyambada's assumption of the accessibility of friends from all cultures. Moreover, the homosociality of cross-cultural friendships becomes more complex to pinpoint, because the social references from different contexts get blurred in the very intimacy of the meeting. This is particularly true for face-to-face interactions, rather than the more recent virtual friendships and intimacies on the electronic networks, which raise new issues in determining the erotics of anonymity. However, if two friends from different cultures do meet physically, on whose ground is the friendship negotiated and explored? Also, does the cultural context of the ground determine the friendship, or do the cross-cultural intimacies of the friendship define the ground?

For example, when we read Surendranath's highly engaging memoir of Okakura, we are struck by the fun that these men had together, travelling across India. Who is the foreigner here? Or, who is more foreign than the other? Surendranath is ostensibly the guide, but given his woefully inadequate grasp of Indian languages beyond Bengali, he is hardly in a position to request clear instructions for the ancient university of Nalanda while trekking with Okakura through the wilderness of rural Bihar. I particularly enjoy, in this regard, Surendranath's ironic reference to his 'Calcutta Hindi',[52] which gets him nowhere. Nalanda is never found.

There are, however, other escapades which are the very stuff of tourism, and it is Okakura who takes the initiative here rather than Surendranath. Meekly, if not sheepishly, he follows the orders of his adopted sensei as, for instance, when he dons a kimono with capacious pockets in order to smuggle bottles of saké from a Japanese liner. Here Surendranath passes as a Japanese in India, which is almost as incongruous as Okakura wearing a dhoti (which he dutifully did while entering temples). There is also another wonderful anecdote involving Okakura's addiction to Bombay duck, the stench of which was apparently sufficient to ward away all passengers while they travelled by train. While Surendranath's 'native' positioning is undermined through the trials of travel, it is Okakura who tackles Indian heat and dust with Japanese equanimity, most notably by boiling himself rice gruel when he gets dehydrated.

At the end of this vivid description of vernacular cosmopolitanism, Surendranath swiftly summarizes Okakura's second visit to India, when nothing is quite the same because he is almost haunted by a premonition of his imminent death. Here we confront the pathos of misunderstanding in a deeply human register:

At the end, we are seated alone together in the railway restaurant, half-an-hour before Okakura's train is due to start. For the first time, I see him depressed. He is toying with the food before him, hardly eating anything.

'Are you not feeling well?'—I ask him, none too cheerful myself. He looks up at me with a mournful smile. 'Can't you understand?' is all he says.[53]

In the next paragraph, Surendranath announces Okakura's death, and in the same breath mentions Okakura's 'parting presents' (for which he had left detailed instructions with Priyambada): Japanese bathrobes and obis for Surendranath's mother and sister, whom he called Didimoni. These gifts are, at one level, sentimental gestures, steeped in highly ritualized conventions, but they also reveal Okakura's considerable thoughtfulness, because in his letter to Priyambada, he had taken pains to enclose a cheque so that the customs duties on the gifts could be duly paid, thereby freeing his Indian friends from any possible inconvenience. The courtesy is exemplary, but, as Okakura puts it very simply, 'I want to make them [Surendranath's family] happy even for a moment'.[54] Is it any surprise that Surendranath should end his seemingly whimsical memoir on a deeply emotional note when he affirms that his family can 'never think of [Okakura] as lost to us'?[55]

The intensity of friendship, and particularly of so-called 'lifelong' friendships, has no direct relationship to the available evidence that can authenticate the friendship in question. The smallest memory, the most trivial gift, the slightest misunderstanding, the most ridiculous joke, the most persistent source of irritation are all elements that can contribute to the endurance of friendship, even while they singularly fail to explain it. Therein lies the enigma of friendship: even as it matters deeply in making everyday life pleasurable, and in enhancing self-recognition through the other, it is also intangible in its tangibility, elusive in its immediacy.

WAR AND FRIENDSHIP

It could be argued that what I have provided is a liberal perspective on friendship, which somehow survives almost all historical considerations and obstacles. However, when is friendship put to the test? Indeed, at what point does it break? In Tagore's life, there were 'difficult' friendships, such as his troubled relationship with Edward Thompson, the Wesleyan minister and educationist, whose 'alien homage' has been masterfully analysed by his son, the Marxist critic E.P. Thompson.[56] This is yet another instance of deep intercultural misunderstanding that was bound to enter the poet's life, given the varied expectations and demands that were made of him through his freewheeling associations, not to mention his own hypersensitivity to what he perceived as irresponsible or vindictive criticism. However, the tensions afflicting troubled relationships could be elided through a discreet parting of ways. What then about friendships in which such discretion was not possible? At what point was misunderstanding perceived as betrayal? When did it become impossible for Tagore to sustain the idea of friendship itself?

In his eventful life, there is perhaps no more painful instance of a broken friendship than his harsh exchange of letters with the Japanese poet Noguchi Yonejiro (1874–1943), whom he had befriended on his first trip to Japan in 1916. What brought these men together was their specific love for the English Romantic poets and a general resistance towards 'Westernization', though even then Tagore should have been a little more wary of Noguchi's need to 'jealousy guard our spiritual insularity'.[57] Noguchi's early fame with the publication of his English poems *From an Eastern Sea* (1903), written while he was based in London, never amounted to very much, but he remained a loyal friend, and was one of the few poets to counter the critical onslaught on Tagore's reading of nationalism. It is surely ironic then that their break-up was directly related to Noguchi's significantly altered reversion to nationalism in 1938.

The immediate provocation for the correspondence,[58] which was initiated by Noguchi, was Tagore's unequivocal condemnation of the Japanese invasion of China. Once again, the spectre of Asia, which has been somewhat muted in the previous sections of this book, re-enters the narrative with virulence. While denying Japan's invasion in terms of a 'slaughtering madness', Noguchi claimed that it was 'the inevitable means, terrible it is though, for establishing a new great world in the Asiatic continent, where the "principle of live-and-let-live" has to be realized' (834). He went on to describe this diabolical principle as 'the war of "Asia for Asia"' (834).

Nothing could have been more devastating for Tagore, because not only was Noguchi defending war, he was defending it on specifically Asian grounds. The poet's immediate rejoinder was steeped in a language of disbelief, which was nonetheless impregnated with anger and grim prophecy:

You are building your conception of an Asia which would be raised on a tower of skulls... The doctrine of 'Asia for Asia' which you enunciate in your letter, as an instrument of political blackmail, has all the virtues of the lesser Europe which I repudiate, and nothing of the larger humanity that makes us one across the barriers of political labels and divisions. [837]

Once again, we return to the affirmation of 'one' in a broadly universalist rather than internationalist register. Now, more under threat than ever before, 'civilization' was increasingly singularized, even as the poet continued to qualify his terms in arguably partisan ways:

[I]n launching a ravening war on Chinese humanity, with all the deadly methods learnt from the West, Japan is infringing every moral principle on which civilization is based.   [837]

In this statement, Tagore could be quoting Takeuchi Yoshimi, who, in the aftermath of the war, believed that Japan had lost its moral ascendancy to China. Yet, unlike Takeuchi, who did not seek a humanist solution to the devastation of the war, Tagore had only one ground on which to counter the machinations of the realpolitik: humanity.

One such machination was the Chinese army's deliberate flooding of the River Hwangho in order to escape certain defeat by the Japanese forces. The consequence of this suicidal gesture was that 'thirty hundred thousand' Chinese soldiers had drowned, and at least 'one hundred thousand village houses' were destroyed in the mass flooding (834). In addition to this 'mass-suicide', Noguchi also attempted to expose the Chinese government's chicanery through the use of false photographs depicting 'Japanese atrocities' on 'Chinese civilians', which were used as propaganda material by the Allied forces and even reprinted in progressive journals like *Modern*

Review published in Calcutta (840). On these charges of Chinese propaganda, and Noguchi's boastful dismissal of the 'fabricated story' surrounding Japan's alleged 'poverty' (835), the poet's response was sharply astute. Almost echoing Noam Chomsky's 'manufacture of consent' thesis, he challenged Noguchi's glowing picture of a united Japan responding to the paternalistic vigilance of a caring government: 'Do you not know, my friend, that there is no propaganda like good and noble deeds, and if such deeds be yours, you need fear no "trickery" of your victims' (844).

To add insult to injury, Noguchi made the mistake of attempting to justify his war of 'Asia for Asia' on religious grounds, notably by invoking the 'Three-headed Siva' from whom he had derived his 'lesson of destruction as [the] inevitable truth of life' (841). Kali is another of Noguchi's mentors. In front of her image in Kalighat, Calcutta, Noguchi had 'knelt', drawing from her 'face smeared in madness, with three wild eyes', a premonition of 'forthcoming peace' (841). Tagore's response could not have been more wry: 'I must thank you for explaining to me the meaning of our Indian philosophy and pointing out the proper interpretation of Kali and Shiva... I wish you had drawn a moral from a religion more familiar to you and appealed to the Buddha for your justification' (844). And yet, there could be no consolation in this riposte for Tagore, because he knew only too bitterly how Japanese priests and artists were erecting colossal figures of the Buddha in order 'to bless the massacre of [their] neighbours' (844). Would Tagore's response have been any different to the savagely macabre mantra used in post-Independence India to hail its successful nuclear tests: 'The Buddha is Smiling'?

At the heart of Tagore's distress was the fact that artist–friends like Noguchi, rather than opposing the politics of violence and genocide, were endorsing it, and thereby playing into 'the betrayal of intellectuals', which Tagore regarded as a 'dangerous symptom of our Age' (838). The abdication of 'moral conscience', for Tagore, was symptomatic of the 'modern intellectual's betrayal of humanity' at large to which poets like Noguchi were merely capitulating through a 'philosophy of escapism' (838). To this charge, Noguchi in turn hurled the accusation that Tagore was simply surrendering to the politics of 'quiescence', to use his archaic vocabulary. In this hurling of accusations and counter-accusations, there was no possibility of reconciliation. At best, Noguchi and Tagore could agree on the most professional way of representing their differences, and that was to make their correspondence public in newspapers. In the process, their friendship was thrown into the anonymity of the public domain.

Even so, there can be no question that both men suffered enormously from the 'betrayal' of the times. There were personal stakes in this betrayal, if not a deep humiliation of long-cherished ideals. As Tagore acknowledged, 'I suffer intensely not only because the reports of Chinese suffering batter against my heart, but because I can no longer point out with pride the example of a great Japan' (844). The poet had lost face in the eyes of the world, as he perceived his predicament. It would have been easier, though no less intolerable, had the war been fought exclusively among Western powers. However, with Japan's aggression, in what way could Asia be considered different? How could this Asia be 'one'? The brutal military reality reinforcing Noguchi's rationale for 'reconstructing the new world in Asia' (842)—a sinister, though refracted, echo of the very different affirmations of New Asia today—had totally smashed Tagore's transcendental vision of Asia. Now, at best, it was possible, and indeed necessary, to separate Asian nations from one another, and redeem the virtue of one against the sins of the other.

It is in this context that Tagore upheld China, affirming its 'inherently superior moral stature'. With this endorsement he was also compelled to remember another friend, who, unlike Noguchi, was still compellingly alive in his memory: '[T]oday I understand more than ever before the meaning of the enthusiasm with which the big-hearted Japanese thinker Okakura assured me that *China is great*' (839). Significantly, Okakura reappears in this book as it comes to an end, within the context of war. His reappearance is at once moving and troubling: moving, because Tagore still remembers him affectionately; troubling, because we know that what made Okakura venerate China was not just its inherent moral values (as he had apotheosized China's 'communism' in his opening paragraph of *The Ideals of the East*). By the time Okakura had rediscovered China towards the last years of his life, it was intrinsically connected to the treasures of a relatively untapped art market in which he was speculating unashamedly on behalf of the Museum of Fine Arts, Boston. We need to keep this background in mind in order to contextualize, at least partially, Okakura's enthusiasm for a 'great' China.

Noguchi was quick to pick up on Tagore's reference to Okakura, because in his second letter to the poet he complimented the inclusion of Okakura only to vindicate his own position: 'I am glad that you still admire Kakuzo Okakura with enthusiasm as a thinker. *If he lives today, I believe that he will say the same thing as I do*' (840, my emphases). This assertion is chilling to say the least because it challenges any cultural historian to make an overall estimate of Okakura's position on less militarist grounds. Was Noguchi correct in intuiting that Okakura would support his militarist logic, or was he merely taking advantage of the fact that Okakura was not around to combat his position? In 1938, the year of Tagore's correspondence with Noguchi, Okakura had been dead for almost a quarter of a century, but in that very year, his inflammatory *The Awakening of the East* was resurrected from oblivion and published in Japan, thereby contributing to his image as an ultra-nationalist. While Okakura cannot be blamed for this image and the propaganda surrounding it, at what level is he posthumously complicit in the justification of the war? Also, conversely, to what extent is his appropriation by nationalist forces a betrayal of his legacy?

We are compelled at this point to return to a question that I had raised early in this narrative: If Okakura had lived — not till 1938, but even as early as 1916, when Tagore had delivered his lectures against nationalism in Japan — would their friendship have lasted? This is a difficult question to answer conclusively. To acknowledge that the friendship would have survived would imply, at some level, the idealistic assumption that it was capable of transcending all historical, political, and ideological differences. On the other hand, to assume that it could not have survived, would mean the total annihilation of the very idea of friendship on which Tagore and Okakura had based their foundation for 'the ideals of the East'. Without this friendship, their Asia would have had no ground on which to survive.

Needless to say, we have entered an area of hypothesis here, as we speculate on the survival of the Tagore–Okakura friendship, and the multiple possibilities for its interpretation today. As we are thinking hypothetically, we may as well push its limits. If I had to be asked to state my position, however ambivalently, I would risk saying that this friendship could have survived Tagore's critique of nationalism and the outbreak of the war, but it would need another ground of understanding. Pushing the time-frame of my hypothetical thinking further into some imaginary space following the devastation of Hiroshima—indeed, this could be the dramaturgical point of departure for an extraordinary dream play—how would Tagore and Okakura meet in this post-atomic space? By this time both of them would be dead. They would be spectres to each other. I cannot imagine this meeting marked by joy or nostalgia for a lost Orient. Rather, this reunion of old friends would be haunted by an overwhelming sense of remorse. This, indeed, is the closing word of the Tagore–Noguchi correspondence: 'remorse'.[59] Their friendship, I would speculate, could last only through a critical engagement with this remorse and out of deep lamentation for what has happened to the world.

Most emphatically, in my dramaturgical imaginary, this friendship would not be renewed to herald the 'ideals of the East', still less to reconstruct a 'new Asia'. Some other universal principle of human coexistence would need to be affirmed to counter the damage of the war of 'Asia for Asia'. While, at some level, this principle would reaffirm Tagore's universal humanism, I would also speculate that Okakura himself would have arrived at a more personally nuanced cosmopolitan humanitarianism. Within the logic of this hypothesis, it is Okakura who would have to undergo some kind of transformation from his earlier nationalist avatar. This is not so far-fetched as it may seem, because these transformative signs were already evident from 1908 onwards through the mellowing of his nationalism through cosmopolitanism. However, only in the last year of his life, in 1913, and primarily through his correspondence with Priyambada, do we find more conclusive evidence of his emergent humanism.

In his last letter to Priyambada dated 21 August 1913, written from Akakura Springs, Echigo (Niigata prefecture), situated thousands of feet above the sea, Okakura looked back on 'the wild reckless career of [his] youth'.[60] However, rather than lacerating himself with self-accusations, there was a sense of openness to the wonder of the world: 'Yet, I am in perfect peace with the universe and grateful, oh, so grateful for what it has granted me of late. I am perfectly content and even boisterously happy. I laugh at the clouds that sweep in and swirl round my pillow.'[61] The delirium of a dying man? I would prefer to be less cynical and trust the self-reflexivity through which Okakura had arrived at a new ideal for himself: 'To be a man, a human being first, before being a minister of Society, to me seems essential. Let us strive for realization within our limitations.'[62] It would be disingenuous to deny the romantic idiom of this self-transformation, but I am tempted to give Okakura the benefit of the doubt that he would have continued to evolve as a person.

While the longevity of the Tagore–Okakura friendship remains speculative, what cannot be denied is the intensity with which it was celebrated. In the posthumous praise that Tagore showered on Okakura following his death, it becomes clear that it was 'that personal relationship, personal influence, in which he represented the best of Japan'.[63] The 'personal' was absolutely vital for Tagore's appreciation of Okakura, and though I have already indicated several valid reasons why Tagore should have opposed Okakura politically on issues relating to nationalism and imperialism, the point is that he saw something 'unique' in Okakura; something that could not be substituted by another Asian expert from Japan. Okakura was special, 'one of [his] intimate friends',[64] and I daresay that Tagore was equally venerable in Okakura's eyes, even though they hardly kept in touch after their first meeting in 1902.

When they finally did meet again in Boston for the second and last time in their lives, shortly before Okakura's death, which Tagore appears to have sensed, this meeting was precious in its own right. There were no professional tie-ups, no Japanese funding for Santiniketan, no additions of Indian art to the Boston collection, no preface for each other's books, not even an exchange of books, to the best of our knowledge. Nothing concrete in terms of 'exchange', but the friendship was solemnized and revisited, leaving Okakura, in Tagore's departure, with a sense of 'sudden loneliness'.[65] While the elegiac quality of the final meeting between Tagore and Okakura may seem overly etherealized, there is some reason to invoke that memorable statement made by the French philosopher Montaigne, which, as Allan Silver informs us, was not understood in his time, perhaps because it was too romantic a perspective on 'unconditional friendship founded solely on elective affinity between two irreplaceable selves'.[66] In its very refusal to explicate the terms of its intimacy, this statement provides some insight into what brought Tagore and Okakura together:

If you press me to tell why I loved him, I feel this cannot be expressed, except by answering: because it was he, because it was I.[67]

Epilogue

Today Okakura has become something of a cult figure in Japan, and, almost inevitably, his memory has been museumized. Most appropriately, he is commemorated in two remarkable institutions—the exquisitely designed and landscaped Tenshin Memorial Museum of Art, and the less extravagant, though no less beautiful Izura Institute of Art and Culture—both of them situated in the remote coastal town of Izura in Ibaraki prefecture to the north of Tokyo. If the Museum is a treasure house of paintings in the *morotai* (hazy) style exemplified by Yokoyama Taikan, Hishida Shunso, Shimomura Kanzan, and others, the institute is perhaps most memorable for its graceful maintenance of Okakura's memoribilia and cultural legacy. His former residence remains a model of elegant sobriety testifying to the exemplary taste underlying his art of living. More breathtaking is his meditative space-cum-study in which he wrote his love letters to Priyambada: the hegaxonal Rokkakudo jutting out on a promontory, lashed by waves on three sides.

When one visits Izura today, one realizes the sheer finesse and scale of Okakura's vision. The landscape itself is inspired, the Pacific Ocean lashing the rocky shore of Izura and stretching outwards into infinity, suggesting a great Beyond. The power of nature here is palpable, evoking a certain grit and rough magic that are not always perceptible in Okakura's excessively ornate and mannered style of writing. Far away from metropolitan Tokyo with its glittering art galleries and department stores, Izura is secluded, and yet, it defies provinciality. Far from being the mere backwaters of a summer retreat, it was the strategically selected site for an avant-garde art colony. The fact that Okakura realized the importance of setting up this colony in the seclusion of Izura, to actively nurture contemporary art practice in Japan, is inspirational. Indeed, it has close parallels in its intensity of vision and alertness to the ecological principles of creativity underlying Tagore's Santiniketan.

The crucial difference, however, is that while the vision of Okakura has been artistically nurtured and sustained with enormous funding, so much so that the Tenshin Memorial Museum of Art has become a haunt for art lovers and Okakura fans worldwide, Santiniketan today falls far short of the poet's vision. I am being euphemistic here, because any honest estimate of Visva-Bharati today would have to acknowledge that the poet's dream-university has become a bureaucratic nightmare, inextricably linked to academic institutionalization and dependency on Central Government funding. At one level, one can fall back on the inevitable First World/ Third World economic divide to account for the staggering difference in the sheer quality and maintenance of the institutions identified with Okakura and Tagore. I do, however, believe that this is a materialist argument that Tagore himself would deride. What he would ask of us is to respect our cultural inheritance with the vigilance of daily care: not just his memoribilia (which have been stolen from the premises of the university itself), but works of art that were inspired by the very soil and spirit of Santiniketan itself.

Today, one of the greatest frescos of modern Indian art, Binode Bihari Mukherjee's epic rendering of Indian saints in a broad national framework of struggle and everyday life, which was meticulously constructed in the Hindi Bhavan at Visva-Bharati, is corroding and disintegrating. The ceiling on top of the fresco is leaking, the plaster on the walls is damp, and the floor is cracked and layered with dust. It is a crying shame to see this blatant neglect; a sign of the philistine vandalism of contemporary India, marked by political indifference and sheer bureaucratic prevarication.

This vandalism hurts almost more than the shocking robbery of Tagore's memorabilia in Santiniketan in 2004: a theft that left a deep sense of shame in Bengal, now covered up with amnesia and silence. At one level, one could argue the obvious fact that the memory of Tagore is far greater than the sum of his relics. What after all does it matter if his Nobel Prize medallion has been stolen? Isn't it more important that we try to activate the poet's principles and ideals, instead of holding on to his relics? Arguably, Tagore had already become something of relic before he died, even as his artistry fought this crass deification. On his death, when his body was paraded through the streets of Calcutta, rather like a medieval saint, it is well known that it was subjected to the frenzied devotion of his fans. That body, which had been so protected and etherealized in his lifetime, was now exposed to the violence of idolatory—not the worship of the Nation, which Tagore despised, but more ignominiously, the deification of the Poet.

Today, Tagore's death anniversary continues to be commemorated year after year with solemn devotion.[1] Despite the routine sentimentalization of the occasion, the grief is real as Tagore is claimed once again as Bengal's deepest patrimony, now shared across the border with Bangladesh, where his memory is perhaps more ardently invoked and recycled through numerous publications, cassettes, videos, and CDs. Over the years, and particularly after the lifting of the copyright on Tagore's writings, which had been controlled by Visva-Bharati University, Tagoreana has become a major industry. Even so, just even as the poet's works have been globalized through new digital and computerized technologies, his regionalization seems to have intensified, perhaps most emphatically through the commodification of his memory by a widening diaspora of *probashi* Bengalis. With long-distance nationalism, there is also long-distance nostalgia for a lost Bengal, which lends itself to being manufactured with a zeal that is often out of joint with the indeterminaces of migrant life. Despite substantial attempts by a few scholars and institutions to perpetuate Tagore's memory in more critically nuanced ways outside the subcontinent and South Asian diasporic constituencies, the poet remains one of the least known and shared of universal thinkers in the world. This continues to be the dominant reality of his legacy; an incomplete translation of staggering proportions given the scale of his multi-genre oeuvre.

And yet, within Bengal itself, and more specifically, within the multitudinous energies of its language, Tagore lives as no other poet does. His songs in particular have entered the minds and hearts of millions of people, even those who disagree with the somewhat too rapturous vision of his universal humanism. He is the language in which love continues to be dreamed, and struggle—including the struggle of revolutionary violence, which he condemned—continues to be imagined. In this crucial sense, as I had mentioned earlier, he remains something of a 'revolutionist' by his own self-definition, even though we sorely lack an appropriate imaginary of revolution to accommodate his own.

Against this living internalization of his memory, we can perhaps draw some consolation in the fact that the museumization of memory pales in comparison. This is not to say that museums don't matter, but they tend to fossilize and sanitize memory in specific ways. On my last visit to Jorasanko, Tagore's ancestral home, which also serves as a museum, I specifically wanted to see a new wing devoted to Okakura, funded by a grant from Mitsubishi—a pittance by Japanese standards, but a generous amount in the Indian context. The Okakura collection was everything that I feared it would be: a totally amateur juxtaposition of prints and poorly reproduced photographs, with inaccurate signs, names misspelt, and some atrocious pieces of Santiniketan kitsch. Even so, along with this amateurism, there was also sincerity and good feeling that I only wish could compensate for the obvious absence of an appropriately nuanced creative response to the poet's legacy.

As I walked out of the museum, past the thick *bakul* tree that is thrivingly alive, into the congested Jorasanko Lane that winds its way towards Central Avenue, I was struck by the density of street life, which seemed to resonate in almost direct proportion to the desuetude of the museum. A native of Calcutta, for all my cosmopolitan wanderings, I was compelled to recognize the hyperreality of the street with its dense imbrication of sounds and smells, and the multitudinous activities embracing the business of everyday life. Suddenly Jorasanko seemed to glow with life. I cannot claim to have experienced anything like an illumination of the street, on the lines of Tagore's mystical experiences when, on one occasion in Sudder Street, he 'found the world bathed in a wonderful radiance, with waves of beauty and joy swelling on every side'.[2] The chaos in Jorasanko was too unsettled and messy to qualify as 'joy', at least in a Tagorean sense, but it seemed to embrace a quotidian sense of beauty, which was all the more startling because, unlike the museum, it had no pretensions of an aesthetic.

If there was one element that Tagore and Okakura shared it was the value given to beauty: not merely the formal aspects of beauty in art and literature, for which both of them had exacting standards, but the beauty of the ordinary, startling in its matter-of-fact materiality. It is our loss that none of the conversations of Tagore and Okakura on beauty have been recorded, because we would surely have been enlightened in these matters. However, there are infinitesimal clues embedded in their very few references to each other, from which we can imagine their larger conversations.

There is at least one joyous moment spliced into Tagore's posthumous tribute to Okakura, where, out of the blue, he provides this insight: '[Okakura] would often buy some very cheap things, like simple clay oil-pots that peasants use, with ecstasy of admiration, some things in which we had failed to realize the instinct for beauty...'[3] In that moment, I see both Tagore and Okakura sharing the beauty of ordinariness embodied in a clay pot. The Japanese traveller is pointing out something that his Bengali host has taken for granted: perhaps the texture of the mud, or the perfect contours of the form of the pot. They are one in the sharing of the rasa of that moment. At this point we need to leave them alone, while acknowledging that the history of that day, *sedinkar itihas*, is waiting to be imagined.

Notes

Preface

[1] For a background on my writings on inter/intra-culturalism in theatre, read *Theatre and the World: Performance and the Politics of Culture* (New York and London: Routledge, 1993) and *The Politics of Cultural Practice: Thinking through Theatre in an Age of Globalization* (London: Continuum Books, and Hanover: The University Press of New England, 2000). On inter-Asian theatrical experimentation, read my monograph *Consumed in Singapore: The Intercultural Spectacle of 'Lear'* (Singapore: Pagesetters, 2000). See also the first section of my essay 'Foreign Asia/Foreign Shakespeare: Dissenting Notes on New Asian Interculturality, Postcoloniality and Recolonization', *Theatre Journal*, vol. 56, no. 1, March 2004, pp. 1–15.

[2] A succinct overview on the discourse of Asian Values is available in the special issue of *Sojourn*, 14:2, Oct. 1999, entitled 'Asian Ways: Asian Values Revisited'. Read, in particular, Clive Kessler's lead article on 'The Abdication of Intellectuals', ironically subtitled 'What Everybody Needed to Know about "Asian Values" that Social Scientists Failed to Point Out'. On the Asian Renaissance, read Anwar Ibrahim's formulation in his book *Asian Renaissance* (Singapore: Times International Publishing House, 1997). On the 'global city of the arts', read 'Foreign Asia/Foreign Shakespeare', pp. 6–8.

[3] While Ashis Nandy's brief but influential intervention 'A New Cosmopolitanism: Towards a Dialogue of Asian Civilizations', *Trajectories*, ed. Kuan-Hsing Chen (London: Routledge, 1998) endorses a civilizational discourse, he is more frequently read in the context of communitarianism, with an explicitly anti-modern and anti-secularist bias.

[4] The 'knowledge-based economy' is contextualized in 'Foreign Asia/ Foreign Shakespeare', pp. 3–8, from which the material in this paragraph has been drawn.

[5] For excerpts from this essay, read David J. Lu's *Japan: A Documentary History* (London: M.E. Sharpe, 1997), pp. 351–3.

[6] Ibid. p. 353.

[7] Fukuzawa Yukichi's category, and its elaborations by Matsumoto Kenichi, are discussed by Tessa Morris-Suzuki in her presentation of 'Asia is One: Visions of Asian Community in Twenty-First Century' at a seminar on *Okakura Tenshin: Exploring Art, Nationalism and Ideals of Asian Community*, New Delhi, Dec. 2002. Typescript, p. 6.

[8] Ibid., p. 6.

[9] Ibid., p. 6.

[10] The notion of 'symbiosis' is included in Matsumoto's intervention 'Okakura Tenshin and the Ideal of Pan-Asianism', presented in the seminar mentioned above. Typescript pp. 12–13. See also Matsumoto's essay 'Will the Era of Asia Come', *Reitaku Journal of Interdisciplinary Studies*, vol. 5, no. 1, March 1997.

[11] William Radice, personal correspondence with author, 29 July 2005.

Prologue

[1] Okakura Tenshin, 'Nature in East Asiatic Painting', *Okakura Kakuzo: Collected English Writings*, vol. 2, ed. Sunao Nakamura (Tokyo: Heibonsha, 1984), p. 150.

[2] For the primary facts of Okakura's life sketched in this prologue, I draw on F.G. Notehelfer's 'On Idealism and Realism in the Thought of Okakura Tenshin', *Journal of Japanese Studies*, vol. 16, no. 2, 1990, pp. 309–55, which sifts through an impressive range of material drawn from the nine volumes constituting Okakura's oeuvre, *Okakura Tenshin zenshu* (Tokyo: Heibonsha, 1981) and at least two dozen biographies, of which Yasuko Horioka's *The Life of Kakuzo* (Tokyo: Hokuseido Press, 1963) remains the only full-length biography in English. An engaging analysis of Okakura's cosmopolitanism, within the larger social context of Boston Brahminism, can be read in Christopher Benfey's *The Great Wave: Gilded Age Misfits, Japanese Eccentrics, and the Opening of Old Japan* (New York: Random House, 2003), pp. 75–120.

[3] A more elaborate account is available in Krishna Dutta and Andrew Robinson's biography *Rabindranath Tagore: The Myriad-Minded Man*

(Calcutta: Rupa, 1995), pp. 17–19. For the basic facts relating to Tagore's life in this section, I have drawn on Krishna Kripalani's *Rabindranath Tagore: A Biography*, 2nd edn (Calcutta: 1980).

[4] It appears that even though Tagore's international reputation as a poet had not been confirmed, he had already been described as a 'world poet' by the religious and political activist Brahmabandhav Upadhyay in an article in English entitled 'The World Poet of Bengal'. This article was published in the short-lived *Sophia*, 1 Sept. 1900. I am grateful to Sankho Ghosh for pointing out this relevant but obscure fact.

[5] Sumit Sarkar's authoritative study of *The Swadeshi Movement in Bengal 1903–8* (New Delhi: People's Publishing House, 1973) remains a classic in the field. Ostensibly on grounds of 'administrative efficiency', the Government of India, emblematized in the figure of Lord Curzon, announced its decision on 19 July 1905 to create a new province of 'East Bengal and Assam', including the Chittangong, Dacca, and Rajshahi divisions, Hill Tippera, Malda, and Assam (p. 9). The formal proclamation of partition was made on 1 September 1905, followed by the actual partition of Bengal on 16 October 1905.

[6] This somewhat unauthenticated exchange, attributed to Pravrajika Atmaprana, but drawn from Josephine MacLeod's memoirs, has been quoted by Inaga Shigemi in 'Okakura Kakuzo's Nostalgic Journey to India and the Invention of Asia', *Nostalgic Journeys: Literary Pilgrimages between Japan and the West* (Vancouver: Institute of Asian Research, 1999), p. 120.

[7] 'Okakura Kakuzo: Some Reminiscences by Surendranath Tagore', appendix to Dinkar Kowshik's *Okakura: The Rising Sun of Japanese Renaissance* (New Delhi: National Book Trust India, 1988), p. 75. All references to Okakura in the following paragraph are drawn from this source.

[8] Ibid., p. 76.

[9] This reference to 'corner warehouse' does not stop Okakura from telling Priyambada Devi Banerjee that 'Kakuzo means Intelligence or one who attained Knowledge'. See *Okakura Kakuzo: Collected English Writings*, vol. 3, p. 190.

[10] In *The Ideals of the East with Special Reference to the Art of Japan* (1903), included in *Okakura Kakuzo: Collected English Writings*, vol. 1, Okakura had spelt out the basic ethos of the Nihon Bijutsuin: '[T]he old art of Asia is more valid than that of any modern school, inasmuch as the process of idealism, and not of imitation, is the *raison d'être* of the art-impulse. The stream of ideas is the real: facts are mere incidents. *Not the thing as it was, but the infinitude it suggested to him*, is what we demand of the artist' (p. 124, my italics).

[11] Christopher Benfey, *The Great Wave*, p. 89.

[12] Okakura Tenshin, letter to Priyambada Devi Banerjee, 3 March 1913, *Okakura Kakuzo: Collected English Writings*, vol. 3, p. 182.

[13] Ibid., letter to Priyambada Devi Banerjee dated 28 June 1913, p. 207.

[14] From Stephen N. Hay's *Asian Ideas of East and West: Tagore and His Critics in Japan, China, and India* (Cambridge: Harvard University Press, 1970), we learn that when Tagore arrived in Tokyo station 'a throng estimated at between twenty and fifty thousand persons crowded as close they could to catch a glimpse of the Nobel Laureate' (62). However, when Tagore embarked at Yokohama in February 1917 on his return from the US, 'only Yokoyama Taikan and a lone newspaper reporter were waiting at the dock to greet him' (80). Tagore received no press coverage whatsoever on his ignominious return to Japan.

[15] All references in this paragraph are drawn from 'On Oriental Culture and Japan's Mission', Tagore's address to the members of the Indo-Japanese Association, Tokyo, 15 May 1929. Included in *The English Writings of Rabindranath Tagore*, vol.3, ed. Sisir Kumar Das (New Delhi: Sahitya Akademi, 1996), pp. 604–10.

1. Asia

[1] Read, for instance, Peter A. Jackson's two essays 'Space, Theory, and Hegemony: The Dual Crisis of Asian Area Studies and Cultural Studies' (2003) and 'Mapping Poststructuralism's Borders: The Case for Poststructuralist Area Studies' (2003), both of them published in the same issue of *Sojourn*, vol. 18, no. 1, 1–88. For a more pragmatic and materialist overview of the future of Area Studies in the thick of globalization and the post-Cold War, read Masao Miyoshi and H.D. Harootunian's edition of *Learning Places: The Afterlives of Area Studies* (Durham: Duke University Press, 2002).

[2] Sister Nivedita, 'Introduction', *The Ideals of the East*, p. 11.

[3] Naoki Sakai, 'You Asians: on the historical role of the West and Asia binary', *We Asians: Between Past and Future*, ed. Kwok-Kian Woon, Indira Arumugam, Karen Chia, and Lee Chee Keng (Singapore: Singapore Heritage Society, 2000), p. 213. All references to Sakai in the following paragraphs are drawn from this source and paginated accordingly.

[4] Ashis Nandy, 'A New Cosmopolitanism', p. 143.

[5] Ibid., p. 148.

[6] This position adopted by Yamamuro Shin'ichi is represented by Morris-Suzuki in 'Asia is One', p. 9.

[7] In this reference, Morris-Suzuki represents the minoritarian cultural politics of the South Korean citizen Kang Sangjung, who is a resident of Japan and a critical interlocutor of its nationalist politics. See Suzuki, 'Asia is One', p. 9.

[8] For a clear exposition, read Oguma Eiji's chapter on 'The Debate on Mixed Residence in the Interior', (pp. 16–30) in his excellent textbook on Japanese ethnicity and nationalism entitled *A Genealogy of 'Japanese' Self-images* (Melbourne: Trans Pacific Press, 2002), translated from the Japanese by David Askew.

[9] Carol Gluck, *Japan's Modern Myths: Ideology in the Late Meiji Period* (Princeton: Princeton University Press, 1985), p. 136.

[10] Quoted in Oguma Eiji's 'The Debate on Mixed Residence in the Interior', p. 23.

[11] Tessa Morris-Suzuki, *Re-inventing Japan: Time, Space, Nation* (London: M.E. Sharpe, 1998), p. 105.

[12] Ibid. It is very unlikely that Tagore was aware of the ethnic massacres following the Great Kanto Earthquake of 1923, or else, on his second visit to Japan in 1924, he would surely have been somewhat more circumspect in praising the Japanese for accepting the 'tribulation' (of the earthquake) with 'courage' and 'indomitable resourcefulness'. As the poet philosophized, 'Disasters only become absolutely disastrous when we know not how to deal with them'. Clearly, the ethnic killings following the earthquake were disastrous in their own right, but the poet did not seem to be aware of their existence. See Tagore's address on 'International Relations', in *The English Writings of Rabindranath Tagore*, vol. 3, pp. 470–6.

[13] Michael Weiner, *Race and Migration in Imperial Japan* (1994), p. 80. Quoted by Morris-Suzuki, *Re-inventing Japan*, p. 105.

[14] Naoki Sakai, 'You Asians — on the historical role of the West and Asia binary', (2000), p. 235.

[15] Ibid.

[16] Okakura Tenshin, *The Ideals of the East*, p. 13. All quotations from this book are included in my text with the appropriate page numbers.

[17] The 'magnetic triangle' is how the artist–scholar K.G. Subramanyan described it to me in conversation, even though this phrase is not usually used in the numerous references to Okakura's three principles in artistic composition. One reading of the principles is provided by Satyajit

Choudhury in his essay 'Nandalal Bose and Indian Modernity', *Nandalal Bose: A Collection of Essays* (New Delhi: Lalit Kala Akademi, 1983), pp. 37–9.

[18] Tessa Morris-Suzuki, 'Asia is One', p. 8.

[19] Ibid., p. 9.

[20] Okakura Tenshin, *The Awakening of Japan* (Tokyo: Sogensha), p. 5. Italics included.

[21] Referring to Okubo Takaki's theory on how 'Okakura appropriated Vivekananda's idea of Advaitism', Inaga Shigemi (1999) somewhat overstretches the assumed parallels between 'Vivekananda's spiritual synthesis of world religions and Okakura's idea of self-realization and the actualization of Oriental art history' (pp. 121–2). Not only are there significantly different stakes in the syntheses of 'world religions' and 'Oriental art history', which Inaga appears to conflate, this reading rests on a mere rhetorical similarity between Okakura's claim that 'Japan is located at the point where all the different currents mingle' and Vivekananda's idea that 'all different paths' ultimately lead to God (pp. 121–2). Not only is this a gross simplification of Sri Ramakrishna's central maxim *joto mot, toto poth* ('as many truths, so many paths'), it elides the more complex reading of Vivekananda's appropriation of Ramakrishna for his own proselytizing ends—a dimension that is absent in Inaga's reading.

[22] This position by Kawakatsu Heita, premised on the notion of viewing global culture through 'large civilizational blocks', is sharply interrogated by Tessa Morris-Suzuki in 'Re-inventing Japan', p. 152.

[23] Ibid., p. 153.

[24] Mimi Hall Yiengpruksawan, 'Japanese Art History 2001: The State and Stakes of Research', *The Art Bulletin*, March 2001, p. 107.

[25] Ibid. To provide a brief cross-cultural perspective on the situation in Bengal, it should be pointed out that the first Bengali art history, Shyamcharan Srimani's *Suksa Shilper Utpatti o Aryajatir Shilpa-chaturi* was published in 1874, a year after the word *'bijutsu'* (fine art) came into existence in Japan. However, it should also be kept in mind that the affirmation of 'fine art' in Bengal was fraught with tensions, not least because, in the context of the actual pedagogy of art at the Government School of Art in Calcutta in the 1870s, the fine arts were assumed to be the prerogative of Western artists, while Indian artists were expected to find their raison d'etre in the 'applied arts', which provided better employment opportunities.

Even as Srimani was advocating the need for cultivating a taste for the fine arts, he was compelled to earn his living as a teacher of geometrical and mechanical drawing.

For a highly informative and contextualized background on the tensions of fine arts/applied arts in Bengal, which were strategically countered by the reformist art pedagogy of Ernest Binfield Havell in the 1890s and the subsequent affirmation of an authentically 'Indian' aestheticism by painters like Abanindranath Tagore, read Ch. 5 in Tapati Guha-Thakurta's *Monuments, Objects, Histories: Institutions of Art in Colonial and Postcolonial India* (New Delhi: Permanent Black, 2004), pp. 140–71.

[26] Anne Nishimura Morse, 'Promoting Authenticity: Okakura Kakuzo and the Japanese Collection of the Museum of Fine Arts, Boston', *Okakura Kakuzo: Okakura Tenshin and the Museum of Fine Arts, Boston*, catalogue published on 23 October 1999. This essay provides a thorough perspective on the changes at work in the museum even before Okakura arrived in Boston. All references in this paragraph are drawn from this text, p. 145.

[27] Ibid., p. 145. It is worth pointing out here that even as Matthew Prichard assumed the existence of a 'public' within the spectatorship of the Museum of Fine Arts, Boston, this was precisely the lacuna in the museological culture of India around the same time. As Tapati Guha-Thakurta emphasizes in her chapter on 'The Museum in the Colony', in *Monuments, Objects, Histories*, 'The gulf [between knowing and seeing] was symptomatic of a critical absence: the absence of an educated general public that could occupy the interstitial space between ignorance and erudition and smoothen the museum's passage from a "Wonder House" to "an institution of the culture of the people"' (p. 82). This viewpoint is based on Guha-Thakurta's historiographical evidence, notably the records of the Museum Conference in Madras, January 1912, which acknowledged that that while '[Indian] museums are places of recreation where one can *see and wonder*', the 'recreative point of view' needed to be supplemented by a more 'dignified object than the temporary amusement of the crowd' (p. 80).

Arguably, even today in the twenty-first century, the Indian Museum of Calcutta, which continues to be called *Jadu Ghar* (Magic House) by thousands of visitors from neighbouring rural areas, has yet to evolve a sufficiently educated public. The old methods of display in the nineteenth century tradition of the South Kensington model continue to be affirmed, with cavernous rooms containing fossils and rocks identified with handwritten inscriptions in Latin. The point is that the considerable gulf that existed between the museological culture inherited by Okakura in

Boston and his Indian counterparts continues to deepen through the very absence of a sufficiently evolved museum culture in the Indian subcontinent today.

[28] In a famous formulation, Naoki Sakai has viewed the mutual imbrication of 'Japan' and the 'West' within the larger interrelation of universalism and particularism. In 'Modernity and its Critique: The Problem of Universalism and Particularism', *The South Atlantic Quarterly*, Summer 1998, he states: 'Japan did not stand *outside* the West. Even in its particularism, Japan was already implicated in the ubiquitous West, so that neither historically nor geopolitically could Japan be seen as the *outside* of the West. This means that in order to criticize the West in relation to Japan, one has necessarily to begin with a critique of Japan. Likewise, the critique of Japan necessarily entails the radical critique of the West. One can never escape the dominion of the universalism–particularism pair' (p. 495).

[29] For a brief background on Yanagita Kunio, read Oguma Eiji's chapter, 'The Birth of an Island-Nation's Folklore', *A Genealogy of 'Japanese' Self-images*, pp. 175–202.

[30] See Tessa Morris-Suzuki's succinct summarization of Yanagita Kunio's principles and beliefs in her section on 'Yanagita Kunio and the Redefinition of Bunka', *Re-inventing Japan*, pp. 67–72.

[31] This statement by Yanagita Kunio is quoted by Morris-Suzuki, *Re-inventing Japan*, p. 71.

[32] Ibid., p. 70.

[33] Ibid., p. 72.

[34] Okakura Tenshin, *The Ideals of the East*, p. 123.

[35] Read Inaga Shigemi's elegant and meticulously researched 'Claude Monet: Between "Impressionism" and "Japonism"', *Monet and Japan*, National Gallery of Australia, 2001, pp. 65, 69.

[36] Inaga Shigemi, 'The Making of Hokusai's Reputation in the Context of Japonisme', *Japan Review*, no. 15, 2003, p. 78.

[37] Inaga Shigemi, 'Cognitive Gaps in the Recognition of Masters and Masterpieces in the Formative Years of Japanese Art History, 1880–1900: Historiography in Conflict', *Japanese Hermeneutics: Current Debates on Aesthetics and Interpretation* (Honolulu: University of Hawaii Press, 2002), pp. 116–8.

[38] Okakura Tenshin, *The Ideals of the East*, pp. 107–8.

[39] Quoted in Inaga Shigemi's 'Claude Monet: Between "Impressionism" and "Japonism"', p. 72.

[40] Ibid., p. 73.

[41] Quoted by William Sturgis Bigelow in his introduction to 'On the Method of Practising Concentration and Contemplation', a document written by Chi Ki, a monk of the Tendai sect, translated by Okakura. Included in *Okakura Kakuzo: Collected English Writings*, vol. 2, p. 221.

[42] Tessa Morris-Suzuki, 'Re-inventing Japan', p. 58.

[43] Ibid. An incisive analysis of Watsuji Tetsuro's reading of India through the concept of *fudo* has been provided by Naoki Sakai in *Translation and Subjectivity: On 'Japan' and Cultural Nationalism* (Minneapolis and London: University of Minnesota Press, 1997), pp. 129–45. Though the actual details of Watsuji's trip to India in 1928 are extremely vague, it did not stop him from perceiving a 'plaintiveness' underlying Indian festivity, and a 'profound lack of will' and 'submission to oppression' in 'the Indian' himself (p. 130). Sakai correctly reads this critique of resignationism as an endorsement of 'British colonial authority and of nineteenth-century European Orientalism' (p. 130). Watsuji seemed less concerned with attributing Indian oppression to British colonialism than to blaming it on 'the transhistorical essence of India's national character', which was itself shaped by the oppressively humid monsoon climate of India.

Although Watsuji himself suffered from what he perceived as racial discrimination while he was living in Europe, and was therefore, in a position to identify himself with the colonized, he '*decided*', as Sakai puts it forcefully, 'to identify himself with the West' (p. 135). Rejecting any romanticized notion of Asian family resemblance, he invariably posited the Japanese 'self' as 'the *other*' of the Chinese and Indian. In contrast, as I shall examine in the following section, Okakura's sense of cultural exclusivity was mediated through a more intricate sense of 'othering', based on an idealized sense of relationality, if not intimacy, with 'other' Asians.

[44] Okakura Tenshin, *The Ideals of the East*, p. 21.

[45] Okakura Tenshin, 'Modern Problems in Painting', *Okakura Kakuzo: Collected English Writings*, vol. 2, 1984, p. 81.

[46] Okakura Tenshin, *The Awakening of Japan*, 1984, p. 116.

[47] Okakura Tenshin, *The Ideals of the East*, p. 15.

[48] Okakura Tenshin, *The Awakening of Japan*, p. 116, my emphases.

[49] Ibid., my emphases.

[50] Naoki Sakai, 'Subject and Substratum: On Japanese Imperial Nationalism,' *Cultural Studies* 14 (3/4), 2000, p. 464.

[51] Okakura Tenshin, *The Awakening of the East* included in *Okakura Kakuzo: Collected English Writings*, vol. 1, 1984, p. 141. All references to this text in the following section are marked with the appropriate page numbers.

[52] Carol Gluck, *Japan's Modern Myths: Ideology in the Late Meiji Period*, 1985, pp. 135–6.

[53] Tessa Morris-Suzuki, *Re-inventing Japan: Time, Space, Nation*, p. 69.

[54] Ibid.

[55] Surendranath Tagore, 'Okakura Kakuzo: Some Reminiscences', pp. 77–8.

[56] The inclusion of a 'foreigner' in the quintessentially Bengali context of the *adda* does stretch the intimate homosociality of its bonds, as elaborated by Dipesh Chakrabarty in his critical insider's perspective on *'Adda, Calcutta: Dwelling in Modernity'*, *Public Culture* 11 (1), 109–45. Associated with stalwarts of Bengali culture ranging from communists like Hiren Mukherjee to film-makers like Satyajit Ray, the institution of the adda would seem to deny entrance to non-Bengalis. Okakura, I would suggest, challenges this protocol, by catalysing the adda in Surendranath's residence, where he was most hospitably accommodated. In one respect, however, this adda was no different from any other, insofar as its participants were exclusively male. It would be difficult to imagine Sister Nivedita, for instance, sharing the 'wildly exhilarating' discussions around Okakura's table in his room, still less to see him sprawling 'over a bolster on his bedstead'.

[57] Sister Nivedita, *The Complete Works of Sister Nivedita*, vol.3, 1967–8, p. 65.

[58] Inaga Shigemi, 'Okakura Kakuzo's Nostalgic Journey to India and the Invention of Asia', 1999, p. 129.

[59] Letter to Josephine MacLeod written by Sister Nivedita on 20 April 1902. Quoted in App. IV of Dinkar Kowshik's *Okakura*, 1988, p. 106.

[60] Sumit Sarkar, *The Swadeshi Movement in Bengal, 1903–1908*, p. 313. There were many claimants to the religiosity of the swadeshi movement, including moderate leaders like Surendranath Banerji, who in his autobiography 'claimed the credit for having originated the swadeshi vow: the pledge before a Hindu deity to abstain from foreign goods' (311). Hemchandra Kanungo, however, emphasized that it was Debabrata Basu (later Swami Prajnananda) who first convinced Aurobindo of the need to 'give revolutionary politics a spiritual colour' (485). Whatever the source, the impact of Hindu religiosity, according to Kanungo, was negative, insofar as it intensified Muslim separatism, enhanced 'the cult of self-sacrifice for its own sake', and replaced 'rational planning' with 'mystical effusions' (314–15).

All other references to the swadeshi movement in this paragraph are drawn from Sarkar's *The Swadeshi Movement in Bengal*, p. 486.

[61] Vivekananda's reference to Okakura as *khudo* is included in Dinkar Kowshik's *Okakura: The Rising Sun of Japanese Renaissance*, p. 44.

[62] The intimacy of Nivedita and Okakura builds to a climax in Sunil Gangopadhyay's unabashedly populist rendition of their relationship in his blockbuster novel *Prothom Alo*, first published in Bengali in 1996, and translated into English by Aruna Chakravarti as *First Light* (New Delhi: Penguin Books India, 2001). The setting is Okakura's somewhat decadent abode in the fashionable Chowringhee area where he is seen reclining on an easy chair drinking brandy and smoking a cigar. While Nivedita reads from her edited version of *The Ideals of the East*, he creeps behind her chair and makes a pass at her only to confront her speechless rage. A consummate actor, Okakura then sinks to the floor and begs her hand in marriage. By this time, the *brahmacharini* (celibate) Nivedita lashes out at him, accusing him of flagrant flirtations with Bengali women: 'Are you here, in this country, to help spark off a revolution? Or are you here to make love?' She then proceeds to elaborate on Okakura's betrayal of the Asian project.

The problem with this melodrama is not simply its particularly awkward depiction of sexuality, but its misleading encapsulation of future events which, in actuality, evolved over a period of time. If one turns to the most important document relating to Nivedita's last days with Okakura, which are meticulously described in her letter to Josephine MacLeod dated 10 September 1902, we learn that far from being captive to his lures in Chowringhee, Nivedita had invited Okakura to her home at 17, Bosepara Lane. Here, in a self-consciously maternal mode, Nivedita had tried to restore the depleted spirits of an obviously exhausted Okakura, who had just returned from his month's sojourn around India with Surendranath. 'I am trying soup—better distribution of food—rest and happiness,' as Nivedita confided to Josephine MacLeod. Only after Okakura's departure from India at the end of September 1902 can we trace the beginnings of Nivedita's sense of Okakura's betrayal, but even here the letters indicate a slow process of her disenchantment, which has less to do with Okakura's mythical sexual advances (invented by Gangopadhyay) than with the absence of a professional and political follow-up to the Asian project. If Okakura had invited Nivedita to Japan, as he had promised, I do believe that their friendship might have lasted.

[63] Quoted in Inaga Shigemi, 'Okakura Kakuzo's Nostalgic Journey to India and the Invention of Asia', p. 125.

[64] Sister Nivedita, *The Letters of Sister Nivedita*, vol. 2, 1982, pp. 705–6.

[65] Okakura Tenshin, *The Awakening of Japan*, p. 17.

[66] Ibid., p. 98.

[67] Sister Nivedita, *The Letters of Sister Nivedita*, vol. 1, p. 130.

[68] Ibid.

[69] Sister Nivedita, 'Preface', *The Ideals of the East*, p. 9.

[70] Ibid.

[71] Ibid., p. 12.

[72] The full title of Leo Ching's essay is 'Yellow skin, white masks: race, class, and identification in Japanese colonial discourse', *Trajectories*, ed. Kuan-Hsing Chen, 1998, pp. 65–86.

[73] Ibid., p. 69.

[74] Ibid., p. 70.

[75] Rabindranath Tagore, *Creative Unity*, Macmillan India, 1st edn 1922, rpt 1995.

[76] Rabindranath Tagore, *Sadhana: The Realization of Life*. Delhi: Rupa, pp. 40–1.

[77] Ibid., p. 41.

[78] Ibid. Refusing to confine his reading of 'one' within the confines of 'textbook Vedantism', Tagore had no difficulty in alchemizing the concept of *atma* so that it assumed many manifestations as a 'sovereign creative agent' rather than a metaphysical absolute. Thus, in a particularly resonant formulation, Tagore could affirm that 'the *Atma* needs its love for the son in order to express itself' (*atma jaar prakasher janya putrasneher prayojan*), and that he as an individual poet was in possession of this atma to facilitate the 'desire for self-expression'. See Ranajit Guha's *History at the Limit of World History* (New Delhi: Oxford University Press, 2002), pp. 84–7.

[79] See William Radice's excellent introduction to *Rabindranath Tagore: Selected Poems*, p. 24, for a cogent differentiation between Tagore's *jiban-debata* and Rammohan Roy's more rational Unitarian connotation of the notion of One God.

[80] Ibid., p. 24.

[81] Leo Ching, 'Yellow skin, white masks', p. 70.

[82] Ibid., p. 80.

[83] Ibid.

[84] Ibid.

[85] Ibid.

[86] Dipesh Chakrabarty, Floor Discussion following Opening Keynote Address on '"Asia" and the Twentieth Century: What is "Asian Modernity"?', *'We Asians': Between Past and Future*, 2000, p. 38.

[87] Partha Mitter, *Art and Nationalism in Colonial India 1850–1922: Occidental Orientations* (Cambridge: Cambridge University Press, 1994), p. 289.

[88] Okakura Tenshin, 'Nature in East Asiatic Painting', *Okakura Kakuzo: Collected English Writings*, vol. 2, ed. Sunao Nakamura (Tokyo: Heibonsha, 1984). All references to this essay are included in the text with the appropriate page numbers.

[89] It is telling that Okakura consciously refrains from using the word *utsukushii* in contrast to *omoshiroi*. While the former word denotes the 'beautiful', particularly in its external manifestations, omoshiroi connotes a sense of interest or curiosity drawn out of something that may or may not be beautiful in itself. Why Okakura inscribes omoshiroi as an aesthetic category in his description of landscape and nature paintings is that he wishes to work against the purely external reproduction of natural beauty, preferring a stylistic rather than a naturalistic representation of nature, by which it can be evoked in our minds through memory. I am grateful to Hori Madoka, Richard Emmert, and Stephen Dodd for their edification of this elusive term.

On a more startling note, it is significant to point out that the word *omo* is also used for 'mask' as in Noh drama; *shiroi* means 'white', as Okakura explains the etymology of the word, though discreetly editing what the gods were actually doing to entice the Sun-Goddess out of the cave. In one version of the story, it seems that they were performing some kind of a striptease to lure the goddess from her seclusion. This 'interesting' detail is tactfully avoided by Okakura, who divests the entrance of the Sun-goddess of any sexual motivation. I am grateful to my friend and Noh expert, Richard Emmert, for this visceral insight into omoshiroi.

[90] Dipesh Chakrabarty, '"Asia" and the Twentieth Century', p. 31.

[91] Ibid., p. 32.

[92] Partha Mitter, *Art and Nationalism in Colonial India 1850–1922*, p. 291.

[93] Ibid.

[94] From Ralph Mayer's *The Artist's Handbook of Materials and Techniques* (New York: Viking Press, 5th impression, 1973), we learn that 'The term "scumbling" refers to the use of thinly applied opaque colours instead of transparent glaze colours. ...[It] is done over a coat of paint which has become dry to the touch or over an isolating varnish, with either glaze medium or straight opaque oil colour. The paint may be applied either with a brush and the surplus wiped off with a rag, leaving a uniform coating of the desired tone, or it may be stippled or rubbed on with a brush, dabber, rag, or with the fingers.'

Against the specificity of such technical detail, it becomes obvious that Abanindranath was not practising the 'scumbling' technique, any more so than he was imitating the *morotai* style. However, by pointing it out as a painterly resemblance, K.G. Subramanyan indicates the cross-cultural complexities that meet the eye in the study of any painting. These subtleties of vision cannot be explained through historiography alone and demand a different kind of aesthetic perception.

[95] Shigemi Inaga, 'Claude Monet: Between "Impressionism" and "Japonism"', *Monet and Japan*, National Gallery of Australia, 2001, p. 66.

[96] Ibid., pp. 67–8. The importation of colours and their effect on *ukiyo-e* prints have also been discussed by Henry Smith and Gary Hickey.

[97] Shigemi Inaga, 'The Making of Hokusai's Reputation in the Context of Japonisme', *Japan Review*, 15, 2003, p. 83.

[98] Dipesh Chakrabarty, '"Asia" and the Twentieth Century', p. 31.

[99] A thorough examination of Havell's pedagogy and paternalistic patronage of Abanindranath within the symbiosis of nationalism and 'new orientalism' can be read in Tapati Guha-Thakurta's *The Making of a New 'Indian' Art* (Cambridge: Cambridge University Press, 1992). More recently, Guha-Thakurta has provided a more discursive reading of Abanindranath's aesthetics through an analysis of his small tract entitled *Bharat Shilpa*, published in 1909, which is clearly influenced by Havell's *Indian Sculpture and Painting* (1908). In their affirmation of a spiritualized and authentic Indian art, the British guru and his Indian *shishya* supported each other, with Abanindranath providing Havell with interpretations of traditional Hindu iconography and commentaries on Sanskrit texts, and Havell acknowledging Abanindranath's Indian genius with an endorsement of indigenous modernity. See sections on 'The Reconstitution of an Aesthetic Sphere' and 'New Claims to Authority and Authenticity', in Guha-Thakurta, pp. 154–67.

[100] Partha Mitter, *Art and Nationalism in Colonial India, 1850–1922*, pp. 290–1.

2. Nationalism

[1] Okakura Tenshin, *The Awakening of Japan*, 122.

[2] Ibid.

[3] Ibid.

[4] Ibid., 123.

[5] Karatani, Kojin, 'The Discursive Space of Modern Japan', *Japan in the World: Boundary 2*, Fall 1991, 205.

[6] From the Rabindra-Bhavana archives in Santiniketan, I was able to confirm this fact through one crucial letter included in the file on Okakura. This letter, dated 5 December 1936, was written by Okakura's son Kazuo to Rabindranath, requesting him to write a few lines of recommendation for a Japanese edition of *The Awakening of Japan*. In the letter, Kazuo had emphasized that permission to reprint the book had already been obtained from the original publisher in New York and that Rabindranath would be receiving a copy of the first chapter. From these details, it becomes obvious that *The Awakening of Japan*, written just a year after the publication of *The Ideals of the East*, had not been distributed either in India or Japan. More crucially, Rabindranath would be reading the text for the first time more than 34 years after it had been published. I am grateful to Pulak Dutta for following up on this valuable archival evidence.

[7] Surendranath Tagore, 'Okakura Kakuzo: Some Reminiscences', p. 78.

[8] Sumit Sarkar has elaborated at length on 'constructive swadeshi', in *The Swadeshi Movement in Bengal 1903–8*, pp. 47–62.

[9] The most useful source in this regard is Sabyasachi Bhattacharya's finely edited *The Mahatma and the Poet: Letters and Debates between Gandhi and Tagore 1915–41* (New Delhi: National Book Trust, India), 1997.

[10] All references to *Swadeshi Samaj* in this essay, which are marked with the appropriate page numbers, are drawn from the *Rabindra-Rachanabali*, vol. 2, published on the occasion of the poet's 125th birth anniversary (Calcutta: Visva-Bharati Granthan Bibhag, 1988), pp. 625–41. This particular quotation is to be found on p. 631. All translations of *Swadeshi Samaj* quoted in this text are by Bhaskar Mukhopadhyay.

[11] Carol Gluck, *Japan's Modern Myths: Ideology in the Late Meiji Period*, p. 143.

[12] Ibid., p. 144.

[13] Ibid., p. 282.

[14] Harry Harootunian, *Overcome by Modernity: History, Culture, and Community in Interwar Japan* (Princeton and Oxford: Princeton University Press, 2000), p. 44.

[15] Carol Gluck, *Japan's Modern Myths*, p. 283.

[16] Quoted in Sumit Sarkar, *The Swadeshi Movement in Bengal 1903–8*, p. 315.

[17] Ibid., p. 316.

[18] A cogent description of the different manifestations of the Bharat Mata figure can be read in Ch. 8 of Manu Goswami's *Producing India: From Colonial Economy to National Space* (Chicago: University of Chicago Press, 2004), p. 256–65.

[19] Quoted in Manu Goswami, *Producing India*, p. 263.

[20] Ibid.

[21] The description in this paragraph is drawn from *Swadeshi Samaj*, pp. 632–3.

[22] All quotations from *Gora* are taken from Sujit Mukherjee's translation published by the Sahitya Akademi, New Delhi, in 1997. I quote from the first paperback edition, 2003. This quotation is from page 134. All other quotations are paginated in my text.

[23] Quoted in Sumit Sarkar, *The Swadeshi Movement in Bengal, 1903–8*, p. 58.

[24] Ibid., p. 60.

[25] All the references to Takeuchi Yoshimi are drawn from two articles by Naoki Sakai, 'Modernity and its Critique: The Problem of Universalism and Particularism', *The South Atlantic Quarterly* 87:3, Summer 1998, and '"You Asians"—on the historical role of the West and Asia binary' (2000). Takeuchi's reference to 'Japan is nothing' is drawn from the first article, p. 499.

[26] Naoki Sakai, 'Modernity and its Critique', *The South Atlantic Quarterly*, Summer 1998.

[27] Ibid.

[28] Ibid.

[29] Naoki Sakai, '"You Asians"—on the historical role of the West and Asia binary', p. 215–6. The phrase 'overcoming the modern' refers specifically to a famous conference held in Kyoto in July 1942 on the crucial issue of how to 'overcome the modern' (*kindai no chokoku*) within the larger context of the war. I will elaborate on this conference with reference to Tagore's modernism later in the chapter.

From Karatani Kojin's 'The Discursive Space of Modern Japan', 1991, we learn of Takeuchi's attempt to re-evaluate this conference in the 1950s within the context of the 'dual nature of the war'—simultaneously, 'a war of aggression against Asia and a war to liberate Asia from the Western powers'. This was not grasped as an 'aporia', and consequently, the discourse of the conference merely got dissipated into 'an analytic version of state military discourse' (97).

[30] I am grateful to Manas Ray for pointing this out to me and also for emphasizing the literary device of the *deus ex machina* through which Tagore strategizes Gora's self-realization. Indeed, if Gora had not been the orphaned child of Irish parents adopted by a Hindu couple—at some level, an extremely artificial piece of evidence inserted into the novel in the last

pages—would it have been that easy for Tagore to structure Gora's *anagnorisis* ('opening of eyes')? It could be argued that by being established as a foreigner by birth, Gora can afford to transcend the dictates of Hindu *samaj*. At a communitarian or religious level, he is not obliged to circumvent the divisions of 'Hindu, Muslim, Khrishtan, Brahmo.' But, as Manas Ray has emphasized (personal communication with the author), the Hindu *samaj* will continue to adhere to these divisions, even as Gora stands outside of its sectarian limits. This could be described, according to Ray, as 'the prestige of the secular'. Even if one doesn't necessarily accept this interpretation, the point is that *Gora* could have been a more profoundly ambivalent novel if the protagonist had been born a Hindu. Tagore, however, chooses an alternative narrative strategy, which, arguably, is ambivalent in its own right.

[31] All references to Tagore's lectures on nationalism paginated in my text are drawn from *Nationalism*, first published by Macmillan in 1917, and subsequently reprinted several times. I draw on the second impression of the paperback by Rupa, New Delhi, 1994. This particular reference is to be found on p. 99.

[32] Ashis Nandy, *The Illegitimacy of Nationalism: Rabindranath Tagore and the Politics of Self* (New Delhi: Oxford India Paperbacks, 3rd imp., 1998).

[33] Stefan Tanaka, *Japan's Orient: Rendering Pasts into History* (Berkeley: University of California Press, 1993), p. 4.

[34] Ibid., p. 22.

[35] Ibid., p. 23.

[36] Ibid., p. 22.

[37] Ibid., p. 234. Tanaka elaborates at length on the pioneering role of Shiratori Kurakichi in building an Orientalist research network of 'pure' scholars beginning with the incorporation of the Toyo Kyokai (Oriental Society, founded in 1898) into his Aija Gakkai (Asia Society), in 1907.

[38] Ibid., p. 12.

[39] The inner contradictions of *toyo* are perhaps best exemplified in the critique provided by Tsuda Sokichi, a former student of Shiratori. As Tanaka explicates Tsuda's position, 'The concept of *toyo* always places Japan in an inferior position relative to both the West and China. To the West, Japan is Oriental; yet *toyo* is similar enough to the Western Orient that it allows the placement of Japan within the latter category, again making Japan inferior to the West. To the Chinese, Japan's use of China's past allows them to see Japan as only a derivative of China with Western learning, thus eliminating

the need for the Chinese to learn from Japan' (279). By attempting to release Japan from its dependency on the pasts of China and Europe, Tsuda 'altered the dichotomy between the Orient and the Occident', and in the process, tried to 'free Japan from a rigid concept of itself and its future' (280).

[40] Okakura Tenshin, *The Ideals of the East*, p. 122; quoted by Tanaka, *Japan's Orient*, p. 13.

[41] Stefan Tanaka, *Japan's Orient*, p. 13.

[42] Okakura Tenshin, *The Awakening of the East*, p. 144.

[43] Rabindranath Tagore, *Talks in China*, edited by Sisir Kumar Das (Santiniketan: Rabindra-Bhavana, Visva-Bharati, revised and enlarged edn, 1999), pp. 15–6.

[44] Ibid., p. 24.

[45] Ibid., pp. 181, 182.

[46] Stefan Tanaka, *Japan's Orient*, p. 266.

[47] Rabindranath Tagore, *Talks in China*, p. 17.

[48] Okakura Tenshin, *The Awakening of the East*, p. 146.

[49] Tessa Morris-Suzuki, *Re-Inventing Japan*, p. 24.

[50] Carol Gluck, *Japan's Modern Myths*, p. 254.

[51] Ibid.

[52] Okakura Tenshin, *The Book of Tea* (Tokyo: Sogensha), p. 141.

[53] Christopher Benfey, *The Great Wave*, p. 105.

[54] Ibid.

[55] Rabindranath Tagore, 'Crisis in Civilization', *The English Writings of Rabindranath Tagore*, vol. 3, p. 723.

[56] Ibid.

[57] In the introduction to his edition of Tagore's *Selected Poems*, William Radice briefly sketches the poet's temperamental difference from the legacy of the Young Bengal movement, which converged around a radical group of students devoted to a charismatic Eurasian teacher in Hindu College called Henry Louis Vivian Derozio (1809–31). For all his radical experiments in poetry and assertion of religious social reform, Tagore did not share this legacy of 'free-thinking, agnosticism and pragmatism', expressed in aberrant cultural practices like 'drinking parties' and the 'revolt' against 'arranged marriage'. See Radice, p. 22.

[58] Rabindranath Tagore, 'Civilization and Progress', *Talks in China*, p. 87.

[59] Ibid., p. 82.

[60] Ibid., p. 81.

[61] Ibid., p. 87.

[62] Ibid., p. 85. The sources for Tagore's story of the Mahsud are drawn from the *Nation* and *The Times* (London). Dates not indicated in the original text.

[63] These lines from an earlier draft of Tagore's lecture on 'Nationalism in Japan' are quoted by Stephen N. Hay, *Asian Ideas of East and West*, p. 64.

[64] Ibid.

[65] Karatani Kojin, 'The Discursive Space of Modern Japan', p. 197.

[66] See, for instance, Arjun Appadurai, 'Patriotism and its Futures', *Modernity at Large: Cultural Dimensions of Globalization* (New Delhi: Oxford University Press, 1977).

[67] Ashis Nandy, *The Illegitimacy of Nationalism*, p. 81.

[68] Ibid.

[69] Ibid., p. 87.

[70] Ibid., p. 86. Nandy adds that Bangladesh is the 'only Islamic state ever to have a national anthem written by a non-Muslim', thereby raising the complex question of whether Tagore's Bengali identity transcends the idea of religion altogether.

[71] Rabindranath declined to compose the second verse of *Bande Mataram* on the grounds of its Hindu religiosity that could offend Muslim sentiments. See my chapter on 'No More Utopias? Re-mapping the Present', in *In the Name of the Secular: Contemporary Cultural Activism in India* (New Delhi: Oxford University Press. 1998), p. 163.

[72] See 'Obituary of Tagore by Mahatma Gandhi', included in *The Mahatma and the Poet*, p. 216.

[73] I have dealt with this theoretical challenge in my book *The Politics of Cultural Practice* in specific response to Frantz Fanon's important but elusive distinction between the 'national' and 'nationalism'. Read Ch. 1, p. 29.

[74] Ashis Nandy, *The Illegitimacy of Nationalism*, p. 83.

[75] Stephen Hay, *Asian Ideas of East and West*, p. 107.

[76] Ibid.

[77] Ibid., p. 117. This was the verdict arrived at by a professor of Keio University, Kanogoki Kazunobu, who, according to Hay, was 'actually arrested in India because he was agitating for Indian independence'.

[78] Ibid., p. 93.

[79] Ibid., p. 76.

[80] See Sisir Kumar Das's extremely informative background included in Rabindranath Tagore's *Talks in China*, p. 176.

[81] This statement was made by Yun Daiying (1895–1931), editor of *Xin Qingnian* (The New Youth) and the director of the department of propaganda of the Communist Youth League. His comments followed an impassioned critique entitled 'Our Expectations from Tagore', published in the journal *Juewu* (Consciousness), written by Mao Dun, who specifically emphasized 'the weakness of the modern Chinese youth'. See Sisir Kumar Das's commentary, pp. 164–6.

[82] Quoted by Sisir Kumar Das in his commentary on *Talks in China*, p. 179.

[83] Quoted by Stephen N. Hay in *Asian Ideas of East and West*, p. 170.

[84] Carol Gluck, *Japan's Modern Myths*, p. 17.

[85] The reference to the circulation of the *Taiyo* magazine is drawn from Marilyn Ivy's 'Formations of Mass Culture', *Postwar Japan as History*, ed. Andrew Gordon (Berkeley, Los Angeles, Oxford: University of California Press, 1993), p. 243. The reference to book production is taken from Carol Gluck, *Japan's Modern Myths*, p. 12.

[86] Harry Harootunian, 'Introduction,' *Japan in Crisis: Essays on Taisho Democracy*, ed. Bernard S. Silberman and H.D. Harootunian (Princeton: Princeton University Press, 1974), p. 15.

[87] Letter of Rabindranath to Abanindranath, dated 8th *Bhadra* 1323, included in *Nandan*, vol. IX, 1986, pp. 40–1, published by Department of History of Art, Kala Bhavana, Visva-Bharati, Santiniketan.

[88] Quoted by Stephen N. Hay in *Asian Ideas of East and West*, p. 75.

[89] From Swapan Chakravorty's finely inflected and precise translation of *Adhunik Kabya* (Modern Poetry), included in *Rabindranath Tagore: Selected Writings on Literature and Language*, pp. 280–92, it becomes clear that the category of 'modernism' (in the literary sense) is also conflated with 'modernity', testifying to the blurred space contained within the Bengali word *adhunikata*, which can be used for both 'modernity' and 'modernism'.

The complexities of nomenclature increase when Tagore upholds the 'modern', as he does in his valorization of the Chinese poet Li Po (AD 701–62), whose 'vibrant' and 'natural' idiom is set against the more aggressive and iconoclastic distortions of verisimilitude to be found in some poems by T.S. Eliot and Ezra Pound. Instead of defining a specifically 'indigenous' form of modernism, Tagore upholds 'pure modernity', which involves the capacity 'to see the world with dispassionate absorption, free of personal attachment', with a 'scientific' focus on the 'selfhood of the object'. In Tagore's conclusion to the essay, he acknowledges that Europe has achieved this 'dispassionate mind' in its investigation of science, but not in its exploration of literature.

In this complex essay, one realizes how far Tagore has travelled from his preliminary comments on 'modernism' in *Nationalism*. Nonetheless, it is possible to trace some embryonic elements of his later position in the lecture upholding the independent mind, a freedom from temporal constraints and European models, and a respect for science in terms of its 'pure' illumination of the object, without a 'wrong application' to life in general.

[90] For a dense contextualization of these charges against modernity, within the specific biographies and ideologies of the participants in the Kyoto symposium, read Harry Harootunian's *Overcome by Modernity: History, Culture, and Community in Interwar Japan* (Princeton and Oxford: Princeton University Press, 2000), pp. 34–94.

[91] This position adopted by a member of the Romantic faction, Kamei Katsuichiro, is quoted at length by Harootunian in *Overcome by Modernity*, p. 41. The 'return to "Oriental religious practice"' to affirm a counter-freedom to 'Western individualism' was advocated by the Kyoto philosopher Nishitani Keiji. See pp. 35–6.

[92] This position adopted by the film critic Tsumura Hideo is discussed in Harootunian, *Overcome by Modernity*, pp. 62–3.

[93] Ibid., p. 49.

[94] Ibid., p. 46.

[95] Ibid., p. 45.

[96] Okakura Tenshin, 'Modern Problems in Painting', *Okakura Kakuzo: Collected English Writings*, vol. 2, p. 77.

[97] Ibid., p. 80.

[98] Ibid.

[99] Ibid., pp. 77–8.

[100] Ibid., p. 78.

[101] Quoted in Stephen N. Hay, *Asian Ideas of East and West*, p. 67. The second quote in the same paragraph is drawn from the same source.

[102] Documented in Sabyasachi Bhattacharya's *The Mahatma and the Poet*, pp. 86, 91.

[103] Dipesh Chakrabarty, *Provincializing Europe: Postcolonial Thought and Historical Difference* (Princeton: Princeton University Press, 2000).

[104] E.P. Thompson, 'Introduction', to *Nationalism*, p. 14.

[105] Ibid.

[106] Ian Buruma and Avishai Margalit, *Occidentalism: The West in the Eyes of its Enemies* (New York: The Penguin Press, 2004).

[107] Ibid. p. 6.

[108] Ibid., p. 49.

[109] Ibid., p. 12.

[110] This statement is made by a nationalist demagogue fictional character in Michael Dibdin's novel *Dead Lagoon*. Endorsed by Samuel Huntingon, with no attempt to mediate the politics of fiction, the character's position is upheld as a political truism: 'The unfortunate truth in these old truths cannot be ignored by statesmen and scholars.' See Samuel P. Huntingon, *The Clash of Civilizations and the Remaking of World Order* (New York: A Touchstone Book, Simon & Schuster, 1997), p. 20.

[111] Ian Buruma and Avishai Margalit, *Occidentalism*, pp. 123–5.

[112] All references to *Bharatbarsher Itihas* are drawn from *Rabindra-Rachanabali*, vol. 2, published on the occasion of Tagore's 125th birth anniversary (Calcutta: Visva-Bharati Granthan Bibhag, 1988), pp. 703–9. I am grateful to Bhaskar Mukhopadhyay for translating the relevant sections of the text from which I summarize and occasionally quote.

[113] Ibid., p. 705.

[114] Ibid.

[115] Ibid., p. 707.

[116] Ranajit Guha, *History at the Limit of World-History* (New Delhi: Oxford University Press, 2002). All references to this book have been marked with the appropriate page numbers in my text.

[117] While 'history' signifies both event and the representation of that event, more specifically, the past and the study of the past, 'historiography' refers more specifically to the 'study of the study of history', more often than not based on the academic scholarship in a particular field, authenticated through evidence and established research methodologies. While history can exist without historiography, it is harder to imagine historiography without history. I am grateful to Vinay Lal for these useful discriminations, which are elaborated in his book *History of History: Politics and Scholarship in Modern India* (Delhi: Oxford University Press, 2003).

In contrast, 'historicity', literally the quality or the state of being historical, is a far more difficult term to define, insofar as 'it has to be seen both as a unity and in its historical development', which Dipesh Chakrabarty specifically invokes as a 'conceptual gift of Europe' in his book *Provincializing Europe* (2000). The challenge of historicity lies in the need to avoid the teleological propensity of seeing the present as a culmination of the past, as well as to avoid the historical determinism of what Karl Popper has described as *The Poverty of Historicism*. Frederic Jameson's imperative 'to always historicize' can be read as an imperative to recognize the historicity of the situation, and thereby to save it from historicism. This can best be realized by acknowledging the contextual specificities and contradictions of a particular moment in history and its mutation and interpretive possibilities over a period of time. For sharing his thoughts with me on this complex cluster of terms, I am extremely grateful to Lee Weng Choy.

[118] Rosinka Chaudhuri, 'Historicality in Literature: Subalternist Misrepresentations', *Economic and Political Weekly*, 16 Oct. 2004, pp. 4658–63.

[119] The troubled history of *Sahitye Aitihasikata* is very competently summarized by Rosinka Chaudhuri, 'Historicality in Literature', *EPW*, pp. 4659–60.

[120] Ibid., p. 4659. Chaudhuri draws on Nepal Majumdar's *Bharate Jatiyata O Antarjatikata Ebong Rabindranath* (Indian Nationalism and Internationalism and Rabindranath), vol. 6, (Calcutta: Dey's Publishing, 1996), p. 313.

[121] Accurately, Chaudhuri highlights Dipesh Chakrabarty's dualistic assumptions of the 'prosaic' and the 'poetic' as distinct narrative modes in relation to history. In contrast to Tagore's poetry, Chakrabarty interprets Tagore's stories as being 'amenable to historicist and objective treatment', without sufficiently exploring the blurred zones of poetry and prose, the imaginative and the ordinary, the apparently sublime heights of creativity in solitude and the trials and tribulations of everyday life. Describing Chakrabarty's dichotomies as 'pedantic', Chaudhuri adds that, '[I]t is this sort of historical reading [Tagore] is reacting to when he had said, as he might have to Chakrabarty if he had been a contemporary, "*dur hok ge tomar itihas*" ("to hell with your history")', pp. 4661–2.

[122] Rabindranath Tagore, 'Talks in China', p. 174.

[123] Ibid., p. 171.

[124] '*Rabindrik nation ki?*' appeared in the Puja Edition of *Baromas*, Calcutta, 2003, pp. 7–25; *Rabindrik nation prasange aro du-char katha*, which appeared in *Baromas*, Autumn 2004, pp. 48–59, was written as a rejoinder to two interventions in response to Chatterjee's earlier article, Prasun Bandopadhyay's '*Abar Rabindranath: Sampratik Samajtattikder Alochanar Prekkhite*' (Rabindranath, once more: In the Context of the Discussion of Contemporary Social Theorists), *Kirtinasa 3*, Dec.–Jan. 2004–5, pp. 5–29; and Debesh Ray's *Partha Chattopadhayer Rabindrik Nation* (Partha Chatterjee's Rabindrik Nation), *Bangla Boi* 63, March 2004, pp. 1–3.

I am grateful to Bhaskar Mukhopadhyay for calling my attention to these articles and to Rajarshi Chakrabarty for his considerable assistance on the translation. For the purpose of my discussion, I will not be providing a detailed discussion of this debate but simply summarizing some of its relevant exchanges, with a focus on Chatterjee's interpretation of Tagore's nation.

[125] Partha Chatterjee, *'Rabindrik nation ki?'*, p. 8.

[126] Rabindranath Tagore, *Nationalism*, p. 51.

[127] Partha Chatterjee, *'Rabindrik nation ki?'*, p. 23.

[128] Ibid.

[129] See discussion in Partha Chatterjee, *'Rabindrik nation prasange aro du-char katha'*, pp. 51–2.

[130] Ibid., p. 52.

[131] Partha Chatterjee, *'Rabindrik nation ki?'*, pp. 23–4.

[132] Partha Chatterjee, *'Rabindrik nation prasange aro du-char katha'*, p. 56.

[133] Samir Amin, 'The Social Movements in the Periphery: An End to National Liberation?', in *Transforming the Revolution: Social Movements and the World-System*, ed. Samir Amin et al., (New York: Monthly Review Press, 1990).

[134] Quoted in Partha Chatterjee, *'Rabindrik nation prasange aro du-char katha'*, p. 54, in response to Prasun Bandopadhyay's description of Tagore's nationalism.

3. Cosmopolitanism

[1] Quoted by E.P. Thompson in his 'Introduction' to *Nationalism*, p. 11.

[2] Stephen N. Hay, *Asian Ideas of East and West*, p. 91.

[3] Christopher Benfey, *The Great Wave: Gilded Age Misfits, Japanese Eccentrics, and the Opening of Old Japan* (New York: Random House, 2003). Read in particular the chapter on 'The Boston Tea Party'.

[4] Homi Bhabha's 'vernacular cosmopolitanism' and James Clifford's 'discrepant cosmopolitanisms' are among the most inflected constructions in the growing literature on 'other cosmopolitanisms'.

[5] Okakura Tenshin, *The Ideals of the East*, p. 129.

[6] This position is put forward by Martha C. Nussbaum in her widely circulated critical provocation on 'Patriotism and Cosmopolitanism', in *For Love of Country: Debating the Limits of Patriotism* (Boston: Beacon, 1966), p. 4. According to Sheldon Pollock (see 'Cosmopolitan and Vernacular in History', *Cosmopolitanism*, ed. Carol A. Breckenridge, et al., 2002), Nussbaum exaggerates the role of classical cosmopolitanism: 'The word *kosmopolites*, for instance, seems to occur only in the much-cited (Greek) utterance attributed to Diogenes in Diogenes Laertius's biography, as in the work of

Philo, the (Greek) Jewish philosopher of Alexandria. Neither the word itself nor any of its derivatives (nor even *cosmopolis*) occurs in Classical Latin' (50).

My problem with Nussbaum's position is the way in which she assumes the universalist pertinence of classical cosmopolitanism in opposition to the politics of ethnicity prevailing in the US (and, more specifically, in university academia). More problematically, she relates cosmopolitanism all too emphatically to the universal humanism of Rabindranath Tagore. Particularly troubling, in this regard, is Nussbaum's reading of Tagore's position through one text, *Home and the World*, and the reductive equation of Nikhilesh's position with uninflected cosmopolitanism. The fact that Nikhilesh opposes the tyranny of swadeshi worship does not necessarily mean that he is, *ipso facto*, a cosmopolitan.

[7] My understanding of the 'cosmopolitical' has been largely influenced by *Cosmopolitics: Thinking and Feeling beyond the Nation*, ed. Pheng Cheah and Bruce Robbins (Minneapolis and London: University of Minnesota Press, 1998). See, in particular, Pheng Cheah's introduction 'The Cosmopolitical — Today', pp. 20–41.

[8] I am thinking in particular of Partha Chatterjee's strategic choice in freezing 'civil society' as a term associated with a specifically Eurocentric epistemology, history, vocabulary, and process of institutionalization, against which he has attempted to formulate a 'political society' which is shaped by the struggle for democracy adopted by marginalized sections of the population who are denied access to the ostensibly universal privileges of civil society and citizenship. For his most recent articulation on the subject, see *The Politics of the Governed: Reflections on Popular Politics in Most of the World* (New York: Columbia University Press, 2004).

[9] Bruce Robbins, 'Comparative Cosmopolitanisms', *Cosmopolitics*, p. 260. The reference to Donna J. Harraway is drawn from 'Situated Knowledges: The Science Question in Feminism and the Privilege of Partial Perspective', *Simians, Cyborgs, and Women: The Reinvention of Nature* (London: Free Association, 1990), p. 191.

[10] Both the edited volumes of *Cosmopolitics* (1998) and *Cosmopolitanism* (2002) prioritize the notion of the 'beyond'. While Pheng Cheah and Bruce Robbins focus on states of being 'beyond the nation', the editors of *Cosmopolitanism* adopt a somewhat more freewheeling tactic in their attempt to work against predetermined models of cosmopolitanism. '[W]hat if we were to try to be archivally cosmopolitan and to say, "Let's simply look at the world across time and space and see how people have thought and acted

beyond the local"'. (italics mine, p. 10). This emphasis seems to neglect the rich possibilities of acknowledging and deciphering an entire gamut of local cosmopolitanisms.

[11] Sheldon Pollock, Homi K. Bhabha, Carol A. Breckenridge, and Dipesh Chakrabarty, 'Cosmopolitanisms', *Cosmopolitanism*, p. 1.

[12] Amanda Anderson, 'Cosmopolitanism, Universalism, and the Divided Legacies of Modernity,' *Cosmopolitics*, p. 289.

[13] Naoki Sakai, '"You Asians" — On the Historical role of the West and Asia Binary', p. 234.

[14] Quoted by Ackbar Abbas, 'Cosmopolitan De-scriptions: Shanghai and Hong Kong', *Cosmopolitanism*, p. 211.

[15] Ibid.

[16] Ibid., pp. 226–7.

[17] Ibid., p. 226.

[18] Ibid.

[19] Walter D. Mognolo, 'The Many Faces of Cosmo-polis: Border Thinking and Critical Cosmopolitanism', *Cosmopolitanism*, p. 174.

[20] See James Clifford, 'Travelling Cultures', *Cultural Studies*, ed. Lawrence Grossberg, Cary Nelson, and Paula A. Treichler (New York: Routledge, 1992).

[21] This ironic, but serious, criticism of Clifford's self-defined 'role of *ex officio* scribe to our scribblings', has been raised by Paul Rabinow in his essay 'Representations Are Social Facts', *Writing Culture: The Poetics and Politics of Ethnography* (Berkeley: University of California Press, 1986).

[22] Abanindranath Tagore, 'On Okakura', extract from *Jorasanker Dhare*, translated by Kanti Ghosh, included in an appendix in Dinkar Kowshik's edition of *Okakura*, p. 85. All references to this text are drawn from this source with the appropriate pagination.

[23] Partha Mitter, *Art and Nationalism in Colonial India 1850–1922*, p. 285. In the thick of the swadeshi movement, in March 1904, Abanindranath, on Havell's instigation, had also provided an ornamental motif — Buddha and the Wounded Swan — for the Calcutta Ladies' Congratulatory Address to Lady Curzon, on her return to Calcutta after a severe illness. See Mitter, p. 294.

[24] Ashis Nandy, *The Illegitimacy of Nationalism*, p. 73. Drawing on autobiographical sources from Tagore's *Jibansmriti* and *Chhelebela*, Nandy emphasizes that it was this 'second-order, fragile but oppressive, immediate authority [of the servants] that Tagore first learnt to negotiate in life'.

[25] The sharpest reading on this point has been provided by Pheng Cheah in his critique of liberal postcolonial readings of migrancy: '[I]t is doubtful

whether transational migrant communities can be characterized as examples of cosmopolitanism in the robust normative sense. ...It is unclear how many of these migrants feel that they belong to a world. Nor has it been ascertained whether this purported feeling of belonging to a world is analytically distinguishable from long-distance absentee national feeling' ('The Cosmopolitical—Today', p. 37).

[26] Ann Nishimura Morse, 'Promoting Authenticity', p. 148.

[27] Ibid.

[28] Krishna Dutta and Andrew Robinson, *Rabindranath Tagore: The Myriad-minded Man*, p. 201, 203. All the facts pertaining to Tagore's American financial deal are drawn from this source.

[29] Quoted in Lloyd Rudoph, 'The Occidental Tagore', *The Boston Review*, vol. XIX, no.5, Oct.–Nov. 1994.

[30] The category of the 'half-way house' is suggested in the closing lines of the obituary written on Okakura's death by William Sturgis Bigelow and John Ellerton Lodge, who believed that Okakura 'invalidated' Kipling's notorious views on 'East is East, and West is West'. According to Bigelow and Lodge, 'They met in Okakura Kakuzo'. (See obituary included in *Okakura Kakuzo: Okakura Tenshin and the Museum of Fine Arts, Boston*, p. 14.)

[31] Okakura Tenshin, 'Exhibition of Recent Acquisitons in Chinese and Japanese Art', *Okakura Kakuzo: Collected English Writings*, vol. 2, p. 157.

[32] Ibid., pp. 156–7.

[33] Ibid., p. 158.

[34] Ibid., p. 159.

[35] Quoted by Anne Nishimura Morse in her article on 'Promoting Authenticity', p. 147.

[36] Mimi Hall Yiengpruksawan, 'Japanese Art History 2001: The State and Stakes of Research', p. 112.

[37] These statements by Tadao Ogura and Malcolm Rogers are included in the Foreword to the catalogue of the exhibition. See *Okakura Kakuzo: Okakura Tenshin and the Museum of Fine Arts, Boston*, p. 2–3.

[38] Quoted in F.G. Notehelfer's 'On Idealism and Realism in the Thought of Okakura Tenshin', p. 327.

[39] Ibid., p. 328.

[40] Quoted in Emma Tarlo, *Clothing Matters: Dress and Identity in India* (Chicago: University of Chicago Press, 1996), p. 60.

[41] Ibid., p. 92. Tarlo correctly points out the problematic shift in Gandhi's attitude from his 'original thesis that people must be worthy of khadi to a

new one that through wearing it people could actually become more worthy. In other words, the mere act of wearing khadi was so virtuous in itself that it could purify the wearer' (91). This kind of diehard swadeshi sartorial purism was anathema to Tagore, who feared the infiltration of the notion of untouchability in the public domain.

[42] This is the verdict of William Radice, one of Tagore's most dedicated translators, who puts it very directly, 'I do not believe you can translate songs... Tagore himself said in *Creative Unity* (1922) that a song without its melody is like a butterfly whose wings have been plucked, and in *My Reminiscences* we read of his reluctance to publish books of the words of his songs, for that very reason.' See 'Introduction' to Radice's edition of Tagore's *Selected Poems*, p. 28.

[43] For elaboration on Okakura's 'inferiority complex toward Japan, the Japanese language, and the Japanese portion of his identity', read F.G. Notehelfer, 'On Idealism and Realism in the Thought of Okakura Tenshin', p. 316–17.

[44] For a fuller context of this trip and Okakura's multilingual education, read ibid., pp. 314–16.

[45] Okakura Tenshin, *The Book of Tea*, p. 162.

[46] For a fuller context on *Sur*, read Ketaki Kushari Dyson, *In Your Blossoming Flower-Garden: Rabindranath Tagore and Victoria Ocampo* (1988), pp. 31–6, from which I draw my information in this section.

[47] The Tagore–Ocampo relationship in Argentina, intensified by the virile presence of Tagore's secretary Leonard Elmhirst, has been meticulously analysed by Ketaki Kushari Dyson (1988). Her investigation of this *ménage à trois*, built through fact-finding minutiae encompassing dates, statements, letters, misunderstandings, and the the erotics of gesture and movement, borders, in my view, on an obsessive overkill of biographical research. Yet, ironically, for all the passion invested in the relationship between Tagore and Ocampo, Dyson is not entirely prepared to see them as friends: 'Like most male heterosexual artists even up to this day, [Tagore] needed women more as sources of inspiration, as sources of *shakti* for his own creativity, than as friends on equal terms' (5). If this is not judgemental enough, Dyson then proceeds to make a wider generalization: 'Nor, to be realistic, is it easy to imagine how friendship on completely equal terms as we understand it today could have been developed and sustained between the two across the linguistic, cultural and geographical distances that separated them, not forgetting the generation gap of twenty-nine

years' (5). Dyson concludes that if the 'gaps' between the relationship could have been 'closed', the relationship could have been enriched.

I have quoted Dyson's position at some length because its premise is almost antithetical to the intercultural reading of friendship offered in the next section of my book. Suffice it to say that the 'gaps' in any friendship could be the very stimulus of its intimacy: a paradoxical intimacy that is not always subject to rational or critical scrutiny. A more measured reading of the Ocampo–Tagore friendship can be read in Sankho Ghosh's *Ocampor Rabindranath: bhumika, anubad, anushango* (Calcutta: Dey's Publishing, Shravan 1380, Aug. 1973).

[48] All references to the Tagore–Ocampo controversy surrounding the translation of the poem *Kankal* (A Skeleton) are drawn from Krishna Dutta and Andrew Robinson's *Rabindranath Tagore: The Myriad-minded Man*, 254–9. The references in my text are paginated accordingly.

[49] Bruce Robbins, 'Comparative Cosmopolitanisms', p. 261.

[50] Rabindranath Tagore, 'Crisis in Civilization', p. 726.

[51] F.G. Notehelfer, 'On Idealism and Realism in the Thought of Okakura Tenshin', p. 355.

[52] Rabindranath Tagore, 'An Indian Folk Religion', *Creative Unity*, p. 77. All references to the 'ascetic woman' Sarva-khepi are to be found on this page.

[53] Ibid., p. 77.

[54] See 'The Sense of Beauty' (*Soundaryabodh*), translated from the Bengali by Swapan Chakravorty, included in *Rabindranath Tagore: Selected Writings on Literature and Language*, ed. Sisir Kumar Das and Sukanta Chaudhuri (New Delhi: Oxford University Press, 2001), pp. 164–78. In this essay, Tagore emphasizes the foundational values of discipline and restraint for the creation of beauty, as opposed to any dependency on austerity or obsession. Another important consideration concerns the 'surplus gain' of beauty, insofar as it 'exceeds what is necessary' (172). Refusing to see any credence in the argument that the most skilled creators of beauty have not been models of temperance, Tagore counters: '[W]hy do we trust reality so much?' (168). Likewise, he debunks the legitimacy of keeping ethics and aesthetics apart. For him, beauty is at once intrinsically good and true: the categories are, at some level, coterminous, encompassing the Keatsian equation of truth and beauty, their embodiment in the sacred figure of Saraswati, further sanctified by the belief of the Upanishads in *anandarupamamritam* (joyous and immortal in form).

Against the sheer normative weight of these categories, supplemented by a total denial of the aesthetics of the ugly, the intemperate, and the contradictory, one is almost tempted to recall many characters, temperaments, and moods in the poet's oeuvre which are beautiful precisely because they challenge the norms of an essentialized truth and beneficence.

[55] Rabindranath Tagore, 'An Indian Folk Religion', p. 80.

[56] Letter to Priyambada Devi Banerjee, 1912, no date or month mentioned, *Okakura Kakuzo: Collected English Writings*, vol. 3, p. 175.

[57] Ibid., 20 Feb. 1913, p. 178.

[58] Ibid., 4 March 1913, p. 183.

[59] Ibid., 4 February 1913, p. 176.

[60] This famous extract drawn from Hugo of St Victor's *Didascalion* is quoted by Edward W. Said in the penultimate paragraph of *Culture and Imperialism* (London: Vintage Books, 1993), p. 407. In his reading of the extract, Said takes pains to work against the valorization of exile by emphasizing that, 'Hugo twice makes it clear that the "strong" or "perfect" person achieves independence and detachment by *working through* attachments, not by rejecting them. Exile is predicated on the existence of, love for, and a real bond with one's native place; the universal truth of exile is not that one has lost that love or home, but that inherent in each is an unexpected, unwelcome loss' (407). While these qualifications are nuanced, the difficulty is that Said's own autobiographical inscription of exile and the sheer theoretical weight of his enunciation almost compel him to privilege the state of exile over other domesticated, nation-bound forms of existence. Arguably, the evolution of the self, traced by Hugo in three stages, has less to do with exile in the modern sense than with the metaphysics of what Tagore would describe as *sadhana* (self-realization).

[61] Letter to Priyambada Devi Banerjee, 3 March 1913, included in *Okakura Kakuzo: Collected English Writings*, vol. 3, p. 182.

4. Friendship

[1] The semi-divine and supernatural quality of the fox has been dramatized in numerous plays in the traditional Japanese repertoire. Okakura's opera itself seems to be inspired by the life of the diviner Abe no Seimei (c. ninth to tenth century), the son of Abe Yasuna and a white fox. Yasuna is, indeed, the name of Okakura's protagonist, while his wife Kuzunoha appears in the well-known play *Ashiya Doman Ouchi Kagami* (also

referred to as *Kuzunoha*), which is performed in both the *kabuki* and *bunraku* performance traditions.

The most famous fox play in the *noh* tradition is *Kokaji* in which the fox god Inari (also the word used for Japanese 'fox shrines') comes down from heaven to help the swordsmith Kokaji make a sword-blade for the emperor. The most famous kabuki/bunraku play featuring the fox is *Yoshitsune Senbonzakura* in which Shizuka carries a small *kotsuzumi* hand-drum which is made out of the hide of the fox's parents. The fox constantly follows Shizuka but appears to her not as a fox but as one of Yoshitsune's retainers, who is there to look after her. All Shizuka needs to do is to play her drum and the retainer appears: the retainer who is actually a fox pretending to be the retainer. Such a typical kabuki/bunraku complication is not to be found in noh.

I am extremely grateful to Richard Emmert for this valuable performance history of the fox.

[2] Okakura Tenshin, *The White Fox, Okakura Kakuzo: Collected English Writings*, vol. 1, p. 348. All references to this opera in my text are marked with the appropriate page numbers.

[3] These phrases are drawn from Priyambada Devi Banerjee's letters to Okakura and two notebooks in which she inscribed her love in a diverse spectrum of moods and impressions. All quotations from Priyambada's writings, excerpted from *Okakura Kakuzo: Collected English Writings*, vol. 3, are indicated by the initials PB and paginated in my text with the appropriate page numbers.

[4] Okakura Tenshin, letter to Priyambada Devi Banerjee, written while journeying on the 'Indian Ocean,' 15 Oct. 1912. Included in *Okakura Kakuzo: Collected English Writings*, vol. 3, p. 170.

[5] Ibid., 25 May 1913, p. 202.

[6] Ibid.

[7] Ibid., 17 May 1913, p. 199.

[8] In her letter to Okakura dated 24 June 1913, Priyambada begins by saying, 'Latterly your letters have come intact, the seals have not been tampered with at all'. In an earlier letter dated 25 May 1913, Okakura had dealt with the matter engagingly, 'Why should they tamper with our mails, I wonder? Surely the people who were overcurious must have been amused at the vast foolishness in them (I speak for myself). They contain dangerous matter,—very dangerous to myself.' See *Okakura Kakuzo: Collected English Writings*, vol. 3, pp. 201–2, 261.

[9] The reason why this translation 'works' is that the song is re-imagined within the framing of a contemporary novel of love, Sunetra Gupta's *Memories of Rain* (1992). The longing for Calcutta in the novel is vividly evoked through snatches of Rabindrasangeet, which are rendered freely without any false obligation to be 'faithful' to the original text of the song.

[10] Okakura Tenshin, letter to Priyambada Devi Banerjee, dated 25 May 1913, included in *Okakura Kakuzo: Collected English Writings*, vol. 3, p. 202.

[11] Quoted by Christopher Benfey, *The Great Wave*, p. 96.

[12] Ibid., p. 98.

[13] Ibid., p. 96.

[14] See Maitraye Devi's evocative memoir *Tagore by Fireside* (Calcutta: Rupa), pp. 220–1, translated from the original Bengali work *Mungpute Rabindranath* (1943) by the author herself.

[15] I draw the concept of 'sexual panic' from Eve Kosofsky Sedgwick's brilliant exposition of 'homosexual panic' in her book *Between Men: English Literature and Male Homosocial Desire* (New York: Columbia University Press, 1985). See Ch. 5 in particular.

It is possible to read such panic in the reaction of the painter Abanindranath Tagore to a nude (English) male model, which has been documented by Partha Mitter in *Art and Nationalism in Colonial India 1850–1922*: 'For life drawing, [Charles Palmer, an English artist appointed to teach Abanindranath oil painting] hired a young English soldier from the neighbouring barracks as a nude model. On arrival, the youth began to take off his clothes in order to pose. Abanindranath grew alarmed and pleaded with him not to remove his undergarment' (275). Though Mitter adds that 'nudes were rare in art schools [in Bengal]', it is also possible to read in Abanindranath's reaction some trace of sexual panic in upholding an intrinsically bhadralok bourgeois propriety. The painter's 'squeamishness' towards objects like the human skull (for studies in anatomy) has been more accurately interpreted by Mitter as originating from 'a subliminal [upper-caste] fear of pollution' (275).

[16] Krishna Dutta and Andrew Robinson, *Rabindranath Tagore: The Myriad-minded Man*, cited above.

[17] Maitraye Devi, *Tagore by Fireside*, pp. 154–5.

[18] Partha Chatterjee, '*Rabindrik nation prasange aro du-char katha*', pp. 49–50.

[19] Eve Kosofsky Sedgwick, *Between Men: English Literature and Male Homosocial Desire*, By problematizing the field of homosociality through 'desire', Sedgwick acknowledges that she is consciously attempting to mark its

'discriminations and paradoxes'. In the process, 'homosocial desire' needs to be read as an 'oxymoron' (1).

[20] Ibid., p. 19.

[21] Ibid., p. 1.

[22] Inserted without elaboration in Christopher Benfey's 'Tea with Okakura', *New York Review of Books* (vol. 47, no. 9), 25 May 2000. While Benfey's sparkling biographical account of 'Gilded Age Misfits', in *The Great Wave* is full of such tantalizing details, he does not always follow up on them. At best, Bigelow's sexuality is suggested through facts such as his 'male-only retreat on Tuckernuck Island' (66) off the coast of Nantucket, and his apparent penchant for 'a rougher, rawer version of Old Japan' (67), represented in his passion for jujitsu, sword fighting, sumo wrestling. Neither does Benfey fully elaborate on the companionship that Bigelow shared with Edward Morse, whose 'sexual alienation' is briefly indicated as one possible reason for his retreat to Japan from the 'modern metropolis' of Boston (66). As for the artist John La Farge, who shared a particular intimacy with Okakura, we have to fall back on his much-reiterated dedication in his *Artist's Letters from Japan*: 'And you too, Okakura San...for a time you were Japan to me' (86).

What is missing in Benfey's reading is precisely an exploration of the continuum between the 'homosocial' and 'homosexual', as pointed out by Eve Sedgwick. In the process, the book seems to legitimize the heterosexual protocols of the Boston Brahmins without sufficiently troubling their sexually ambivalent relationships.

[23] Eve Kosofsky Sedgwick, *Between Men*, p. 3. In her Introduction, Sedgwick specifically states that 'Our own society is brutally homophobic; and the homophobia directed against both males and females is not arbitrary or gratuitous, but tightly knit into the texture of family, gender, age, class, and race relations' (3–4).

[24] I have argued this point in my essay 'Towards a Politics of Sexuality: Critical notes on *Spider Woman* and *Fire*', *The Politics of Cultural Practice*, pp. 89–91.

[25] Eve Kosofsky Sedgwick, *Between Men*, pp. 1–2.

[26] Ibid. On the question of female homosocial desire and its linkage with friendship, there is an intriguing acknowledgement in one of Priyambada Devi Banerjee's letters to Okakura: 'My foreign lady friend [who remains unnamed] is sweet. She is half Irish and half Italian, and is naturally and unconsciously a lover of the beautiful, passionately fond of

art and full of romance and poetry. She is gentle and good, with soft dreamy eyes, pretty ways, a sweet smile and is always charmingly dressed. I am sure you will like her if you met [sic] her. I am fond of her, but I am ashamed to own she is ever so much fonder of me. Whenever she can, [she] runs aways from home and spends whole days with me. Everyone laughs at her for her over-fondness of me, but she does not mind that in the least. Mother likes her very much. You can well understand why' (*Okakura Kakzuo, Collected English Writings*, vol. 3, p. 267). The keyword here is 'over-fondness', which could be related not only to 'homosocial desire', but to the more intriguing fact that Priyambada is unselfconsciously sharing her friendship with a 'foreign lady', totally confident that her mother and Okakura will 'like' her.

[27] Rabindranath Tagore, *A Visit to Japan*, translated from *Japan Jatri* by Dr Shakuntala Rao Sastri (New York: East West Institute, 1961), p. 58.

[28] Ibid.

[29] Ibid., p. 59.

[30] Ibid.

[31] Ibid.

[32] Ibid.

[33] My discussion on friendship in the 'modern' context draws heavily from the valuable contribution of Allan Silver, particularly 'Friendship and Trust as Moral Ideals: An Historical Approach', *Archives européenes de sociologie* 30, pp. 274–97, and 'Friendship in Commercial Society: Eighteenth-Century Social Theory and Modern Sociology', *American Journal of Sociology*, vol. 95, no. 6, May 1990, pp. 1474–1504. I am grateful to Bhaskar Mukhopadhyay for calling my attention to these articles.

[34] Allan Silver, 'Friendship and Trust as Moral Ideals', p. 274.

[35] Ibid. The reference to Aziz in *A Passage to India* is to be found in 'Friendship in Commercial Society', p. 1477. Silver quotes a few statements by Aziz to substantiate the point that 'friendship is diminished in moral quality if friends consciously monitor the balance of exchange between them'. For a different perspective on the Aziz–Fielding friendship in the context of 'intimate enemies' and Orientalism, read my early essay on 'Forster's Friends', *Raritan*, Fall 1987.

[36] Allan Silver, 'Friendship and Trust as Moral Ideals', p. 274.

[37] Rabindranath Tagore, *Chaturanga*, translated from the Bengali by Asok Mitra (New Delhi: Sahitya Akademi, 1993), p. 11. The original novella was first published serially in *Sabuj Patra* in 1915 and in book form in 1916 by Indian Press, Allahabad.

[38] Ibid., pp. 11, 13.

[39] Rabindranath Tagore, *Gora*, p. 64.

[40] Ibid., p. 89.

[41] Ibid., p. 323.

[42] Ibid., pp. 324–5.

[43] Ibid., p. 477.

[44] Rustom Bharucha, 'Forster's Friends', p. 48.

[45] Rabindranath Tagore, 'Crisis in Civilization', p. 725.

[46] Ibid., p. 726.

[47] Rabindranath Tagore, 'East and West', *Creative Unity*, p. 101.

[48] Ibid., p. 100.

[49] Ibid.

[50] Ibid., pp. 100–1.

[51] Priyambada Devi Banerjee, 'Priyambada Devi's Notebook', *Okakura Kakuzo: Collected English Writings*, vol. 3, p. 293.

[52] Surendranath Tagore, 'Okakura Kakuzo: Some Reminiscences', *Okakura*, p. 78. All references to Surendrath's travels with Okakura are drawn from this source.

[53] Ibid., p. 82.

[54] Okakura Tenshin, letter to Priyambada Devi Banerjee, 11 Aug. 1913, *Okakura Kakuzo: Collected English Writings*, vol. 3, p. 216.

[55] Surendranath Tagore, 'Okakura Kakuzo: Some Reminiscences', p. 83.

[56] E.P. Thompson, *Alien Homage: Edward Thompson and Rabindranath Tagore* (New Delhi: Oxford University Paperbacks, 1993).

[57] Stephen N. Hay, *Asian Ideas of East and West*, p. 86.

[58] The correspondence, involving an exchange of four letters between Noguchi and Tagore, was initiated by Noguchi in a letter dated 23 July 1938. Tagore's second letter, which closed the correspondence, was dated 27 October 1938. This intense exchange has been recorded by Sisir Kumar Das in *The English Writings of Rabindranath Tagore*, vol. 3, pp. 834–45. Pagination of the different excerpts is included in the text.

[59] Ibid., p. 845. Rabindranath's closing words in his last letter to Noguchi: 'Wishing your people whom I love, not success, but remorse.'

[60] Okakura Tenshin, *Okakura Kakuzo: Collected English Writings*, vol. 3, p. 217.

[61] Ibid.

[62] Ibid., p. 206.

[63] Rabindranath Tagore, 'On Oriental Culture and Japan's Mission', p. 605.

[64] Ibid., p. 606.

[65] Okakura Tenshin, letter to Priyambada Devi Banerjee, *Okakura Kakuzo: Collected English Writings*, vol. 3, p. 182.

[66] Allan Silver, 'Friendship and Trust as Moral Ideals', p. 291.

[67] Ibid.

Epilogue

[1] In his splendid essay 'On civil and political society in postcolonial democracies' (2002), Partha Chatterjee reflects ironically on this fact of contemporary Bengali cultural history by contextualizing Tagore's deification against his earlier support of civic condolence meetings to mourn the dead. On the occasion of Bankimchandra Chattopadhyay's death in 1894, Tagore had provided a canonical tribute in the memorial meeting, which had been boycotted by the poet Nabinchandra Sen on account of its foreign, Westernized artificiality. In reaction to Nabinchandra's suggestion that the dead should be deified by transforming their birthplaces into places of pilgrimage, Tagore had defended the need for secularized public rituals in order to educate the public. Today, however, even as public culture has been more regulated in cities like Calcutta, the irony is that Tagore's birthplace has been transformed into a place of pilgrimage. In his closing statement, Chatterjee imagines Nabinchandra 'chuckling with delight' over the poet's 'predicament'.

[2] Quoted by Krishna Dutta and Andrew Robinson, *Rabindranath Tagore: The Myriad-minded Man*, p. 83.

[3] Rabindranath Tagore, 'On Oriental Culture and Japan's Mission', p. 605.

References

Abbas, Ackbar (1998): 'Cosmopolitan De-scriptions: Shanghai and Hong Kong', *Cosmopolitanism: Thinking and Feeling beyond the Nation* (Minneapolis and London: University of Minnesota Press).

Amin, Samir (1990): 'The Social Movements in the Periphery: An End to National Liberation?' *Transforming the Revolution: Social Movements and the World-System*, ed. Samir Amin et al. (New York: Monthly Review Press).

Anderson, Amanda (1998): 'Cosmopolitanism, Universalism, and the Divided Legacies of Modernity', *Cosmopolitics: Thinking and Feeling beyond the Nation* (Minneapolis and London: University of Minnesota Press).

Appadurai, Arjun (1997): 'Patriotism and its Futures', *Modernity at Large: Cultural Dimensions of Globalization* (New Delhi: Oxford University Press).

Bandopadhyay, Prasun (2004): '*Abar Rabindranath: Sampratik Samajtattikder Alochanar Prekkhite*', *Kirtinasa* 3, Dec.–Jan. 2004–5.

Banerjee, Priyambada Devi (1984): 'Priyambada Devi's Notebook,' *Okakura Kakuzo: Collected English Writings*, vol. 3.

——— (1984): 'Letters to Okakura,' *Okakura Kakuzo: Collected English Writings*, vol. 3.

Benfey, Christopher (2003): *The Great Wave: Gilded Age Misfits, Japanese Eccentrics, and the Opening of Old Japan* (New York: Random House).

Bharucha, Rustom (1989): 'Forster's Friends', *Raritan*, Fall 1987.

——— (1993): *Theatre and the World: Performance and the Politics of Culture* (London: Routledge).

——— (1998): *In the Name of the Secular: Contemporary Cultural Activism in India* (New Delhi: Oxford University Press).

Bharucha, Rustom (2000a): *The Politics of Cultural Practice: Thinking Through Theatre in an Age of Globalization* (London: Continuum Books, and Hanover: The University Press of New England).

_____ (2000b): *Consumed in Singapore: The Intercultural Spectacle of 'Lear'* (Singapore: Pagesetters).

_____ (2004): 'Foreign Asia/Foreign Shakespeare: Dissenting Notes on New Asian Interculturality, Postcoloniality and Recolonization', *Theatre Journal*, vol. 56, no. 1, March 2004.

Bhattacharya, Sabyasachi, ed. (1999): *The Mahatma and the Poet: Letters and Debates between Gandhi and Tagore 1915–1941* (New Delhi: National Book Trust, India).

Bigelow, William Sturgis (1984): Introduction to 'On the Method of Practising Concentration and Contemplation', a document written by Chi Ki, a monk of the Tendai sect, trans. by Okakura. Included in *Okakura Kakuzo: Collected English Writings*, vol. 2.

Bigelow, William Sturgis and John Ellerton Lodge (1999): Obituary of Okakura, included in *Okakura Kakuzo: Okakura Tenshin and the Museum of Fine Arts, Boston*.

Buruma, Ian and Avishai Margalit (2004): *Occidentalism: The West in the Eyes of its Enemies* (New York: The Penguin Press).

Chakrabarty, Dipesh (2000a): '*Adda*, Calcutta: Dwelling in Modernity', *Public Culture* 11: 1.

_____ (2000b): *Provincializing Europe: Postcolonial Thought and Historical Difference* (Princeton: Princeton University Press, 2000).

_____ (2000c): Opening Keynote Address on '"Asia" and the Twentieth Century: What is "Asian Modernity"?', *'We Asians": Between Past and Future*, ed. Kwok-Kian Woon, Indira Arumugam, Karen Chia, and Lee Chee Keng (Singapore: Singapore Heritage Society).

Chatterjee, Partha (2002): 'On civil and political society in postcolonial democracies', *Civil Society*, ed. Sudipto Kaviraj and Sunil Khilnani.

_____ (2003): '*Rabindrik nation ki*? (What is Tagore's nation?)', Puja Edition of *Baromas*, Calcutta.

_____ (2004a): '*Rabindrik nation prasange aro du-char katha* (A few more words about Tagore's nation)', *Baromas*.

_____ (2004b): *The Politics of the Governed: Reflections on Popular Politics in Most of the World* (New Delhi: Permanent Black).

Chaudhuri, Rosinka (2004): 'Historicality in Literature: Subalternist Misrepresentations', *Economic and Political Weekly*, 16 October 2004.

Ching, Leo (1998): 'Yellow skin, white masks: race, class, and identification in Japanese colonial discourse', *Trajectories*, ed. Kuan-Hsing Chen (London: Routledge).

Choudhury, Satyajit (1983): 'Nandalal Bose and Indian Modernity', *Nandalal Bose: A Collection of Essays* (New Delhi: Lalit Kala Akademi).

Clifford, James (1992): 'Travelling Cultures', *Cultural Studies*, ed. Lawrence Grossberg, Cary Nelson, and Paula A.Treichler (New York: Routledge).

Devi, Maitraye (2002): *Tagore by Fireside*, trans. from the original Bengali work *Mungpute Rabindranath* (1943) by the author herself (Calcutta: Rupa).

Dutta, Krishna and Andrew Robinson (1995): *Rabindranath Tagore: The Myriad-minded Man* (Calcutta: Rupa).

Dyson, Ketaki Kushari (1988): *In Your Blossoming Flower-Garden: Rabindranath Tagore and Victoria Ocampo* (New Delhi: Sahitya Akademi).

Gandhi, Mahatma (1999): 'The Great Sentinel', *The Mahatma and the Poet*, ed. Sabyasachi Bhattacharya (New Delhi: National Book Trust, India).

Gluck, Carol (1985): *Japan's Modern Myths: Ideology in the Late Meiji Period* (Princeton: Princeton University Press).

Goswami, Manu (2004): *Producing India: From Colonial Economy to National Space* (Chicago: University of Chicago Press).

Guha, Ranajit (2000): *History at the Limits of World History* (New Delhi: Oxford University Press).

Guha-Thakurta, Tapati (1992): *The Making of a New 'Indian' Art* (Cambridge: Cambridge University Press).

────── (2004): *Monuments, Objects, Histories: Institutions of Art in Colonial and Postcolonial India* (New Delhi: Permanent Black).

Gupta, Sunetra (1992): *Memories of Rain* (New Delhi: Penguin Books).

Harraway, Donna J. (1990): 'Situated Knowledges: The Science Question in Feminism and the Privilege of Partial Perspective', *Simians, Cyborgs, and Women: The Reinvention of Nature* (London: Free Association).

Harootunian, H.D. (1974): 'Introduction: A Sense of an Ending and the Problem of Taisho', *Japan in Crisis: Essays on Taisho Democracy*, ed. Bernard S. Silberman and H.D. Harootunian (Princeton: Princeton University Press).

Harootunian, Harry (2000): *Overcome by Modernity: History, Culture, and Community in Interwar Japan* (Princeton and Oxford: Princeton University Press).

Hay, Stephen N. (1970): *Asian Ideas of East and West: Tagore and His Critics in Japan, China, and India* (Cambridge: Harvard University Press).

Horioka, Yasuko (1963): *The Life of Kakuzo* (Tokyo: Hokuseido Press).

Huntington, Samuel P. (1997): *The Clash of Civilizations and the Remaking of World Order* (New York: A Touchstone Book, Simon & Schuster).

Ibrahim, Anwar (1997): *Asian Renaissance* (Singapore: Times International Publishing House).

Inaga, Shigemi (1999): 'Nostalgic Journey to India and the Invention of Asia', *Nostalgic Journeys: Literary Pilgrimages between Japan and the West*, ed. Susan Fisher (Vancouver: Institute of Asian Research).

_____ (2001): 'Claude Monet: Between "Impressionism" and "Japonism"' *Monet and Japan* (National Gallery of Australia).

_____ (2002): 'Cognitive Gaps in the Recognition of Masters and Masterpieces in the Formative Years of Japanese Art History, 1880–1900: Historiography in Conflict', *Japanese Hermeneutics: Current Debates on Aesthetics and Interpretation* (Honolulu: University of Hawaii Press).

_____ (2003): 'The Making of Hokusai's Reputation in the Context of Japonisme', *Japan Review*, no. 15.

Ivy, Marilyn (1993): 'Formations of Mass Culture', *Postwar Japan as History*, ed. Andrew Gordon (Berkeley, Los Angeles, Oxford: University of California Press).

Jackson, Peter A. (2003a): 'Space, Theory, and Hegemony: The Dual Crises of Asian Area Studies and Cultural Studies', *Sojourn*, vol. 18, no. 1.

_____ (2003b): 'Mapping Poststructuralism's Borders: The Case for Poststructuralist Area Studies', *Sojourn*, vol. 18, no.1.

Karatani, Kojin (1991): 'The Discursive Space of Modern Japan', *Japan in the World, Boundary* 2, Fall 1991.

Kowshik, Dinkar (1988): *Okakura: The Rising Sun of Japanese Renaissance* (New Delhi: National Book Trust, India).

Kripalani, Krishna (1980): *Rabindranath Tagore: A Biography*, 2nd edn (Calcutta).

Lu, David J. (1997): *Japan: A Documentary History* (London: M.E. Sharpe).

Mahbubani, Kishore (2004): *Can Asians Think?* (Singapore: Times Editions).

Majumdar, Nepal (1996): *Bharate Jatiyata O Antarjatikata Ebong Rabindranath* (Indian Nationalism and Internationalism and Rabindranath)', vol. 6 (Calcutta: Dey's Publishing).

Matsumoto, Ken'ichi (1997): 'Will the Era of Asia Come', *Reitaku Journal of Interdisciplinary Studies*, vol. 5, no. 1, March 1997.

_____ (2002): 'Okakura Tenshin and the Ideal of Pan-Asianism', typewritten manuscript, presented at seminar on Okakura Tenshin: Exploring Art, Nationalism and Ideals of Asian Community, New Delhi, Dec. 2002.

Mitter, Partha (1994): *Art and Nationalism in Colonial India 1850–1922: Occidental Orientations* (Cambridge: Cambridge University Press).

Miyoshi, Masao and H.D. Harootunian (ed.) (2002): *Learning Places: The Afterlives of Area Studies* (Durham: Duke University Press).

Mognolo, Walter D. (1998): 'The Many Faces of Cosmo-polis: Border Thinking and Critical Cosmopolitanism', *Cosmopolitanism: Thinking and Feeling Beyond the Nation* (Minneapolis and London: University of Minnesota Press).

Morris-Suzuki, Tessa (1998): *Re-inventing Japan: Time, Space, Nation* (London: M.E. Sharpe).

_____ (2002): 'Asia is One: Visions of Asian Community in Twenty-First Century', typewritten manuscript, presented at seminar on Okakura Tenshin: Exploring Art, Nationalism and Ideals of Asian Community, New Delhi, Dec. 2002.

Morse, Anne Nishimura (1999): 'Promoting Authenticity: Okakura Kakuzo and the Japanese Collection of the Museum of Fine Arts, Boston', *Okakura Kakuzo: Okakura Tenshin and the Museum of Fine Arts, Boston*, catalogue published in Japan on 23 Oct. 1999.

Nandy, Ashis (1998a): 'A New Cosmopolitanism: Towards a Dialogue of Asian Civilizations,' *Trajectories*, ed. Kuan-Hsing Chen (London: Routledge).

_____ (1998b): *The Illegitimacy of Nationalism: Rabindranath Tagore and the Politics of Self* (New Delhi: Oxford India Paperbacks, third imp.).

Notehelfer, F.G. (1990): 'On Idealism and Realism in the Thought of Okakura Tenshin', *Journal of Japanese Studies*, vol. 16, no. 2.

Nussbaum, Martha C. (1996): 'Patriotism and Cosmopolitanism', *For Love of Country: Debating the Limits of Patriotism* (Boston: Beacon).

Oguma, Eiji (2002): *A Genealogy of 'Japanese' Self-images*, trans. from the Japanese by David Askew (Melbourne: Trans Pacific Press).

Okakura Tenshin (1981): *Okakura Tenshin zenshu*, nine vols (Tokyo: Heibonsha).

_____ (1984a): *Okakura Kakuzo: Collected English Writings*, vols 1–3, ed. Sunao Nakamura (Tokyo: Heibonsha).

_____ (1984b): *The Ideals of the East with Special Reference to the Art of Japan* (1903), included in *Okakura Kakuzo: Collected English Writings*, vol. 1.

_____ (1984c): *The Awakening of the East*, included in *Okakura Kakuzo: Collected English Writings*, vol. 1.

_____ (1984d): *The White Fox*, included in *Okakura Kakuzo: Collected English Writings*, vol. 1.

_____ (1984e): Letters to Priyambada Devi Banerjee included in *Okakura Kakuzo: Collected English Writings*, vol. 3.

Okakura Tenshin (1984f): 'Modern Problems in Painting', *Okakura Kakuzo: Collected English Writings*, vol. 2.

_____ (1984g): 'Exhibition of Recent Acquisitions in Chinese and Japanese Art', *Okakura Kakuzo: Collected English Writings*, vol. 2.

_____ (1984h): 'Nature in East Asiatic Painting', *Okakura Kakuzo: Collected English Writings*, vol. 2, ed. Sunao Nakamura (Tokyo: Heibonsha).

_____ (1984i): *The Awakening of Japan* (Tokyo: Sogensha).

_____ (1984j): *The Book of Tea* (Tokyo: Sogensha).

Pollock, Sheldon (2002): 'Cosmopolitan and Vernacular in History', *Cosmopolitanism*, ed. Carol A.Breckenridge, Sheldon Pollock, Homi K. Bhabha, and Dipesh Chakrabarty (Durham and London: Duke University Press).

Rabinow, Paul (1986): 'Representations are Social Facts', *Writing Culture: The Poetics and Politics of Ethnography*, ed. James Clifford and George E. Marcus (Berkeley: University of California Press).

Radice, William (1987): *Rabindranath Tagore: Selected Poems* (Harmondsworth: Penguin Books).

Ray, Debesh (2004): *Partha Chattopadhayer Rabindrik Nation* (Partha Chatterjee's Rabindrik Nation), *Bangla Boi* 63, March 2004.

Robbins, Bruce (1998): 'Comparative Cosmopolitanisms', *Cosmopolitics: Thinking and Feeling Beyond the Nation* (Minneapolis and London: University of Minnesota Press).

Rudoph, Lloyd (1994): 'The Occidental Tagore', *The Boston Review*, vol. XIX, no. 5, Oct.–Nov. 1994.

Said, Edward W. (1993): *Culture and Imperialism* (London: Vintage Books).

Sakai, Naoki (1997): *Translation and Subjectivity: On 'Japan' and Cultural Nationalism* (Minneapolis and London: University of Minnesota Press, 1997).

_____ (1998): 'Modernity and its Critique: The Problem of Universalism and Particularism', *The South Atlantic Quarterly*, 87:3, Summer 1998.

_____ (2000a): 'Subject and Substratum: On Japanese Imperial Nationalism', *Cultural Studies* 14 (3/4).

_____ (2000b): 'You Asians—on the historical role of the West and Asia binary', *'We Asians': Between Past and Future*, ed. Kwok-Kian Woon, Indira Arumugam, Karen Chia, and Lee Chee Keng (Singapore: Singapore Heritage Society).

Sarkar, Sumit (1973): *The Swadeshi Movement in Bengal 1903–1908* (New Delhi: People's Publishing House).

Sedgwick, Eve Kosofsky (1985): *Between Men: English Literature and Male Homosocial Desire* (New York: Columbia University Press).

Silver, Allan (1989): 'Friendship and Trust as Moral Ideals: An Historical Approach', *Archives européenes de sociologie* 30.

_____ (1990): 'Friendship in Commercial Society: Eighteenth-Century Social Theory and Modern Sociology', *American Journal of Sociology*, vol. 95, no. 6, May 1990.

Sister Nivedita: *The Complete Works of Sister Nivedita*, vol. 3, 1967–8.

_____ (1982): *The Letters of Sister Nivedita*, vol. 2 (Calcutta).

_____ (1984): 'Introduction,' *The Ideals of the East with Special Reference to the Art of Japan* (1903), included in *Okakura Kakuzo: Collected English Writings*, vol. 1.

Sojourn (1999): 'Asian Ways: Asian Values Revisited', 14:2.

Tagore, Abanindranath (1988): *Jorasanker Dhare*, trans. by Kanti Ghosh, included in Dinkar Kowshik's *Okakura: The Rising Sun of Japanese Renaissance* (New Delhi: National Book Trust, India).

Tagore, Rabindranath (1961): *A Visit to Japan*, trans. from *Japan Jatri* by Dr Shakuntala Rao Sastri (New York: East West Institute).

_____ (1986): Letter to Abanindranath, dt. 8th *Bhadra* 1323, included in *Nandan*, 88. vol. IX, 1986, 40–1, published by Department of History of Art, Kala Bhavana, Visva-Bharati, Santiniketan.

_____ (1988a): 'Swadeshi Samaj', *Rabindra-Rachanabali*, vol. 2, published on the occasion of the poet's 125th birth anniversary (Calcutta: Visva-Bharati Granthanbibhag).

_____ (1988b): '*Bharatbarsher Itihas* (India's History)', *Rabindra-Rachanabali*, vol. 2, published on the occasion of Tagore's 125th birth anniversary (Calcutta: Visva-Bharati Granthanbibhag).

_____ (1993): *Chaturanga*, trans. from the Bengali by Asok Mitra (New Delhi: Sahitya Akademi).

_____ (1994): *Nationalism* (New Delhi: Rupa).

_____ (1995a): *Creative Unity* (Calcutta: Macmillan India Ltd, 1st edn 1922, rpt 1995).

_____ (1995b): 'East and West', *Creative Unity* (Macmillan Pocket Tagore Edition, New Delhi).

_____ (1995c): 'An Indian Folk Religion', *Creative Unity*, 1st edn 1922 (Macmillan Pocket Tagore Edition, New Delhi, 1995).

_____ (1996a): *The English Writings of Rabindranath Tagore*, vols 1–3, ed. Sisir Kumar Das (New Delhi: Sahitya Akademi).

_____ (1996b): 'Crisis in Civilization', *The English Writings of Rabindranath Tagore*, ed. Sisir Kumar Das, vol. 3 (New Delhi: Sahitya Akademi).

Tagore, Rabindranath (1996c): 'On Oriental Culture and Japan's Mission', Tagore's address to the members of the Indo-Japanese Association, Tokyo, 15 May 1929. Included in *The English Writings of Rabindranath Tagore*, vol. 3.

―――― (1996d): 'International Relations', *The English Writings of Rabindranath Tagore*, vol. 3.

―――― (1996e): Correspondence with Noguchi, included in *The English Writings of Rabindranath Tagore*, vol. 3 (New Delhi: Sahitya Akademi).

―――― (1997): *Gora*, trans. by Sujit Mukherjee (New Delhi: Sahitya Akademi).

―――― (1999a): *Talks in China*, ed. Sisir Kumar Das (Santiniketan: Rabindra-Bhavana, Visva-Bharati, revised and enlarged edition).

―――― (1999b): 'Civilization and Progress', *Talks in China*, ed. Sisir Kumar Das (Santiniketan: Rabindra-Bhavana, Visva-Bharati, revised and enlarged edition).

―――― (1999c): 'The Call of Truth', included in *The Mahatma and the Poet*, ed. Sabyasachi Bhattacharya (New Delhi: National Book Trust, India).

―――― (2001): 'The Sense of Beauty', *Selected Writings on Literature and Language* ed. Sisir Kumar Das and Sukanta Chaudhuri. (New Delhi: Oxford University Press).

―――― (2002a): *Sadhana: The Realization of Life* (Calcutta: Rupa).

―――― (2002b): *'Sahitye Aitihasikata'* (Historicality in Literature), trans. Ranajit Guha and included in his *History at the Limits of World History* (New Delhi: Oxford University Press).

Tagore, Surendranath (1988): 'Okakura Kakuzo: Some Reminiscences', app. to Dinkar Kowshik's *Okakura: The Rising Sun of Japanese Renaissance* (New Delhi: National Book Trust, India).

Tanaka, Stefan (1993): *Japan's Orient: Rendering Pasts into History* (Berkeley: University of California Press).

Tarlo, Emma (1996): *Clothing Matters: Dress and Identity in India* (Chicago: University of Chicago Press).

Thompson, E.P. (1993): *Alien Homage: Edward Thompson and Rabindranath Tagore* (New Delhi: Oxford University Paperbacks).

―――― (1994): 'Introduction', *Nationalism*, New Delhi: Rupa).

Weiner, Michael (1994): *Race and Migration in Imperial Japan* (London: Routledge).

Yiengpruksawan, Mimi Hall (2001): 'Japanese Art History 2001: The State and Stakes of Research', *The Art Bulletin*, 83, no.1, March 2001.

Index